er:
hai're M'Lady Sharon, owned by Mr. and Mrs. Andrew Clark
nes, Long Island and photographed by Sal Miceli.

er:
Ɔan Brearley and Dawn owned by Madeleine Blush of Bald-
g Island, and photographed by Sal Miceli.

ece:
ɔn O'Boy, photographed by Tauskey at 16 months of age.
on March 8, 1932, O'Boy was retired early in 1938 and died on
945. His obituary in the *New York Sun* was compared to that
War. No other dog had been so honored. O'Boy was handled
ly by Harry Hartnett for owner Mrs. Cheever Porter of New
.

ISBN 0-87666-655-1

y T.F.H. Publications, Inc. Ltd.

this is the
irish sett

by joan mc donald br

t.f.h.

Distributed in the U.S.A. by T.F.H. Publications, Inc., 211 We
Neptune City, N.J. 07753; in England by T.F.H. (Gt. Britain) Ltd
in Canada to the book store and library trade by Clarke, Irwin &
Clair Avenue West, Toronto 10, Ontario; in Canada to the pet
Sartelon Street, Montreal 382, Quebec; in Southeast Asia by
Singapore 14; in Australia and the south Pacific by Pet Imports
2100, N.S.W., Australia. Published by T.F.H. Publications, Inc.
Hong Kong.

Front
Dun La
of St.

Back
Autho
win, L

Frontis
Ch. Mi
Whelpe
June 2
of Man
exclus
York C

© 1975

CONTENTS

What to Teach First. . . The "Down" Command. . . The "Stay" Command. . . The Stand for Examination. . . Formal School Training. . . Advanced Training and Obedience Trials. . . The Companion Dog Excellent Degree. . . The Utility Dog Degree. . . The Tracking Dog Degree

Thenderin The Heir Apparent, owned by Ann Savin and Jane Zaderecki of Westbury, New York.

DEDICATION

for

Anne and Edmond Vianney

who listened with
infinite patience to
all my dog tales during
a life-long friendship
this book on their favorite
breed is dedicated with
deep affection. . .

ACKNOWLEDGMENTS

The author wishes to express her sincere gratitude to the following people who supplied important material for this book. First, to Irene Castle Phillips Khatoonian Schlintz for the statistical records based on her famous Phillips System ratings; to Emily Schweitzer for significant obedience information; to Constance Vanacore for photographs and material on Irish Setters in Russia; to Madeline Blush and her beautiful Irish Setter, Dawn; to Erwin Hutzmann for special assistance; to Dr. Robert R. Shomer, D.V.M. for expert counsel over the years; to Stephen McDonald for additional material; and to Sal Miceli, an extraordinary photographer, for his photographic artistry throughout the book; and to all those who submitted photographs of their dogs so that they may be a part of this permanent record on a glorious breed.

". . . the dogge called the Setter, which layeth
its belly to the ground and creepeth
like a worme. . ."

Caius, 16th Century

ACKNOWLEDGMENTS

ABOUT THE AUTHOR. . .

JOAN McDONALD BREARLEY

Joan Brearley has loved animals ever since she was old enough to know what they were. Over the years there has been a constant succession of dogs, cats, birds, fish, rabbits, snakes, turtles, alligators, squirrels, lizards, etc., for her own personal menagerie. Through these same years she has owned over thirty different breeds of purebred dogs, as well as countless mixtures, since the door was never closed to a needy or homeless animal.

A graduate of the American Academy of Dramatic Arts, Joan started her career as a writer for movie magazines, actress and dancer. She also studied journalism at Columbia University and has been a radio, television and magazine writer, writing for some of the major New York City agencies. She was also a television producer-director for a major network on such shows as *Nick Carter, Master Detective*, and has written, cast, directed, produced and, on occasion, starred in television film commercials. She has written material for such personalities as Dick Van Dyke, Bill Stern, Herman Hickman, Dione Lucas, Amy Vanderbilt and many others prominent in the entertainment world.

Her accomplishments in the dog fancy include being an American Kennel Club approved judge, breeder-exhibitor of top show dogs, writer for various dog magazines, author or co-author of **many** breed books including *This is the Afghan Hound, This is the Shih Tzu, This is the St. Bernard, This is the Bichon Frise, This is the Old English Sheepdog, This is the Siberian Husky, This is the Skye Terrier*, and many others. For five years she was Executive Vice-President of the Popular Dogs Publishing Company and editor of *Popular Dogs* magazine, the national prestige publication for the dog fancy at that time.

Joan Brearley is just as active in the cat fancy, and in almost all the same capacities. She is editor of the Cat Fanciers Association Annual Yearbook and writes for the various cat magazines as well. Joan Brearley speaks at kennel clubs and humane organizations on animal legislation and has received many awards and citations for her work in this field, including an award from the Morris Animal Foundation.

At present Joan lives in a penthouse apartment overlooking all Manhattan in New York City with three dogs and a dozen or more cats, all of which are Best in Show winners and have been professional models for television and magazines. Joan is proud of the fact that in her first litter of Afghan Hounds she bred a Westminster Kennel Club Group winner, Champion Sahadi (her kennel prefix) Shikari, the top-winning Afghan Hound in the history of the breed for many years.

In addition to her activities in the world of animals, Joan Brearley is a movie buff and spends time at the art and auction galleries, the theatre, creating needlepoint (for which she has also won awards), dancing, the typewriter—and the zoo!

1. THE EARLY HISTORY OF THE IRISH SETTER

The only fact that can be stated with perfect certainty regarding the origin of the Irish Setter is that the breed originated in Ireland, the country from which it derives its name.

In Ireland, as well as in every other inhabited part of the earth before the birth of Christ, hunting dogs were essential to man's very existence. Dogs were not used as hunting aids alone; their flesh was eaten and their skins were worn, and they served man well as guard dogs.

Remains of dogs unearthed in Ireland during the Harvard Archeological Expedition in the 1930's, in the crannog of Lagore, near Dunshaughlin, produced three of the oldest types of the early dogs: *Canis intermedius, Canis palustris* and *Canis leineri*, all of which date back to the 7th and 8th centuries AD. The largest of these "species" belonged to a large wolfdog-type. Other remains bore bent forelegs and were more diminutive in size; they had obviously belonged to the toy dog breeds. A third type carried the distinctly domed skull and clearly defined stop which indicated the first evidences of the Water Spaniel common to all of Ireland and therefore the staunchest local contender for the title of ancestor to our Irish Setter.

The fact that these Irish Spaniels were prevalent in the first century is indicated by a reference to them in the ancient tome called *Laws of Howell*, written before the 11th century. The same canine history also presents a strong argument for this common Spaniel's being bred and worked in Spain; there are texts that say that this hairy-tailed, rough-coated dog was proficient at falconry. Called the *chien oysel*, or Spanish Pointer, it was also reputed to be the ancestor of the Poodles and larger Spaniels used all over the known world for hunting small birds and game on both land and water as early as the 14th century. These Spaniels, whose name centuries ago was spelled Spagnel (or Spanyell, as they were referred to in the age of Henry VIII, who decreed that no dogs should be kept in his court except "some small Spanyells for ladies."), actually got their name from

13

Spain, which at that time was spelled Spayne! Actually Spain can be considered the homeland of a Spaniel that later found its way to England and Ireland by way of France, and more centuries later developed into the Irish Setter.

Behind the Spanish Spaniel was the Spanish Pointer, a large, thick, cumbersome, slow-moving dog which historian and dog writer Rowland Johns describes in his book *Our Friend the Irish Setter* as being adequate for hunting in the days when reloading flint-locks took time but less than adequate as firearms improved and the need for speedier dogs became important. Hunters began to seek out the Foxhounds for speed and accuracy, and a blending of the Spaniels and the Pointers ultimately produced the English and Irish Red Setters.

It would be difficult to define the various breeds of dogs indigenous to Ireland from those which were actually brought into Ireland by the Celts from the south of England in the early times. When the Pope gave Henry II of England the go-ahead to invade Ireland in 1154 there had already been a canine, as well as human, integration, because the peoples of Ireland, Scotland and England had begun moving from country to country in sailing ships. In the 16th century a Sir Robert Cecil was importing "setting dogs" from Ireland which he presented with great ceremony to visiting diplomats, so we can be certain that Setters were enjoying a certain degree of recognition and popularity as "Irish-bred" dogs and regarded as something of value even at this early point in time.

There had been dogs of various breeds brought into Ireland from Belgium and the Netherlands also by returning warriors down through the centuries. After the Treaty of Utrecht in 1713 there was obviously even more mixing of breeds, as both the local Irish breeds bred with the mixed breeds that came to Ireland from as far away as what is now known as Germany, and from the Orient. There has been speculation that it might well have been one of the German imports that actually triggered the breeding of self-colored dogs, inasmuch as the German Vorstehund was certainly self-colored and certainly more Setter than Pointer. But whatever the importations and mixtures which might have been either intentional or unintentional, it became an established fact within the fancy that the finest Setters evolved and were perfected in Ireland.

A reasonably safe hypothesis on Irish Setter beginnings would actually suggest a combination of the aforementioned Irish Water Spaniel and Pointer, with a dash of Bloodhound, and further, that the Irish Red Setter descended from the Irish Red and White Setter. However, this theory has been challenged by some who declare that Irish Red and Irish Red and White Setters co-existed throughout Ireland as early as the 1700's. Dr. Erich Schneider-Leyer wrote in 1960 in his book *Dogs of the World* that he tends toward the belief that the Irish Red Setter was developed from the Red and White Spaniels taken to

The Irish Red Setter of 1819, from a drawing by Sir Edwin Landseer.

Ireland from France around 1803 and crossbred with the Pointers.

Others contest the theory by citing that not only did the Irish Red Setter carry the similar stature and conformation of the Irish Red and White Setter but also that many of them had a tendency to resemble the Gordon Setter, especially in coloring, and especially when we consider that the "red" color of that time could better be described as being more a yellow or dun color and not the rich red mahogany shade as we know it today. Yet a third group suggests that the native Irish Red Spaniel, or Modder Rhu as it was called in Gaelic, was behind it all, since it was very much in evidence at the time the Irish Setter was coming into its own as a separate color category at the beginning of the 19th century.

No matter which theory held true at the time, we do know that in the early large kennels there was obviously much mixed breeding going on, along with the concentrated efforts to create a pure strain of self-colored dogs which were to become the Irish Red Setter. It was during the early 1800's that controversy was running high in Ireland as to both the advantages and disadvantages of this solid red dog.

The chief objection to the self-reds was the danger that their color would fade into the surrounding ground and brush color, resulting in their being shot. Feeling was that the flash of white on the Red and White Setters made spotting them easier for the hunter—although it

15

also made them easier for the game to spot! The solid color reds had a better chance at sneaking up on their prey and going on point. Many of those who preferred and bred the self-colored reds but who feared losing sight of their valuable hunting dogs tied a piece of white cloth around their necks to make them stand out against the field, and continued to breed a pure strain of Irish Red Setters. . .

THE SELF-COLORED REDS GAIN IN POPULARITY

While the first written record of a working Setter's being referred to by the name "Setter" was recorded in 1576 in *De Canibus Britannicas*, an 18th century publication called *Rural Sports* revealed just how far the self-colored reds had come in the space of a few hundred years. The story in *Rural Sports* told how two Irish Red Setters had become an integral part of a real estate transaction. It seems an Irishman renewed a 999-year farm lease on his property in Northern Ireland, the sale of which would have netted for him over two hundred and fifty dollars a year. This was a tidy sum in those days, and certainly far more than the purchase price of an Irish Red Setter dog and bitch. . . but the terms of the sale would have forced him to give up his dogs, something he could not bear to do!

Sir Walter Scott in 1823 in his work *St. Ronan's Well* has two characters given to hunting discussing the attributes of both Setters and Pointers. Sir Bingo and Tyrrel are comparing the hunting merits of the two breeds, and Tyrrel goes on to boast of the Setter's advantage of companionship in the home as well as the field. Sir Bingo told Tyrrel that he ". . . had never heard that a Setter was only fit to follow at a poacher's heels." Tyrrel lost no time in setting him straight by saying, "You know it now, then, Sir Bingo, and I hope you will not fall into as great an error again."

A statute recorded in the time of Queen Anne of England as part of the realm's Forest Laws made specific reference to Setters and bore evidence of the first dog licensing and the levying fines for the dogs' misuse. It read as follows: "He who keeps Greyhounds, Lurchers, Setting-Dogs, to kill game, being not qualified, forfeits five pounds, a stipend to the Informer, the other to the Poor."

And so Irish Red Setters' popularity continued to grow as they excelled as both companions and hunting dogs. Their ability in the field was renowned, and more and more frequently they were bred to strengthen what were becoming inherited tendencies to go on point.

In 1872 Charles Darwin's *The Expression of the Emotions in Man and Animals* was published. In it Darwin wrote a piece called "The Tactics of Setting," which read as follows:

"Many carnivorous animals, as they crawl towards their prey and prepare to rush or spring on it, lower their heads and crouch, partly, as it would appear, to hide themselves, and partly to get ready for their rush; and this habit in an exaggerated form has become hereditary in our pointers and setters. Now I have noticed scores of times that when two strange dogs meet on an open road, the one which first sees the other, though at the distance of one or two hundred yards, after the first glance always lowers its head, generally crouches a little, or even lies down. . . that is, he takes the proper attitude for concealing himself and for making a rush or a spring, although the road is quite open and the distance great. Again, dogs of all kinds when intently watching and slowly approaching their prey, frequently keep one of their fore-legs doubled up for a long time, ready for the next cautious step; and this is eminently characteristic of the pointer. But from habit they behave in exactly the same manner whenever their attention is aroused."

In Darwin's *The Origin of Species*, he again expounded on the inherent hunting characteristics which had been so highly developed in these dogs. He wrote:

"It may be doubted whether any one would have thought of training a dog to point, had not some one dog naturally shown a tendency in this line; and this is known occasionally to happen, as I once saw, in a pure terrier: the act of pointing is probably, as many have thought, only the exaggerated pause of an animal preparing to spring on its prey. When the first tendency to point was once displayed, methodical selection and the inherited effects of compulsory training in each successive generation would soon complete the work; and unconscious selection is still in progress, as each man tries to procure, without intending to improve the breed, dogs which stand and hunt best. On the other hand, habit alone in some cases has sufficed —."

Be it habit or training or inherited tendencies, later in this chapter we will reveal the authenticated story of a dog whose skeleton was found in an Irish bog—on point—that had starved to death waiting for his master's command to return!

EARLY BLOODLINES

The Earl of Enniskillen went in for breeding Irish Red Setters in 1796, and in 1812 Jason Hazard (whose name appears in old books on the breed spelled with both single and douzle "z's") from Timaskee County, Fermanaugh, also believed in the attributes of the self-colored dogs and initiated a breeding program. As early as 1770, one of the oldest lines of Red Setters was founded by Maurice Nugent O'Connor. He was a staunch advocate of the solid reds, but his dogs did carry a trace of white on them and in turn produced get which also bore traces of white. O'Connor continued to breed the Red and White Setters also, and his kennel was regarded as an important one, so important that it was taken over by Robert La Touche of Harristown in 1818 when O'Connor died.

By the 1830's Sir St. George Gore had established a large kennel of self-reds, even though the Red and White Setters were continuing to hold their own in popularity among the fanciers. Some breeders were still cross breeding them with Gordon Setters. Gordon Setters were officially known as the Black and Tan Setter in those days and were producing, in many instances, undesirable self-blacks. There was tolerance for slight white markings during this evolution of the self-reds, but black was in no way condoned. Today black means a disqualification in the show ring if even a few black hairs are present.

In his early writings, Stonehenge (actually J.W. Walsh, the acknowledged and foremost dog authority of the day) wrote, "The blood red or rich chestnut or mahogany color is the color of an Irish Setter of high mark. This color must be unmixed with black; studied in a strong light, there must not be black shadows or waves, much less black fringes to the ears, or to the profile of the form."

This specific and emphatic mention of black on the dog would bear testimony to the theory that there was cross-breeding to the Gordon Setter in the breed.

It was during the first half of the 19th century that Captain Allan MacDonald of Scotland, whose name was also associated with the propagation of the Skye Terrier, became active in Irish Red Setters and bred into the early Ahascragh line, as did Jackson Lloyd and a Mr. Evans of Gortmerron, who was well known in Setter circles during this period.

Others who were dedicated to seeing the Irish Red Setter thrive during these important fifty years and can be found mentioned for their achievements in ancient chronicles on the breed are Charles O'Keeffe, Lord Howth, Lord Waterford, Lord Dillon, Lord Lismore, Lord Clancarty, Mr. Dunne of Brittas, Mr. Handy, Mr. Trumble and Mr. Reeves, both of Dublin, Sir Hill Barker, Mr. Oliver of Castle Oliver, Yelverton O'Keeffe, Sir Francis H. Loftus, Lord Anglesey, Lord Rossmore, the Misses Lidwell, Lord Forbes and the man referred to during this era as the "Father of the Breed," John G. King.

The French Park strain was well-known during this time, and no less than three generations of the Lord de Freyne family were active in the breeding of Irish Red Setters. It is also recorded that a brace of Red Setters was sold by a Mr. McCarthy of Spring House for two hundred pounds—a fantastic price at that time, and not bad even for today, more than a century later! The going price for an Irish Red Setter in those days was 100 guineas. This was said to be the going bid for the superior stock belonging to Sir John Blunden, Castle Blunden, County Kilkenny.

THE FIRST RED SETTER SHOW DOGS

It was inevitable that this attractive, active red dog would find its way into the spotlight to excel in yet another field. . . the dog show ring!

Ireland's first dog show was held in Dublin in 1864. The *Irish*

18

SETTER   COCKER

This reproduction of an 1840 print by Lizars illustrates the Setter and Cocker Spaniel of the times. From the collection of the author.

Times newspaper reported that the Dublin event "compared favorably with the English and Scottish shows." The first Irish Red Setter to earn the distinction of winning a first prize in an all-breed event was named simply "Bob." The year was 1860 and the show was the first event held at Birmingham, England, December 3rd and 4th.

Bob was whelped in 1859 and was owned by a Major Hutchinson. Second prize at this dog show went to Mr. Jones Carlo, a dog described as pug-headed and bearing a strong evidence of a cross to a Gordon Setter with its black ear fringes. While this Birmingham show was the first all-breed event for the Red Setters, actually the breed had competed at a show for Setters (27 entries) and Pointers (23 entries) at the Town Hall, Newcastle-on-Tyne, England, in June of 1859.

In addition to Major Hutchinson, Captain Alloway was a familiar figure in the show ring during the 1860's while showing his dogs, Alloways Grouse and Alloways Shot. Dr. Stone, who had been breeding Irish Red Setters for twenty-odd years, was showing a dog named Dash. In 1867 a dog named Ranger was the big show winner, and another of his claims to fame was that his sire was the aforementioned Bob, still held in high regard among Irish Red Setter people.

While there was much difference of opinion at the time on exactly what the ideal Irish Red Setter should look like—with some disagreeing even on the degree of perfection to be found in Bob—there was no denying he was a popular stud and made history as both a stud and as the first show dog of note. He did more than his share of winning even in those days, when ribbons were frequently withheld for lack of quality.

Another well-known Irish Red Setter, well known for many reasons including a most ignoble beginning, was Ch. Palmerston, owned by Mr. Cecil Moore of Omagh, County Tyrone. All of his life Palmerston was a poor eater and considered by Mr. Moore as being too small in size to be of value in his breeding program, and too fragile for the field. At five years of age he could have been purchased for five pounds, for Mr. Moore used the dogs for hunting and his prime concern was for substance and stamina rather than the beauty required for the show ring. Mr. Moore subsequently decided to drown Palmerston. Mr. Moore's friend T.M. Hilliard, a Red Setter enthusiast, pleaded for Palmerston's life at what is reported to have been the psychological moment when the dog was actually approaching a watery grave, and Cecil Moore relented. He gave Hilliard the dog with the provision that the dog be kept solely for show purposes.

Palmerston's championship became a matter of record in record time even though he was no longer considered a young dog suited for a career in the show ring. His ability as a stud dog also became a matter of record in record time. And the thin line of white on the dog's forehead became known as the "Palmerston strip," since it seemed to be a trademark he passed on to his progeny, and soon became the mark of distinction in the breed.

Palmerston is said to have weighed 64 pounds and possessed the now-popular long and narrow head. At least his head was what was considered to be almost excessively long and narrow at that time, since the majority of the Setters carried the thicker Spaniel skull and foreface. Apparently this "new narrow look" caught on, since Palmerston was used widely as a stud and his name appeared on the majority of pedigrees of important dogs during, and long after, his triumphant reign during the second half of the 1870's, thanks to the foresight of his benefactor, Mr. Hilliard.

In 1875 Mr. Hilliard sold a part interest in Palmerston to another Irish Red Setter fancier and dog judge who also recognized the dog's fine qualities and realized that his prepotency as a stud force would assure his place in Irish Setter history as heralding the Irish Setter as a genetically reliable variety of dog. Upon Palmerston's death on September 9, 1880, his head was mounted and displayed at New York City's Waldorf Astoria Hotel, courtesy of Hilliard's son, the hotel's manager. In 1918 it was given to the Irish Setter Club of America.

EARLY FIELD TRIAL IRISH RED SETTERS

Though the first field trial was held in 1865, 1891 is acknowledged to be the beginning of the Irish Red Setter's competing in earnest at official field trials. They had, of course, long been running and hunting with other sporting breeds and hunters and more than holding their own against all competition.

In spite of the many sportsmen who contended that the Reds were stubborn and headstrong, as well as hard to see in the fields, they more than proved themselves as excellent hunters and extremely obedient to their masters. This fact is borne out by the often-told story related in Anna Redlich's book *The Dogs of Ireland*. It tells the unforgettable tale of the finding of an Irish Setter skeleton discovered still "on point" over a year after his owner had lost him in a bog. This story is not too surprising to aficionados of the breed who know just how strong the instinct is. Stonehenge wrote in the early 1800's that he had seen with his own eyes a brace of Lord Foley's dogs remain on their point for indefinite time, or until exhausted for want of food. Others remained on point upwards of six hours. Stonehenge also bore out Darwin's theory by stating that training can induce a state of near catalepsy by a single word.

Field dogs were not then kept in covered runs but were kenneled outdoors, with not more than three or four braced together. Apparently they were so keen on working that if not thoroughly exercised they would pounce on one of the group and literally tear it to pieces. But field trial enthusiasts were a sturdy lot and not apt to be swayed by such happenings, and soon these field events were an established sport.

One of the first famous contenders at the trials was a dog named Wrestler; he competed regularly against any and all comers and was described by his "fans" as a tireless worker.

Just as the famous Ch. Palmerston reigned supreme in the show ring, a famous field dog named Plunket reigned in the fields. He was owned by the Reverend J. Cumming Macdona, a staunch supporter of the Irish Red Setter and a founder of the Kennel Club, London, in April 1873; he won distinction in the dog fancy for being the first Englishman to judge at an American dog show. Rev. Macdona was invited to judge Gordon Setters, Pointers, Mastiffs and St. Bernards at the first Westminster Kennel Club show in New York City in 1877—but not Irish Setters! So he brought some Irish Setters with him, and they were entered at this show.

In all fairness, we must give Plunket his due by allowing for his success in the show ring, but his true value was proved by his performances in the field.

Bred by the Reverend Robert O'Callaghan, Plunket was whelped in 1868 and was sired by a dog called Plunket's Beauty *ex* Macdona's Grouse. Grouse was a Bob daughter, and her mating with Beauty

At extreme left is Rev. J.C. Macdona at an early 19th century dog show with four of his Irish Setters depicted in this reproduction of an ancient lithograph.

brought together the valuable Hutchinson and La Touche bloodlines which proved to be such a winning combination. This combination also produced a dog called Rover, used by Stonehenge to illustrate the perfect example of the Irish Setter in his book *Dogs In The British Islands*.

Plunket was later purchased by Mr. R.L. Purcel Llewellin for 100 guineas. It was Mr. Llewellin who is credited with having created the field trial strain of English Setters at the time. He then sold Plunket for export to America at a net profit to Mr. Llewellin of 100 pounds!

The Rev. Robert O'Callaghan, in addition to Plunket, bred quite a roster of field trial winners before his demise in 1897. One of the greats was a bitch named Ch. Aveline, referred to as "the beautiful Aveline." Others were Fingal, Ch. Fingal III, Ch. Geraldine II, Ch. Shandon II and Ch. Boyne. This pack of worthy contenders were frequently run against those of his good friend C.C. Ellis of Suffolk. The Ellis pack consisted of Drogheda, Dartrey, Rossmore, Tarbat, Harlech and his most famous of all field dogs, Mac's Little Nell, bred by a Mr. MacGoff of Tralee, another prominent field trial enthusiast.

Ch. Milson O'Boy. When retired in 1938, he had a show record of 103 Bests of Breed, 46 Best Sporting Group wins and 11 Bests in Show (including Morris and Essex in 1935). O'Boy was also Best American-bred dog at Westminster in 1935. Handled exclusively by Harry Hartnett for owner Mrs. Cheever Porter of New York.

The Messrs. L.F. and R. Perrin of Kingstown owned a formidable contender named Maid of the West, part of a pack that included dogs named Hecktor, Wee Kate and Ch. Peaceful Times. Mr. J.G. Hawkes of Kenmare entered competition with his Muskerry, Ch. Signal, Miss Signal and a dog called Blue Rock, which boasted a first prize at the 1890 Birmingham show. Old field trial records show the triumphs and field wins of Ch. Ponto and Ch. Drenagh, owned by Major Jameson and of the famous Garryowen, sired by Ch. Palmerston *ex* Belle, owned by Major J.J. Giltrap, a dog judge and one-time Secretary of the Dublin Irish Red Setter Club and one of the authors of the first Irish Red Setter standard. Competition was provided by Captain J.K. Millner's winning line of field dogs; his Airnie made history as the winner of the 1892 Kennel Club Derby.

As the years passed other owners and field dogs made history and further established field trials as a popular outdoor sport in which our gorgeous Irish Red Setters continued to excel. A prominent kennel in the late 1800's was Wickham Market, owned by a Mr. Austin Austin, who made his mark with his Ch. Ben and Ch. Tim Sullivan. Records show a Mr. Swiney worked in the fields with his Ch. Jill and Ch. Donald MacSwine. Recorded also were the names of W.W. Despard of Rathmoyle, Falkiner Nuttall of Cullinamore, County Sligo, Mr. Waterhouse of Killiney, W. Hill Cooper (who owned a famous dog named Isinglass), Dr. Harrison of Bray, Gibbon Hawkes, the original owner of Ch. Punchestown, Mr. Bond of Derry, the Honorable Mrs. Bellew of Enniskerry and James Wright, an Irish gamekeeper who was also an important breeder of Red Setters.

Sir Humphrey F. de Trafford, a baronet, entered the sport at the close of the 19th century with his Barton Kennel Irish Setters. He bred and owned over twenty-five field and bench show champions including Nora, Flush, Judy, Barton Mick, Barton Punch, Ch. Camlough Bloom and the aforementioned and famous Ch. Punchestown, which later went to Dr. R. O'Callaghan, Rev. Robert O'Callaghan's son. Still later Punchestown went to H. Bertrand in Belgium.

The 1894 Birmingham Show cup was won by F.H. Bass's Irish Red Setter Cork's Blossom IV and was acclaimed as the best Setter for that year. In 1896 the Best Setter cup was again won by a Red Setter named Princess, from Dr. Harrison's Bray Kennel.

2. IRISH SETTERS IN ENGLAND IN THE 20TH CENTURY

While the Irish Red Setters were gaining steadily in popularity during the 1890's and into the 20th century in Ireland, genuinely dedicated breeders in England were still rather scarce. The Kennel Club in London registered a scant 289 for the year 1891, for example, and by World War I, registrations had dropped to 25. But once the war was over they once again picked up, and Irish Setter breeders registered over 300 by 1921. The Irish Red Setter boom in the 1930's swelled the ranks to over two thousand. They maintained a healthy balance until World War II, when they went into another decline.

When World War II was over the expected post-war boom which had followed the first World War never came about, since at this time a panic hit the fancy over the serious onset of what was referred to as night-blindness. The breed hit a post-war low in 1956, with a total of only 384 registrations at the Kennel Club. The following decade saw a steady climb back up as researchers conquered breeders' fears, and by the 1970's over 3,000 Irish Setters a year were being recorded.

PROMINENT FANCIERS AND DOGS, 1890-1920

The 1890's saw a decade of great successes for the magnificent Irish Red Setters owned and bred by Mrs. N. Ingle Bepler of Tottenham at her Rheola Kennels, which were to continue for the next three decades. Mrs. Bepler had taken over Rev. O'Callaghan's Brandeston Kennels when the vicar's health failed, and she won her first Challenge Certificate with his bitch named Winifred. Later the bitch became Ch. Winifred and competed for her victories during this important era, when Sir Humphrey was taking breed wins with his outstanding dogs. Winifred's championship was followed by her kennelmate's, Carrig Maid, a lovely bitch bred by A.E. Daintree in 1897.

In addition to Winifred, Carrig Maid and a bitch named Lady Honora, there were so many of Mrs. Bepler's Rheola champions finishing for their titles during this ten-year period that Mrs. Bepler lost count! Besides the bitches already mentioned, there also were Ch. Clancarty Rhu (imported from Holland), Didona, Dione, Daphne, Bryndona and Norma. Some of Mrs. Bepler's prominent males were Toby Bryn, Boniface and Benedict.

Mrs. Bepler's book on the breed, written in the late 1920's, contains the names and photographs of no fewer than eight generations of her breeding, starting with Ch. Winifred in 1898 up to and including Ch. Rheola Bryndona in 1928. Her contribution to the Irish Setter breed during this thirty-year period is truly remarkable and cannot be denied.

It was also Mrs. Bepler who presented the theory in her writings delineating three color varieties in the Irish Red Setter breed: the self-red from the north of Ireland, the red and white predominating in the south and west and the "shower of hail" or spotted variety, with their quarter-inch white spots, found on the west coast of Ireland.

Following the Rheola successes, Mrs. Eileen K. Walker devoted forty years to the breed. Her stock, founded largely on the Rheola dogs, reigned triumphantly for four decades and provided quality breeding which served as the basis of many other kennels during her time. Her Rheola-Loc Garmain breeding produced Hartsbourne Jade in 1927. Competition also came from impressive kennels such as those of Miss S. Lennox and her Brackenfield dogs, the O'Kilner Irish Red Setters owned by W.W. Poole and the Watenlath dogs of W.J. Rasbridge.

Along with the Bepler and Walker dogs which managed to successfully bridge the turning of the century there were the dogs of Mr. P. Flahive, which appeared in the show ring beginning in 1902. He showed Ch. Kerry Palmerston and Ch. Kerry Surprise. A Mr. Nelson, owner of the Carntynes, came along with Ch. Muckross Chief. This prominent Muckross prefix, known even today, was eventually transferred to a Mr. McDougall, owner of Ch. Stewartstown Chieftain. Three outstanding dogs, Ch. Deception, Ch. Peaceful Times and Amaranthus, under the capable piloting of Mr. Perrins of Kingstown, went on to become the foundation stock behind many pedigrees and important winners. Another well-known gentleman, Mr. McNamee, and his Tyrone Princess did their share of winning, and Princess's litter sister, Ch. Florizel, owned by Mr. W.A. McCandless of Londonderry, was among familiar representatives of the breed in the show ring.

The most outstanding bitch right after the turn of the century was Ch. Strabane Sally, whelped in 1904 by Dr. T.A. Baldwin. Described at the time as being "practically faultless," Sally was later sold to a Mr. Judd. A dog named Galahad, owned by Dr. Fuller and sired by Ch. Kerry Palmerston *ex* Strabane Sally, became known as the sire of more field and bench show winners than any other Irish Red Setter of his time.

During the first part of this century an ever-increasing number of dog fanciers became enamoured of the flashy Red Setters. One was J.A. Carbery.

Carbery was both a breeder and a judge and, with Mrs. Bepler, was one of the most important breeders right up to and through the 1920's. Mr. Carbery owned Ch. Oonagh of Boyne, the first recorded Irish Red Setter champion recorded under the rules of the Irish Kennel Club. His Barney of Boyne and Sarsfield of Boyne were champions of record numbers four and six. Mr. Carbery's Ch. Gadeland Neula of Boyne was the remarkable winner of more than two hundred prizes in open competition. Neula eventually went to Mrs. E.M. Baker's Gadeland Kennel, where she produced twelve winners in her first two litters for her new owner.

Neula whelped a litter sired by Ch. Rheola Bryn and also one by a top Bryn son, Ch. Shamus of Ballyshannon (owned by Miss Thorne-Baker). Between the two litters it can be said that these two sires and the dam are behind almost all of the present-day show dogs of the breed in Ireland and Britain.

During this first quarter of a century other breeders and exhibitors came into prominence. George Bennet showed his Ch. Gruagach and Tadg; Judge Monahan's Ravenhill dogs enjoyed great successes in the ring, as did the Corona dogs of P. O'Callaghan and the Glenariffs of S.G. Taylor. Mr. Taylor bred Glenariff Denis in 1912, and this dog was a prominent winner in the fields as well as on the bench. Mr. Taylor was a well-known breeder up until World War I, and had many champions to his credit.

1912 was also the year Runchamp Tab was bred by J. Coward. This bitch was later purchased by the late Hollis Wilson, a prominent American judge active in Irish Setters as a breeder and exhibitor. Hollis Wilson died in 1974 still loving the breed and enjoying especially his Irish Setter assignments.

Show catalogs during this period listed the names of exhibitors such as the Messrs. Quinn and Mortell, Miss Peggy Kelly, Miss M. Kiernan, Captain W. Kennis, T. Clayton, Mrs. M. Dwyer, Mrs. W. Richardson, S. Stewart, Lady Harman, Mr. and Mrs. R.J. Vint and the Marchioness of Waterford.

Another member of the clergy came into prominence at this time also as an exhibitor of Irish Red Setters. He was the Reverend J. McMenamin, and he competed against the breeders mentioned above as well as the W.T. Devenny dogs, those of Mrs. S. Smith, Mr. and Mrs. Dunne, Mr. Shannon, P.J. McNamera and the Matson House Irish Setters bred by Mrs. P. Selwyn.

One of the top competitors was the famous Ch. Menaifron O'Moy. He was a big winner for Mrs. Margery Ogden's Borrowdale Kennels, though the Menaifron kennel name belonged to Mrs. M. Holt. Mr. and Mrs. H.E. Whitwell became famous for their Ardagh prefix, and a Mrs. Morse came on the scene with her Croftdown dogs.

27

Mrs. Florence Nagle, an Irish Wolfhound breeder, who along with her Sulhamstead kennel name is well-known in the Irish Wolfhound fancy in America, was devoted to the handsome red sporting dogs also. Her kennel of Irish Setters stemmed from the Challenge Certificate-winning Ben d'Or, a son of the well-known Gorse of Auburn, who in turn was a son of the celebrated stud dog Galahad, mentioned earlier as having sired more field and bench show winners than any other dog of his day.

Malting was the kennel name of Mrs. I.C. Mathews, and the Cymwrans name identified the dogs of Mr. and Mrs. Yeoward's Irish Red Setters; Hundridge was the name chosen by Lieutenant Colonel F.C. Lewis to carry his bloodlines to prominence in the show ring.

The short time from 1912 until the war broke out in Europe saw several top Irish Red Setters come to fame in the ring. The aforementioned Glenariff Denis started his show ring career in 1912, in 1913 there was Auburn Nellie bred by Dr. L.O. Fuller, and in 1914 Tipperary Bhoy (from the Rheola stock) won a great deal for owner Miss W.L. Dance. During the war (1915) Windsor Sensation was born, bred by Dr. T.A. Baldwin and later owned by T. Clayton; 1916 was marked by the successful breeding which produced Ch. Gruagach, and in 1917 Maga was bred by the Boyne Kennels of Mr. Carbery, later to be sold to Mrs. R. Douglas Deas and become the foundation of her famous Heatherick kennel. In 1919 T.J. Monahan whelped future Ch. Ravenhill Sally. 1919 was also the year J.E. Bayley bred Lady Lustre, owned later by R. Smales.

During this important era in Irish Red Setters we must also include the name of Mr. and Mrs. D.M. Cucksey of the Maydorwill kennel, General and Mrs. R.N. Foote, who exhibited under the Beorcham name, and Mrs. J.M. Roberts with the Corneven line.

The vast number of other breeders, exhibitors and one-dog fanciers who joined the devoted group of Irish Red Setter devotees are too numerous to mention here. Their numbers and accomplishments are legion. Suffice to say that it was also their dedication and endeavor which brought the Irish Red Setter into the prominence it was enjoying around this period.

Then this "run on the Reds" came to a resounding halt, and breeding stopped almost entirely except in the breed's native Ireland. Almost immediately upon cessation of the war, there was new impetus to get back into the fields and show ring once again, to such an extent that the Kennel Club took note and, to protect the breed from deterioration in the face of such fantastic growth in popularity, passed a rule which decreed that no gun-dog could be awarded a championship unless it had first been given a working certificate won in the field, in addition to earning three Challenge Certificates under three different judges at dog shows recognized by the Kennel Club. This the Club believed would assure dogs of sound conformation as well as dogs that possessed the spirit and hunting abilities required of a true sporting dog.

IRISH RED SETTERS IN THE 1920's

The 1920's felt the "boom" of the postwar popularity of the Irish Red Setters. The Rheola and Boyne kennels, important during the first twenty years of the century, really came into their own during this decade, to such an extent that many of their dogs were the basis of the kennels which also came into prominence during the 1920's.

The O'Kilner line, for instance, owned by Mr. and Mrs. W.W. Poole of Lancaster, and J.E. Sayer's Gramsceugh dogs stemmed from the Rheola bloodlines. The Pooles owned Bloompat, an Irish Red Setter which was said to have been stolen from Ireland, since it was valuable for being one of the "shower of hail" fleck-coated Irish Setters indigenous to the west coast of Ireland.

The Ardagh line and the name of H.E. Whitwell came into their own in 1922 at the time when the Boyne Kennels produced the Ch. Oonagh Florrie and Ch. Barney dogs. Ch. Terry of Boyne won his championship title in 1922 and was exported to the United States in 1923. This dog was behind the stock which was to bring the Nutbrown and Wendover kennels to prominence during the 1930's.

Major O'Kelly was breeding top-winning Irish Red Setters during the mid-1920's, and P.J. O'Callaghan's Corona dogs were winning nicely. P.J. O'Callaghan was no relation to the O'Callaghans who had been important several years earlier. Mr. Helliwell came into prominence in the early 1920's with his Norland dogs also.

The 1920's were also the years for the show-winning dogs carrying the Hymany name used by M.L. Colahan, and Mrs. McKeever came along with her Derrycarne Kennels.

A colorful print, published in 1820 by T. McLean of London, featuring Irish Setters of more than a century ago. From the collection of the author.

In 1922 Mrs. C.S. Darley (known at that time as Miss Ward and identified with her Boisdale strain), appeared on the scene with Carrickfergus of the Mill and Watermill Brenda. She bred Brenda herself, and this beautiful bitch was lauded as having one of the best heads at this time. She won many Bests of Opposite Sex wins during her show career, although she carried a little too much weight to take the top win. Brenda was sired by Miyaba *ex* Watermill Bridget. Mrs. Darley, who has put in over fifty years in the breed, has written about her beloved Irish Setters and has served as a President of the Irish Setter Association of England.

W. O'Bolger's Loc Garmain dogs were still very much in evidence during the 1920's, though Mr. Bolger's fame dated back to the 1890's in both Irish Setters and Irish Water Spaniels. He was perhaps best known for his bitch Norland Blossom, but the Loc Garmain bloodline is behind most of England's top Irish Setters today.

The latter years of the decade were winning times for Mrs. A. Ashworth, owner of the Halcana dogs, and for Sir Valentine Grace and his Ch. Ravelhill Meta. Mrs. E.D. Heron also made a mark with some of her O'Crane dogs. In the field W.J. Patterson was winning with his F.T. Ch. Rhu Gorse. The Dodmans from Scotland were part of this winning time and still are active almost fifty years later with their Irish Setters in Scotland.

All of these Irish Setters and their owners were scoring in the rings, but the big boom in the breed was to come. . . the 1930's were to bring the Irish Setter into even greater prominence.

THE 1930's

The W.W. Pooles' Crispian O'Kilner started off the decade with a major triumph for the Irish Red Setters. He won the famous Crufts show, the most important and certainly the biggest dog show in the world. He was the sire of nine Challenge Certificate winners out of six different bitches. Menaifron Pat O'Moy came into his own during this decade, and the Carbery dogs were still winning at the shows.

Gadeland and Hartsbourne dogs of Mrs. E.K. Walker were still much in the show news, as was Miss D. Woodhouse in 1933 for winning Challenge Certificates with her Norma of Settnor bitch, and Miss I. Hoffmann in 1934 with Bridget O'Ivanhoe.

The Wendover Kennels owned by Mr. and Mrs. L.C. James and the Nutbrown Kennels of Miss Manuelle came into their own in the 1930's along with all the others which had managed to build up the fame and successes of this marvelous breed.

Jean Samms won her first Challenge Certificate in 1936 with her lovely bitch Norland Susan. Miss Samms later took the kennel suffix "of Oosh" to identify her dogs, but not until after she had bred her first litter (in 1941). This initial litter produced a dog named Brans-

An English show winner in the 1950's. . . Bodewell Copperlass, daughter of show champion Bodewell Beginagen **ex** show Ch. Copperplate of Ide. Owned and bred by Mr. T.J. Harper, Bodewell Kennels, Kent, England.

English show dog Dallinghoo Ebenezer "looking the field over." Bred and owned by Mrs. C.M. Girling, Dallinghoo Kennels, England.

combe Robyn, which had a considerable influence on the Irish Setters which came along after World War II. She also bred Ch. Giselle of Oosh and Paprika of Oosh. Miss Samms later became the wife of Gilbert Leighton-Boyce.

Gilbert Leighton-Boyce was the son of Mrs. E.F. Leighton-Boyce. Mrs. Boyce registered her first Irish Setter, Red Ginger, in 1932 after her first litter, which produced a quality bitch named Welby Beauty. While Mrs. Boyce never campaigned her Irish Setters extensively, just showing in and around the London area, she was well known as one of the breed's greatest boosters and became a judge for championship shows in 1957. Mrs. Boyce also bred Ch. Norlan Paddy out of a litter sister of Miss Samm's Ch. Giselle of Oosh, named Norlan Odette of Oosh.

With an early childhood attending the famous Crufts and Crystal Palace dog shows by his mother's knee it was only natural for Gilbert Leighton-Boyce to continue in the breed he also admired so much. Mr. Boyce is the author of a book titled *Irish Setters* and in 1952 he became Honorary Treasurer of the Irish Setter Breeders Club, a position he held for about five years. He went on to judging in 1956 and began awarding Challenge Certificates at championship shows in 1969.

Others in the show ring during the 1930's were Mrs. Flora Banks and her Casamia dogs, Mrs. J. Clarke of the Brynmount kennels, Miss B.J. Johnson and the well-known Kyrewood dogs, the Badley dogs of Mrs. E.V.M. Freshwater, Mrs. M. Moody and her Elmford line, Miss Methuen and her Seaforde dogs, Miss Crawford and her Dochra, Miss Moorhouse and her Shaunavon winners.

Also winning their share of the honors were H.T. Stonex with his Lydeard dogs, N.W. Morrish of Stephenshill Kennels, J.G. Petherick, Glyncoed, Mrs. C.E. Rice, Llantarnum, Mrs. V. Richard, Miklebuffe, the Robinsons of Tremont kennels, and Miss Russling of the Minty line.

And the 1930's were the years that Mrs. M.E. Stokes was exhibiting her Marrona dogs, along with her famous bitch, Matsonhouse Mist, bred by Mrs. Selwyn. Any discussion of the 1930's would not be complete without including the names of Mrs. M.V. Christian's Ballymoy dogs, or J.A.L. Wenger's Rattlin line, and the Ide dogs of J.H.J. Braddon. J. Whitaker also did his share of winning with his Gaelge line and Miss R. Lamb introduced her line during the late 1930's.

The Wendovers won Best of Breed at Crufts in 1938 with their Irish import Portlairge Steady of Wendover, and also won with Wag of Wendover.

By the 1930's the gorgeous mahogany Irish Red Setter was firmly established as a breed—almost unchallenged in beauty in the canine world, virtually unexcelled in performance in the field, incomparable in disposition and loyalty, and admired by all who loved dogs.

Then came World War II. Most of Europe and the British Isles felt the crunch. Shows and trials and breeding once again came to a grinding halt with only the very smallest degree of breeding going to preserve the breed. In Europe hungry people were forced in some cases to eat dog meat to prevent their own starvation. Large breeds suffered most and in some cases entire kennels were wiped out by lack of food, and sad owners put down their dogs rather than watch them slowly starve. In some instances breeding was done but only under the veil of secrecy and to preserve valuable bloodlines.

All across Europe it was not until after World War II and almost into the 1950's that the Irish Setters were once again in full swing and conquering the dog show world—on both sides of the Atlantic.

IRISH SETTERS ABROAD FROM THE END OF WORLD WAR II TO NOW

Many of the prominent breeders from the pre-war years were back in the ring again soon after hostilities ceased. There were some newcomers to the breed as well. Mrs. Nagle and Mrs. Laughton-Moore returned to the scene, as did the Myre, Kyrewood and Watermill dogs. Mrs. Thorne Baker was back in the spotlight as a judge at this point in time. The Misses E.A. and F.E. Stokes were active with what they now called their Goonbell Setters. In 1956 a Green Star winner in Ireland named Jane of Sallyrobyn came out successfully with her breeder of long standing, Mr. W.P. Craven.

In addition to the old guard, Eagletop Kennels, owned by I.B. MacQuarrie, entered the picture, as well as the Clympmoor Kennel dogs of Mrs. V. Dennis, most prominent of which was her Biddy of Coppeen. Jean Samms was off to an impressive start with her Paprika of Oosh; Paprika won a Reserve Best of Sex win at Birmingham and two Firsts at Crufts. Pressures of business for both Mr. and Mrs. Gilbert Leighton-Boyce necessitated the withdrawal of Paprika just as she was reaching the peak of her career.

Perhaps one of the most significant events in the Irish Setter world during the 1950's occurred in 1958 when Mrs. Walker imported American Champion Erinhaven Dennis Muldoon from the United States. He was considered a valuable outcross and immediately commanded the highest stud fee in the breed up to that time. Among his impressive offspring was Miss S.J. Lennox's Brackenfield Dandelion, who was successfully tested and found clear of progressive retinal atrophy (PRA). The sire was unfortunately blamed for reintroducing the condition to the breed.

Dennis Muldoon went on to sire six Challenge Certificate winners, in spite of this claim, and was the grandsire of Mrs. J.E. Coates' Musbury Melasande of Twoacres and, through Mrs. V. Page's Orichalc Freyja (also tested clear of PRA), of Ch. Brackenfield Orichalc Juniper.

Musbury Magnus, First Prize winner at Crufts and sire of Musbury Melisande of Two Acres. Melisande is famous in the breed in England as the dam of four show champions in one litter. Owned by the W. Foulds, Musbury Irish Setters, Lancashire, England.

In the 1960's the Brackenfield dogs were to become a major force in Irish Setters. Also the Wendover Kennels continued to excel through the successful results of their carefully-planned long-term breeding program and their Joao and Kevin dogs.

A remarkable succession of winners came along bearing their name, including the 1970's winner Ch. Wendover Gentleman, which may even come to top the record held by their famous stud Wendover Beggar. Mrs. Roberts' bitch, Ch. Cornevon Snowstorm, was shown in 1963 and traced back to several important lines.

Names such as Miss O.M. Hunt and her dog Sowerhill Winsford Robert and the Misses Tomlison with their Ch. Norlan Paddy are capturing ribbons in the ring in the 1970's. When Mrs. Walker died in 1970, her well-known and successful Hartsbourne line was taken over by Miss Lennox, who carried on the famous bloodlines Mrs. Walker had acquired over the many years she was active in the breed.

Other names and kennels popular in the 1970's included Mrs. Parson's Thurnbrook dogs, Mr. and Mrs. Welfore's Lyghe Irish Setters and Mr. and Mrs. Stephen's Bidford dogs. Mrs. Lewis-Murison showed her Gowerlands line, and the H.B. Oakes dog Achates of Thurnbrook came into the limelight. Also Mrs. R.D. Passmore's Kyrene line came to the fore, as did Miss J.M. Russel and her Ballyweston strain. Mrs. Bryden's Scotswood Kennels were represented in the

The English Setter Musbury Mustard, winner of 1 Challenge Certificate and 2 Reserve C.C.'s. Mustard is litter brother to Musbury Meteor, exported to the U.S.A. in 1967. Owned by Mr. and Mrs. W. Foulds, Musbury Kennels, Lancashire, England.

English Champion Raycroft Call Boy was sired by South African Ch. Hartsbourne Kerry **ex** English Ch. Raycroft Bramble. Call Boy is the winner of 17 championships and many Groups. Bred and owned by Mrs. C.E. Furness of Derbyshire, England.

English Champion Bodewell Beginagen, pictured winning at the 1957 Blackpool show. Sired by the famous Ch. Wendover Beggar **ex** Maydorwill Shadow Girl, Beginagen was the winner of 9 Challenge Certificates. Owned by Mr. T.J. Harper, Bodewell Kennels, Kent, England.

English show Champion Raycroft Pirate, bred and owned by Mrs. C.E. Furness, Raycroft Irish Setters, Derbyshire, England. Pirate is the sire of Int. Ch. Raycroft Hoobram Rich Corona, winner of 18 championships. Pirate's sire was Ch. Raycroft Rowdy **ex** Ch. Raycroft Hartsbourne Perdita.

Musbury Muffin, First Prize winner at Crufts, the largest dog show in the world. Owned by Mr. and Mrs. W. Foulds, Musbury Kennels, Lancashire, England. Muffin is litter mate to Musbury Mustard, an English winner, and to Musbury Meteor, exported to the United States in 1967.

English show winner Marrona Malachite of Bodewell, Best in Show winner at the Irish Setter Breeders Club event in 1973. Sired by English Ch. Scotswood Barrabas **ex** Marrona Marstock Witch, Malachite is the winner of 1 Challenge Certificate and 2 Reserve C.C.'s during the 1971-1974 show seasons. Owned by Mr. T.J. Harper of the Bodewell Kennels, Kent, England.

Brackenfield Shamus, winner of 1 Challenge Certificate and 2 Reserve C.C.'s in England. Shamus is the sire of Mr. and Mrs. W. Foulds' Musbury Mustard, Musbury Muffin and Musbury Meteor.

show ring, along with the Joanmas dogs of Mrs. Jarosz; Miss B. Worth showed Ch. Heathcliffe Jason, Miss R. Carruthers had her Viana dogs, G.S. Coupes had the Timadon strain, and Mr. and Mrs. Davis' Castleoak bitches were winners.

The 1970's have also produced winning dogs from the Fernley Kennels of Mr. and Mrs. B.F. Rhodes; Mr. and Mrs. W. Foulds' Musbury line; Mr. and Mrs. L.S. Drage's Birchmoor Irish Setters; Rev. and Mrs. E.B. Grant, Audrey and John Harper, Mr. and Mrs. T.J. Holden with their Rebbin Red Setters, Mrs. June Bush, Rev. C.R.B. Coleman and dogs of the Misses L.J. and E. Coleman breeding, bearing the Hartswelin name. Mrs. H.B. Anderson was maintaining a small kennel of championship show-winning stock, as was Mrs. S.C. Coles and her Vylias line.

English show dog Dallinghoo Candida, by Wendover Superman **ex** Wendover Hope. Candida is owned by Mrs. C.M. Girling, Dallinghoo Kennels, Beds., England. Photographed in 1971.

Three marvelous English Irish Setter puppies bred and owned by Mrs. C.E. Gurness, Raycroft Kennels, Derbyshire, England. Note the great quality and beautiful heads, even at this tender age.

An Irish Setter in Belgium. . . Russetmanor Dame Morgwse, bred and owned by Mr. and Mrs. Guy Francis of Tavier, Belgium. "Suki" is pictured here in the field in the autumn of 1973. Her sire was Belgian Ch. Cornevon Snowstorm *ex* Avalong Sheba. She was whelped in April, 1967.

The 1970's have seen the names of Mrs. V. Banks, Miss C. Besford, Mr. and Mrs. W. Ashton, J. and K. Capstick, Mr. and Mrs, C.M. Girling (Dallyhoo), Mrs. E.A. Holder (Applecourt), Mrs. Yvonne Horrocks (Green Meadows), Mr. and Mrs. D.W. McCartney, Mrs. K. and Miss J. Norman, Mrs. C.F. O'Callaghan, Mr. and Mrs. W. Webb and Mrs. S.M. Webb, the C. Tonkyns, the D.S. Wades, Mr. B.G. Pirie, Mrs. S.M. Rootes, Mrs. M.B. Rampton, and Mrs. M.E. Stokes.

Even in a book of this size it would be impossible to name every one of the exhibitors and breeders who have contributed to Irish Setter progress over the decades. However, we have included the more prominent or active kennels, those with a top winning dog or bitch, and many names of the longtime fanciers as well as those still active in the breed today.

For any that we might have overlooked we regret the omission and assure you it was not deliberate, since we owe a debt of gratitude to everyone who has ever done anything to further the appreciation of this marvelous breed.

3. EARLY FIELD TRIALS ABROAD

When the famous artists of the 17th, 18th and 19th centuries weren't painting royalty in full court regalia, bedecked in their satins, brocades and laces with the crown jewels upon them and holding their little lap dogs, they were devoting their time and talents to painting the lush British countryside with the Pointers and Setters pursuing game they had flushed or on point awaiting their master's commands while hunting in the field.

We know that field competitions have been great sport ever since the first two men and their dogs appeared in a field together to see whose dog could run the game first. However, the first written record of hunting dogs being used for competitive sport appeared in the *London Gazette* in 1681. For the next hundred years these hunting matches were made and came to be a regularly organized sports event in British country life.

Written records are to the effect that these matches between various kennels were for the purpose of testing speed and endurance. The field trials as we know them today only began to resemble today's field trials around 1850 when a Joshua Logan, a birddog enthusiast of that era, made an appeal for officially recognized and officially organized events for sportsmen. He was not successful until after more than a decade of campaigning and editorializing in the sporting journals of the day on behalf of himself and other hunting dog owners. He did receive additional support in 1857, when J.H. Walsh (Stonehenge) became editor of *The Field* and published many editorials calling for field trials. In 1864 a Mr. John Douglas took it upon himself to stage the first officially recognized field trial. He wrote the rules, invited the judges, and put up all the prize money. It was the first positive step in the right direction!

"BREAKING" THE IRISH SETTER FOR THE FIELD IN TIMES PAST

Before 1850 many of the prominent hunters of the day relied on dog-dealers to field train or "break" their dogs, or to supply their packs with dogs which had already been trained and broken. As time went on, many of the owners had become so involved with field work that they actually preferred to break their own dogs, though the methods and procedures on just how to accomplish this were not common knowledge.

However, with the idea of doing their own training, a brand new idea, in the spring of 1858 *The Field* published certain basic observations on how to accomplish this training. Furthermore, it had become an expensive proposition to have dogs professionally trained, and the sportsmen came to the conclusion that they would rather spend the training money on buying quality puppies for their packs and doing their own breaking.

In the beginning they required the assistance and advice of a keeper who had done breaking himself, and who sometimes assisted the sportsmen in seeing to it that they secured only the best possible prospects to begin with.

THE ACTUAL TRAINING

Sportsmen hunted with a brace of dogs, the brace consisting of four dogs. And while the brace was always prepared for hunting in the field there was a brace and a half being trained to supplement the already existing pack. This also allowed for replacements in the existing pack and allowed for dropouts or defects in the dogs going through the training process. These specially chosen puppies were fed according to the best available diet known at the time and were carefully housed and watched over as part of the training for the field.

Training commenced near the end of January each year and continued until each dog was ready to join a pack or was mustered out for lack of ability. The dogs were taken out on virtually empty stomachs in the belief that too much food affected their ability or desire to keep on the scent.

Puppies were "walked out" early and taught as soon as possible to learn their name and that each command would be preceded by their name; they learned to heel, to run forward and to lie down and stay down on command, and were taught strict adherence to orders. Occasionally guns were shot off over their heads to prevent their being gun-shy at maturity.

The trainers, also called "breakers," began teaching the puppies restraint by placing tidbits of food before them and restraining them with the word "toho." Restraint was an important part of the training so that later when they came upon the game in the field they would not damage or devour it, since the dog's instinct or desire for game should be greater than its appetite for food if it was going to be a hunting dog.

This restraint was not as difficult to teach as might be imagined, unless breakers went too far with the dietary limitations and the underfed dogs became ravenous. Just to be sure, if they had any doubts during the early training, they made use of a device known as a puzzle-peg, though do not ask why it was called this. The puzzle-peg prevented the dogs from actually taking the game into their mouths. Its use was limited, since the training for the field was based upon voice commands. Since many puppies were taught with the aid of a check-cord to drop and stay down when guns were discharged, they could be reeled in should they seem to want to pick up the game.

With these preliminaries mastered, the "range" was taught, which was the most difficult aspect of breaking. It is most desirable for the dog to hunt freely; he should range only when and where directed and should not depend on other dogs to find the scent or allow them to detract him from the scent. The younger dogs were taken into the fields with the older, more experienced dogs to learn this routine. And once they had learned the "follow the leader" idea the younger dogs were hunted on their own until they also began to point on their own. Then they were hunted in pairs, and eventually became part of the brace of four.

This did not usually happen until they had also learned to "quarter" the ground, with the dog being "down wind." This assured that the dog was learning to hunt on body scent as well as by foot scent. The good hunter, who waited for orders, with a competent master, managed very well on both counts. But only really proficient hunters and packs were successful, for the instinct to hunt has to be bred into the dog. The master merely develops it and puts it to use. The dog's job was to learn how to find game on its own and to stand steady over it on point.

BREAKING TO RETRIEVE

Even though almost every dog in the world loves to "fetch" — which is another word for retrieve — actual retrieving of game in early times was usually restricted to certain dogs specially trained for this purpose. In addition to pointing they were taught to stay down until given the command "Seek dead," and then to "peg" the bird with a steady point.

The "Seek dead" command was usually used only on injured game and could spoil a dog for pointing if the dog were not ready for such advanced training. Since it was seldom advantageous or necessary to send a dog after wounded or lost game, getting Irish Setters to retrieve was not too widely practiced. The development of the Labrador Retriever and other retrieving breeds made the use of the Setters for this purpose virtually unnecessary, and many believed even then that the use of Setters for retrieving impaired their steadiness for their natural work in pointing. The fetch and carry command, with an inexperienced or hard-bitten Setter, often ruined the game beyond use, as it was brought back between the dog's clenched jaws.

Endless patience is required for field training, and many hours are required for the actual developing of the natural instincts to produce a capable hunting dog that will come anywhere near perfection in the pursuit of a field trial title.

FIELD TRIALS IN 20TH CENTURY ENGLAND

The 1930's and 1940's did not produce much activity in the field trials as far as Irish Setters were concerned. The only notable worker during the 1940's was Boisdale Rococo, an import that scored highly as a dual purpose dog.

Mrs. Holt and her Menaifron dogs and Mrs. Florence Nagle with her Sulhamsteads were most active, though after Mrs. Holt's death her dogs were given over to Mrs. Roslin-Williams. Mrs. Nagle continued to be extremely successful, and a great tribute was paid to her in Gilbert Leighton-Boyce's book, *Irish Setters,* where he said, ". . . Mrs. Nagle had strength enough in her kennel to carry on with the incredible string of successes, almost certain to remain unsurpassed in the British history of the breed, stretching from the 1920's to the 60's."

English Champion Boisdale Boggit on point on partridges. Owned and trained by Mrs. Darling of Devon, England.

It was during the 1960's that Mrs. Nagle decided to curtail her activities upon the retirement of her handler, only to be faced with yet a new generation of potential winners to compete against the rest of the Setters! These dogs were, in most cases, also winning in the show ring!

Dr. Beazley's field trial Ch. Ridge of Firbanks was the perfect example of a show dog which was also an exceptionally good worker in the field. So was Miss S.J. Lennox's Ch. Brackenfield Hartsbourne Bronze and two others, Ridgetor Derrycarne Peach Brandy and her grandsire Derrycarne Red Admiral of Rye.

H.E. Taylor handled Ch. Boisdale Boggit to a First at one trial and to Certificates of Merit at others during 1960. Taylor considered him to be the greatest dual purpose Irish Setter since Ch. Barney of Boyne.

In 1970 the Irish Setter Association elected a field trial sub-committee of five persons in response to a proposal by Colonel Balding, who worked his Irish and English "Flashaway" Setters. The committee consisted of Dr. Beazley, Captain Bennett (Tomani Kennels), Mr. Peter Heard (Dunroon), Mrs. Jarosz (Joanma's), and Mrs. Mason (Acornbank).

While interest continues on a small but dedicated level in England today, it is a matter of record that the English field trial enthusiasts almost always have to "take a back seat" when the Irish trainers come over to England for competition!

IRISH KENNEL CLUB FIELD CHAMPIONS OF RECORD

Two field trials were held by the Irish Kennel Club in their first year in 1922, but it wasn't until June of 1929 that the Irish Kennel Club issued its first field trial championship to an Irish Setter. The dog was Menaifron Meane O'Moy. In 1935 the second Irish Setter, Ann of Aileach, was issued her diploma.

A complete list of Irish Kennel Club recognized Irish Setter field trial champions are listed here up to and including 1973: 1929: Menaifron Meane O'Moy, owner not listed; 1935: Ann of Aileach, owner not listed; 1937: Curraghmore Biddy, Marchioness of Waterford; 1939: Garry of Burton, Mr. A.L. Spiers; 1940: Dunboy Rock, Dr. W.M. O'Sullivan; 1941: Redskin of QU'Appelle, Mr. P.B. Galwey-Foley; 1946: Tremont Dreamland of QU'Appelle, Mrs. Robinson; 1947: Tremont Stut, Mrs. Robinson; 1949: Red Spinner, Mr. R.W. Barry; 1949: The Blacksmith, Mr. P.J. McNamara; 1952: Derrycarne Red Admiral of Rye, Mr. W.T. McMenamin; 1956: Fermanagh St. Rua, Mr. P.F. Goodwin; 1957: Prince of Kilmurray, Mr. D.V. Fitzgerald; 1957: Roscomrobe Red Grouse, Mr. D. McMenamin; 1957: Moanruad Chilly Breeze, Mr. John Nash; 1957: Clanwilliam Rex, Dr. R.D.

Field Trial Champion Sherry Bowl, winner of the Irish Champion Stake at Ballyfin, Ireland, in 1969. Sherry is pictured here on point in the field. Owned and trained by R.P. Stakelum of Tipperary, Ireland. Sherry died recently at the age of 11 years.

Seale; 1957: Sherry, Mr. A.L. Spiers; 1959: Rahard Belle, Mr. P.G. Goodwin; 1960: Punch Bowl, Mr. Thomas J. Kennedy; 1961: Moanruad Admiral, Mr. Peadar Murnane; 1961: Rusty of Televara, Mr. R.P. Stakelum; 1963: Una Moanruad, Mr. John Nash; 1964: Cahir Miss Chips, Mr. Denis Hanley; 1965: Sliev Eibawn Minnie, Mr. R.A. Stewart; 1968: Sherry Bowl, Mr. Robert Stakelum; 1968: Moylrath Blaze, Messrs. R. Stakelum & O'Connor; 1968: Latton Blarney, Rev. L. Marron; 1969: Galtee Grouse, Rev. R.J. Dineen; 1969: Bena of Maytown, Mr. John Nash; 1969: Moanruad Latton Jewel, Mr. John Nash; 1970: Knockmore Mona, Mr. S. Denneby; 1970: Moanruad Sprite, Mr. John Nash; 1970: Moanruad Dan, Mr. John Nash; 1970: Red Revolution of Fallows, Mr. E.J. Cunningham; 1970: Moanruad Kaye, Mr. John Nash; 1972: Cleo of Maytown, name not supplied; 1972: Knockmore Red Molly, name not supplied; 1973: Hopeful Betsey, Mr. Robert Stakelum.

Hopeful Betsey, a successful contender in 1973 for field trial championship in Ireland. She is pictured here with her owner and trainer, Mr. R.P. Stakelum of Tipperary, Ireland, and 13 of the magnificent trophies won during the 1973 season. Mr. Stakelum claims Betsey to be one of the greatest field trialers under Irish conditions despite her small size. Mr. Stakelum is the treasurer of the Irish Red Setter Club in Ireland.

Two other names were supplied by the Irish Kennel Club for field trial champions, those of Heathericks Gaiar and Rhu Gorse, but the year the title was earned and the names of the owners were not included with the rest.

OBEDIENCE TRAINING IN ENGLAND IN MODERN TIMES

Both obedience and field trial work increased in popularity in England after World War II, though in no way could it compare with what we enjoyed in this country when it first caught on in the mid-1930's.

Even though field work had always been popular and widespread, obedience training did provide a challenge to those who kept these active dogs in small houses or apartments with no outdoor kennel facilities. So while there was intent and purpose among a select few, obedience for Irish Setters got off to a rather slow start.

The first obedience awards were won in the mid-1950's by Mrs. Malloch with her dog Boisdale Bob. Miss Cooke was working with Giselle of Oosh and Miss H. Wise had her Copperbright Shaun in training. Mr. Errington had Hartsbourne Pansy and a bitch named Hartsbourne Purros Petula that won her C.D. in 1957 and went on to the C.D.X. in September, 1958 in the Senior B Stakes of the Associated Sheep, Police and Army Dog Society's working trials in Sussex.

By the 1960's there were less than a dozen or so fanciers competing in obedience, but that small group included Mr. and Mrs. Kyffin with their Wonderkip of Norwood, winner of a Reserve Challenge Certificate at the Birmingham show in 1960 and sire of Dr. Jamieson's field trial winner, Noctorum Red Regal. Miss J. Rolfe and Norlan Diarmid joined the ranks of obedience pioneers during this initial period also.

Mr. Foy of the famous Kinsman of Chatham line did perhaps more than anyone else to prove that working Irish Setters in both field and obedience could be successfully accomplished.

4. THE IRISH SETTER IN AMERICA

During the second half of the 19th century, as word of the successes of the beautiful Irish Red Setters in both show and field reached our shores, interest grew in the breed. Americans began descending on Britain and Ireland in droves to buy into this exciting "new" breed. The sky was the limit on the amount of money the American dog fanciers would pay for the foreign show winners. They just about bought up all that was worthwhile on the European market in the hope of setting the dog world on its ear in the U.S.A.

FIRST AMERICAN SHOW APPEARANCES OF IRISH SETTERS

On June 6, 1874 P.H. and David Bryson of Memphis, Tennessee took an ad in the Philadelphia-based *Field and Stream* publication announcing a dog show and field trial to be held on Monday, October 7, 1874, in Memphis, for Pointers and Setters. This inaugural event was the first combined bench and field trial ever held in the U.S.A. and was to be sponsored by the Tennessee Sportsmen's Association.

Similar attempts at staging dog shows were announced for June 2 in Chicago and June 22 at Oswego, New York, but these shows were so poorly attended that judges merely commented on the few dogs present (at one show just two) and returned the prize money. The Illinois State Sportsmens Association also tried to "jump the gun" on the Brysons by holding a show on June 4 of that year. They drew 21 entries of Pointers and Setters. Also, on the very same day as the Bryson's October 7 event, there was also a show held in Mineola, New York; this show was equally unsuccessful.

But the Brysons' show could be said to be successful—especially for the Brysons. On the day of the show Pointers were judged by Mr. P.H. Bryson. He gave Best of Breed to a bitch named May, owned by Dr. D.D. Saunders. Oddly enough, Dr. D.D. Saunders was judging Setters that day and gave Best of Breed to an Irish Setter bitch named Maud, owned by—P.H. Bryson! As the two judges returned to the ring with their dogs for the Best in Show final judging, the atmosphere at the ringside was noticeably tense. The Best in Show judge took his time and gave great consideration to making his selection for his top winner before writing in his judge's book, "Cup for best Setter or Pointer of any age or class of the show, Maud, P.H. Bryson." Maud distinguished herself further that weekend by placing third in the field trial the next day at the same show.

Dog show entries were obviously increasing since these first attempts, and everyone wanted a show winner. This prompted Charles H. Turner, prominent member of the St. Louis Kennel Club, to import the famous dog Elcho from J.C. Cooper of Limerick, Ireland. Elcho became the first Irish Setter to win a championship in the United States (completed on January 26, 1876) and was the first dog of any breed to attain championship in this country. The show was at the Exposition Building in Chicago and featured a class specified for imported Red and Red and White Setters and their progeny. There were also classes listed for "Native" Red or Red and White Setters called Irish, to be judged also by the British Standard Stonehenge had published in 1867. This was the very first show with special classes for our breed.

In addition to the ribbons there was a silver-plated trophy valued at $35.00 offered by the Chicago Kennel Club, holding their very first dog show. In 1925 Group and Best in Show judging was started, and the first Irish Setter to win a BIS was Ch. Modoc Morty Oge at Des Moines on April 3, 1925. That same year the second Irish Setter to win was the imported Ch. Tadg at San Francisco and Oakland, California in May.

OTHER EARLY IMPORTATIONS

In the fall of 1875 Mr. Turner imported Sullivan's Rose and two other Irish Setters named Erin and Frisk. Erin was a top field worker and a worthy sire, but he unfortunately got himself a name for bad disposition (even then uncommon in the breed) after an attack on his trainer. Mr. Turner was also influential and involved with the importation of a bitch named Lou II, a triple winner at Westminster shows, and her son Berkley, as well as other Irish Setters named Sting II and Thorstan, which also were the property of the St. Louis Kennel Club. In those early days it was not at all uncommon for kennel clubs to maintain kennels for both show and field dogs.

Also in 1875 E. Fowler Stoddard of Dayton, Ohio, imported a bitch named Friend which won first place at the 1878 Minnesota Field Trial Club event. When bred to Rufus, Arnold Burges' imported consistent bench show winner, she produced a litter containing four bench show winners. Rufus, whelped in 1873, sired over 22 litters before he was through standing at stud.

The famous dog Plunket was another among the "first" to be imported to this country, also in the second half of the 1870's. He was another import which sired many litters during his lifetime, with several repeat breedings, in spite of the fact that some of his offspring carried more white on them than was desired.

Early in 1877 Dr. William Jarvis, a dentist by profession and a dog judge, sportswriter and hunter as well, acquired Elcho from Charles Turner for his Claremont, New Hampshire kennel. He then imported two fine bitches to be bred to Elcho. One of the bitches, named Rose and purchased from D. Sullivan, was bred to Elcho nine times. The other imported bitch was named Noreen and was bred to Elcho five times. All told, over fifty bitches were bred to Elcho, and the matings produced over 30 bench show winners. Dr. Jarvis is to be credited with recognizing the excellent combination of the Palmerston/Elcho breedings which actually set the foundation for the breed in this country.

In addition to his sexual prowess, which earned him the title of "Prince of Stud Dogs," Elcho became—a point that bears repeating —the first U.S. bench show champion. The first Irish Setter stud dog listed in the American Kennel Club stud book (recorded in 1878), however, was Admiral, entry #534.

IRISH SETTERS AT THE FIRST WESTMINSTER SHOW

Such was their rise to popularity that the Irish Setter made an impressive entry at the first annual New York City Westminster Kennel Club show, held on May 8, 9 and 10th, 1877, just 1½ years after the Chicago show at which Elcho made the first championship in American dog show history. This first Westminster show, held at Gilmore's Garden, was called the First Annual New York Bench Show of Dogs and was held under the auspices of the Westminster Kennel Club. A century later, this show is rated as the most prestigious dog show of them all!! There was an entry of over 130 Irish Setters for judges Dr. L.H. Twaddell and John Davidson, Esquire, plus additional entries in the classes for special prizes. The catalog and the classes read as follows:

Class 2 CHAMPION IRISH SETTER BITCHES. This class listed 6 entries, with first place going to an entry by the St. Louis Kennel Club. It was entered as a red dog named Lou II by Glendenning's Grouse *ex* Nuttall's Maybe and carried a sale price of $350.00.

This Champion Class was specifically for ". . . either Native or Imported Dogs or Bitches that have won First Prizes at any Bench Show in this country or abroad, the Centennial Bench Show at Philadelphia not included."

Class 7 was for IMPORTED IRISH SETTER DOGS and carried 16 listings. Winner of this class was entry #195, owned by W.N. Callender of Albany, New York. Following the name of the owner in the catalogue was the name of the dog, Rory O'More, described as being red, 1 year and 7 months of age, by Burges' Rufus out of Burges' Friend. Mention was made of "full pedigree". . . and the price was $1,000.00.

It is interesting to note than entry number 210 was owned by the Reverend J. Cumming Macdona of Cheadle Rectory (also known for its Beagle packs in days of yore) Cheshire, England. The catalogue stated: "ROVER (brother to Plunket), red, 9 years; by Beauty out of Grouse. Rover has been engraved in the *London Field, Forest and Stream*, and for *Stonehenge Book on Dogs*, as the finest specimen of the Irish Setter. (Not for competition.)" The price was 10,000 pounds!

Other interesting observations on this class were that there was another Irish Setter named Rover, that a dog named Jack was further described as "formerly known as Joe," and that there was another entry named Joe and one named Frank.

Another Class 7 was for IMPORTED IRISH SETTER BITCHES. Nine bitches competed and first place went to T. Medley's Belle, a red and white 3½ years of age by Moyart, out of Brosna. Her price was 10,000 pounds; her owner lived in Picadilly, London.

Yet another Class 7 was for IMPORTED IRISH SETTER DOG PUPPIES (under 12 months). Out of 7 entries the winner was Guy, a nine-month-old red by Plunket out of Carrie, owned by Harry La-Grand Cannon of Fifth Avenue, New York, and was listed as "Not for Sale."

Class 7 for IMPORTED IRISH SETTER BITCH PUPPIES (under 12 months) also had 9 entries. First place went to Kathleen Mavourneen, 11 months and 12 days old, a red sired by Plunket out of Moya. Full pedigree and a price of $500.00 completed her listing.

Class 8 read NATIVE IRISH SETTER DOGS and boasted 49 competitors, by far the largest class of all. The winner was Duke, a three-year-old red by Thompson's Duke out of Belle. Owner B. Bacheller of Essex County, New Jersey listed it as being for sale at $100.00. Second place went to Snipe, also a three-year-old red, but one whose owner wanted $5,000.00. Is is the author's considered opinion that the number one winner might have been quite a bargain! Snipe, by the way, was not the only entry for sale at $5,000.00. A seven-year-old named Frank carried that price, and one other entry was going for a meager $60.00.

Class 8 for NATIVE IRISH SETTER BITCHES had only 19 entries and was won by F.H. Cozzens' Kate. This three-year-old red and white by Frank (the $5,000.00 dog?) out of Nell was not for sale. Her owner, Mr. Cozzens of New York City, was wise to hold onto her if her sire was indeed the Frank that was commanding a $5,000.00 price!

Class 8 for NATIVE IRISH SETTER DOG PUPPIES (under 12 months) listed 17 entries, with the winner being the six-month-old red from Greenwich Street, New York City, by Tar out of Gipsey. Owner W.P. Asten wanted $100.00 for Preston. This class presented an interesting note in that one owner, instead of listing the sire and dam of his puppy, suggested that those interested "See Kennel Register." Another owner was more specific, but not completely, and listed the parentage as ". . . by Bronson's dog, out of Macomber's bitch." He was casual in his price as well. The price was $50.00.

Class 8 for NATIVE IRISH SETTER BITCH PUPPIES (under 12 months) listed 9 entries. These puppies were listed as being both red and red and white, with one listing for a *black and tan* 4-month-old named Topsey. In spite of her color her price was $150.00.

Class number 1 under the SPECIAL PRIZE LIST category specified that competition for this class required: "For the best Setter, of any breed, dog or bitch, in the show. A Silver Cup, presented and manufactured by Messrs. Tiffany & Co., value $150."

Class 17 was. . . "For the best Setter, Dog or Bitch, of any strain, bred in the United States; a split bamboo Black Bass Rod, 3 joints, 6 sections, German silver mounted, extra tip, etc.; manufactured and presented by Messrs. Abbey & Imbrie, No. 48 Maiden Lane. This rod is similar to their Black Bass Fly Rod in construction, with the exception of its having standing guides, and the proper difference in calibre; value $60.00." There were 17 entries for this unusual prize, but the catalogue did not specifiy which Setters were which.

Class 18 required: "For the best Native Setter Puppy, either dog or bitch, either English, Irish or Black and Tan, or Black, Tan and White, a United States Arms Co. 32 Cal. Revolver, 6 chambers, pearl handled, nickle plated and engraved, in case complete, presented by Messrs. Barton & Co., No. 337 Broadway, value $25." 7 Setter owners wanted this prize.

Class 19 was "For the best Irish Setter Puppy, either Dog or Bitch, an ivory enamelled Opera Glass, presented by Messrs. T. Steele & Son, of Hartford, Conn., value $25." Ten opera buffs competed.

The 1877 Miscellaneous Class was #44, for dogs or bitches; while there were seven entries, only one had its breed identified. This was an imported Maltese Lion Dog appropriately named Leo. J.M. Crapo of Albany, New York entered his three-year-old buff dog named Punch, which was for sale for $10,000. Andrew Wagner advertised Nellie, a two-year-old brown female, for $100.00 and noted that: "Bitch born with two legs only; father and mother had four legs each." There was a trick dog class with a single entry, but there was no mention of what tricks the $200.00, four-year-old brown dog named Sprite could perform.

It was this morbid curiosity for the unusual or extraordinary performance that was almost the undoing of the Irish Setter in this country in its early years in this country.

IRISH SETTERS VERSUS THE OPPORTUNISTS

The tremendous success and warm reception of the Irish Setter in America, unfortunately, was marred in some quarters by unscrupulous opportunists. Some of the earliest imports in this country were used as money-makers in sporting events totally foreign to their show and field training and their purpose in life.

In some instances Irish Setters were put up against ponies, as racers, or were raced against other breeds of racing dogs fully trained at the game. In some cases they were made to run in competition with humans in freakish handicap races. Other so-called "sporting" events saw them pulling carts and carriages, often with loads which severely taxed their strength and totally unsuited to their conformation. They were often expected to lose by their unscrupulous owners, who received money for their attempt alone, or by deliberately betting on the opposition.

But the indomitable spirit of the Irish Setter saw some through their trials, though many fell by the wayside, victims of cruel owners. One dauntless dog named Dock, however, managed to overcome adversity and made a lot of money for his owner with his ability to literally "pull a lot of weight." But Dock was the exception to the rule, and the majority of Irish Setters that were used so uselessly led the breed into an early decline that nearly led to its destruction in this country.

Devotees of the breed took matters into their own hands just in time by publicizing the dog as a dual-purpose worker in both the field and show ring and put the dog back where it belonged in the dog fancy and in the public's image. It took years to rebuild what this folly had destroyed, and the fancy can be thankful to people like Mrs. Florence Nagle of the Sulhamstead Irish Wolfhound and Irish Setter kennels who took matters into her own hands in England, along with Mr. H. Dean in Canada and Mr. E. Berolsheimer of the O'Cloister line in this country. They started the lead along the road back to their recovery, and once again the beautiful Irish Setter regained its dignity and its rightful place in the canine world.

FURTHER IMPORTS AND BREEDINGS

It was obvious to all fanciers dedicated to purebred Irish Setters that the imports from abroad were far superior in every way to the native Setters being bred in this country. Breeding was being confined more and more to the imports, with only occasional outcrosses to the native-born dogs, or bred back to the offspring of the imports born in this country.

Most outstanding of these imported dogs was, of course, Elcho, sire of 197 puppies. His greatest offspring was a champion son appropriately named Elcho, Jr. The younger dog's show record, just as his father's did, confirmed his excellence, as Junior went undefeated in more than forty shows from 1882 through 1891. In addition to siring field champions among his quality puppies he sired five bench show champions and was himself shot over in the field, though he never attained a field championship for himself.

Dr. Jarvis, his breeder, sold Elcho, Jr. for $1000 when he was nine years of age. George H. Covert, the new owner, set Elcho Jr. up at his Killarney Kennels in Chicago. Unfortunately, within a year of the transaction both the new owner and the dog were dead. Elcho Jr. died on November 8, 1891.

Elcho and Elcho, Jr. were not the only popular sires of the day, of course. The list of available studs included the names of Rufus, Plunket and Berkley, as well as dogs named Erin, Nimrod, Biz, Norwood, Race, Stoddards Bob, Rory O'More, Brush, and champions Tim, Chief, Kildare, Duke Elcho, Gerald, Mike Swiveler T, Mack N, Kildare Glenore and Glencho.

Ch. Glencho deserves special mention, since he was a litter brother to Ch. Elcho Jr. and sired litters from 55 bitches. He, like Elcho, Jr., was exhibited extensively at the bench shows by W.H. Pierce, his owner.

In addition to Dr. Jarvis and Mr. Pierce, the names of other prominent men, their kennels and top show dogs became known during the 1880's and 1890's. Dr. L.C. Sauveur operated his Seminole Kennels in Philadelphia, where Ch. Tim reigned supreme until his death at thirteen years of age. Tim, a four-time winner of the coveted Westminster Kennel Club Best of Breed award, also sired forty litters.

Also prominent at the time was Max Wenzel, a dog judge as well as one of the founders of the Fisher's Island Field Trial Club. This Club was one of the first and most active organized field trial organizations in the country. Mr. Wenzel's Ch. Chief sired 42 litters, which included six field trial winners. A.B. Truman's Ch. Dick Swiveler was a big winner during his entire ten-year show career during the late 1880's and 1890's though he had to take a second place at the shows to the top-winning Ch. Elcho, Jr.

W.L. Washington owned the Kildare Kennels, and his Ch. Kildare dog was an Irish Setter to be reckoned with during the 1890's. Kildare won over 50 prizes, and among the get from his twenty-seven he produced two champion bitches, Ch. Red Rose III and Ch. Queen Vic. Queen Vic won top bitch awards for six consecutive years at the Westminster Kennel Club show. It was quite a feat at the time, especially for a bitch and with so many newcomers coming along as the breed was managing to take a foothold during these important last two decades in the 19th century.

Other notable breeders and exhibitors were making names for themselves during this period also. F.C. Fowler, owner of the Oak Grove Kennels in Connecticut; Joseph Lewis, also of Connecticut;

and Samuel Coulson in Canada was being heard from, as was I.H. Roberts, Jean Grosvenor, W.N. Callender, A.F. Hochwalt, W. Dunphy and Dr. Gwilyn G. Davis.

Dr. Davis' primary concern was with Irish Setters in the field, and until his demise in 1918 he not only ran his Currer Bell III, Currer Bell IV and Currer Maud at the trials but also served the Irish Setter Club of America as its president from 1895 into 1918, when death called a halt to all of his Irish Setter activities. I.H. Roberts was also running three of his field trial winners at this time.

THE IMPORTANT BITCHES OF THE ERA

We should not forget the importance of the bitches in the dog show world of this period. In addition to the "famous first" imports in Rose, Noreen, Lou II, Ch. Red Rose II and Ch. Queen Vic, there were other show queens which made their contribution to the breed and took their rightful places in the winner's circle at the bench shows and at the field trials.

Names like Ch. Mollie Bawn, owned by Mr. Dunphy; Ch. Laura B; Ch. Norna; Ch. Edna H.; Ch. Ruby Glenmore; Ch. Lady Swiveler; Belle of Orange; Nell; Carrie; Devlin's Moya, Kathleen, Diffenderffers Bess, and Hudson's Stella, a sister to Friend. There was Fannie Fern, owned by the Chicago Kennel Club; Colleen, owned by the Westminster Kennel Club; and Doll, owned by the Toledo Kennel Club. Ch. Hazel and Lady Clare, both Ch. Elcho daughters, were also making their presence known. All these, and all of those mentioned in the Westminster catalogue listings presented earlier in this chapter, as well as many others, each made their mark in some important way in early breed history in this country.

As the 20th century approached and interest continued to build in the breed it was noted that progress was being made. But the importing of top Irish Setters was still the order of the day. Unfortunately, owners and exhibitors of Irish Setters who had worked so hard at establishing the breed in this country began to suffer from "kennel blindness." As dissension rose among them as to the correct interpretation of the Standard, the Irish Setters began to lose a substantial number of its supporters, and some of the original interest and enthusiasm began to wane.

We can all be thankful that some of the old-time loyal die-hards in the breed managed to keep up their dedication; through persistence and the continued importation of the superior specimens from overseas, they maintained the breed until renewed interest once again carried the Irish Setter to its rightful place in the fancy.

Charles T. Thompson helped this cause enormously by importing two important dogs for his Chestnut Hill Kennels. They were Ch. Winnie II and Desmond II, purchased by him from the Reverend Robert O'Callaghan.

A lovely drawing of Vogue by Terry. Owned by the Banshee Kennels in Gardiner, New York.

E.B. Bishop imported a most worthy field trial winner named Coleraine for his Hutchinson, Kansas kennel. Coleraine was the result of a breeding between the much admired Ch. Aveline and her brother Fingal III. S.L. Boggs of Pittsburgh, Pennsylvania, imported Coleraine's litter brother Ch. Finglas in 1891, and in 1892 he was declared Absolute Winner, All-Age Stake at the Columbus, Indiana, American Field Trial Club event. He became a bench show winner and over the years sired seven field trial winners and three bench show champions.

Kennels all over the United States began to see the important contribution that could be made by continuing to import foreign bloodlines. A significant addition to the kennels of F.H. Perry of Des Moines, Iowa, was the purchase of Claremont Patsy, a half brother to the famous Ch. Aveline. Patsy was a great grandson of Ch. Palmerston and renewed the Palmerston bloodline once again in this country. He was also the sire of Chief Red Cloud, one of the foundation dogs in Charles Gale's "Law strain."

Other breeders who imported Irish Setters were F.L. Cheney, owner of the Onota Kennels in Massachusetts and C.M. Rounds of San Antonio, Texas, who obtained the valuable bloodlines of Ch. Palmerston by importing Princess Royal. Still others not mentioned before were J.S. and T. Wall and their Lismore dogs, whose breeding was largely based on the Law strain also; L.L. Campbell, F.M. Thomas and his Thasmo line, G.O. Smith, Dr. J.S. Laycock, Michael Flynn, F.P. Kirby, George Kunkel, A.W. Pearsall and W.H. Eakins.

5. IRISH SETTERS IN AMERICA IN THE 20TH CENTURY

The development of the Irish Setter in America during the first two decades of the 20th century was slow, steady, and significant. While obedience was unheard of and field work sparse and scattered over just about every part of the country where there were Irish Setters, a dedicated core of admirers managed to keep the breed in the running at the dog shows and progress was made.

Charles Gale's Law breeding, imported from Ireland, was the dominant bloodline behind the winning dogs during the first twenty years in the new century. The dog Ch. Ben Law, whelped in 1896, was behind the breeding, and Ben Law managed to win the Breed at the Westminster Kennel Club show in 1901. This noted sire managed to produce 7 champions out of 12 bitches with a total of 50 puppies. A half a dozen of Ben Law's sons can be said to be the foundation stock behind a majority of America's early show dogs.

Dr. William Jarvis also owned a Law dog, Ch. Shan Law, born in 1901. Shan went on to become one of the most famous of Ben Law's sons and was also responsible for a great deal of the quality passed on by the Law strain. Fortunately, the Law bloodlines were well distributed all over the United States, and even in the 1920's more than half of the quality registered Irish Setters were seen to have this valuable Law bloodline in their pedigrees. J.S. and T. Wall of the Lismore Kennels in Brooklyn, M.G. Heim, Charles Esselstyn and N.M. Emerson all took full advantage of the Law lines. Walter McRoberts did especially well with his Ch. Pat Law, whelped in 1903, with 160 puppies sired by his Pat, many of which were campaigned during the early years.

Otto Pohl also owned some of the Law dogs, which he showed in both bench and field trials until his death in 1918. Pohl bred the Law bloodlines to the Morty Oge bloodlines and was successful in breeding some excellent bench and show Irish Setters that were equally skilled in the field and well as of such fine quality they did much winning at the bench shows throughout the midwest.

A dog named Ch. Rheola Clanderrick, imported from Mrs. M. Ingle Bepler in 1914, became a popular sire also. His quality get kept his Clanderrick name prominent in breeding circles for several decades.

On the strength of Clanderrick's excellence, two or more of Mrs. Bepler's dogs were imported the following year. They were Rheola Pedro and Rheola Judy.

Active over a span of thirty years were L.S.A. and Louis Contoit. They established their St. Cloud Kennels in 1889, and before Louis Contoit's death in the early 1930's he was reported to have owned over 5,000 Irish Setters. The Contoits were among the first breeders to advocate line breeding, and their famous lines went back to the early Elcho and Noreen lines. The Contoits were the breeders of Ch. St. Cloud III and Ch. St. Cloud's Fermanagh, later owned and campaigned by Mrs. Cheever Porter of New York City.

Ch. Rosecroft Premier, upon his retirement in June, 1944, had a show record of 124 Bests of Breed, 53 Best Sporting Dog and 12 Bests in Show to his credit. Whelped on April 9, 1938, Premier died on June 12, 1951. His owner was Mrs. Cheever Porter of New York City.

Another important dog was Otto Pohl's McKerry. The pedigrees of several Irish Setter field champions go back to this dog, and he did exceptionally well in the field himself. While McKerry changed hands after Pohl's death, he spent his last years with Fred Lefferdink, at stud, until his death in 1923. By that time he had sired 30 litters which included two field champions.

Other devotees of the breed during the first two decades included Miss Marie Louise Welch, George Thomas, Fred Kirby, Mrs. E. Alban Sturdee, Miss E.L. Clarkson, Michael Flynn, L.L. Campbell, Mrs. Helen Talbot, Miss Elise Ladew, F.A. Johnson, Stacey Waters, Mrs. Nancy Lee Fletcher Nannetti, Mrs. R.W. Creuzbauer, Mrs. Walter Simmons, Mrs. E.B. Chase and Miss E.L. Clarkson.

Mrs. Sturdee started her kennels in 1912 based on Walter Mc-Roberts bloodlines, and Mrs. Olga Neilsen owned the Bergniel Kennels, started around the same time, and bred them until 1926. Mrs. Neilsen is not to be confused with the registered Rosecroft Kennels of C. Frederick Nielson, begun in 1905. This most important Rosecroft Kennel would continue to produce top quality Irish Setters for the next four decades. Perhaps the most famous was Ch. Rosecroft Premier, whelped in 1938 and campaigned to 124 Bests of Breed, 53 Sporting Group Firsts and 12 Bests in Show while owned by the aforementioned Mrs. Cheever Porter of New York City.

In 1909 Warren Delano established his St. Val Kennels, and it was one of his dogs used as the model for a profile bas relief on the Irish Setter Club of America bronze medal.

SETTERS DURING WORLD WAR I

The activity in Irish Setters almost came to a standstill during World War I. . .

Importations stopped and the kennels which had been active up to this point had to get along with what was available to them in this country. However, once the war was over the Law strain had just about run its course; breeders were looking around for new blood, since everyone seemed to sense that the Irish Setter was here to stay and would increase in popularity, and breeding would be greatly accelerated.

This fact was borne out by the tremendous number of dogs which were imported as soon as the wartime restrictions were out of the way. More than two hundred Irish Setters were imported. Everyone seemed to want the famous Boyne dogs bred by J.A. Carbery, Drogheda, Ireland.

In July, 1920 G.O. Smith of Wheeling, West Virginia imported the Bran of Boyne dog that did well in the field and a dog called Tipperary Eamon, who made the Tipperary name famous in field circles. In 1922 Smith imported another dog, Raneagown, of Boyne lineage. Smith, who had imported his first field trial winner, a dog named

Young Signal, in 1893, said Raneagown was the best dog he had ever shot over.

There was no question about it, the breeders felt it necessary to import dogs from abroad since the earlier breeding had been rather scattered and therefore there was great discrepancy in requirements for meeting the Standard. Differences in type and conformation were obvious; fortunately, enough of the serious breeders at the time were willing to do something about it.

Miss Laura Delano and some of her famous Dachshunds and an Irish Setter at her Knocknagree Kennels in Rhinebeck, New York; photographed in 1949.

THE 1920'S

In 1922 C.C. Stillman established his Kenridge Kennels in Cornwall, New York. His Ch. Bergniel Red Helmut was a show winner from 1923 through 1928. He also owned other Best in Show winning Irish Setters. Dr. John D. DeRonde and his Palmerston Kennels in New York City bred some outstanding show winners and imported others during the early 1920's. They competed against Charles Jackson's Londenderry Kennel dogs from New Jersey.

1923 was the year when Emily Schweitzer first got involved with her glorious Irish Setters which bear her Verbu kennel prefix when she bought her first dog from Mrs. A.E. Sturdee, Glencho Ruddy Oogh. Endless patience and hard work over this more than half a century of devotion to the breed has resulted in a highly satisfying and proud heritage for her Verbu dogs. Many bench show champions were bred and owned and shown by Miss Schweitzer, but she is perhaps best known for her work and accomplishments with Irish Setters in obedience.

In the spring of 1936 the Midwest Reserve Kennel Club in Cleveland, Ohio held the first obedience trial in the midwest, open to all breeds. Emily Schweitzer was right there in the thick of it competing with her dogs against all the German Shepherds and Dobermans one could imagine. . . and Emily and her Irish Setter placed first. This was her American and Canadian Ch. Verbu Killeen Oogh. Killeen quickly completed her C.D. title and went on to a C.D.X. She was the first Irish Setter in the breed to accomplish the earning of these titles.

Next there was Canadian and American Ch. Verbu Norna Oogh, who went all the way to a U.D.T. title and was also the first Irish Setter to do so. Her two daughters, Verbu Susie Oogh and Verbu Noreen Oogh, were the second and third Irish Setters to attain the titles. This is a feat Emily Schweitzer can be proud of, since she trained them herself.

Fifty years later, the spring of 1972 saw the crowning of Dual Champion Duffin Miss Duffy, C.D. She was trained and handled in the field by Jake Huizenga of the well-known Oxton Irish Setter kennel in Salinas, California.

There are numerous other Verbu title holders who will always be remembered by Emily Schweitzer as well as others in the fancy who have owned or admired her great intelligent Irish Setters. She is grateful for the happiness they have brought her over the years and can be proud of her part in the fancy as breeder, exhibitor and trainer! She has been especially successful in the obedience rings, and many of the Verbu dogs also were field trained—the kennel over the past 50 years has produced more than a dozen bench show champions. Many of these have gone on to win Canadian championships as well; they go back to the Milson O'Boy lines. Emily Schweitzer is still most active in the 1970's, and her beautiful Irish Setters are still her great love!

Along with the Verbu Kennels in 1923, there was the entry of Laura Delano of Rhinebeck, New York, to the group. She had decided to follow in her father's (St. Val) footsteps by establishing her own Knocknagree Kennels. A remarkable succession of great Knocknagree Irish Setters followed, and Laura Delano's greatly admired Best Team in Show winners at America's most important dog shows became the talk of the breed.

There were other breeds—the Dachshunds, for instance—at the Knocknagree Kennels that gained fame, but the Irish Setter always had a special place in the heart of Laura Delano until the day she died.

It was also in 1923 that the English Champion Terry of Boyne was imported by F.R. Wingerter of Hurdland, Missouri; $2,600 was the price paid for this dog by Wingerter to enhance his Woodbine Kennels. Eight of his get (whelped in Ireland) were also later imported

One of the most impressive photographs in the history of the breed! Emily Schweitzer's enviable accomplishment with her splendid dogs in both the show and obedience rings. . . American and Canadian Ch. Verbu Norna Oogh, U.D.T., Am. and Can. Ch. Verbu Killeen Oogh, C.D.X., Verbu Susie Oogh, U.D.T., Am. and Can. Ch. Verbu Peter Oogh, C.D.X., verbu Noreen Oogh, U.D.T.—all bred and owned by the owner of the Verbu Kennels in Dundee, Illinois.

American and Canadian Ch. Verbu Norna Oogh, U.D.T., and her daughters Verbu Susie Oogh, U.D.T. and Verbu Noreen Oogh, U.D.T. These three bitches, bred, owned and trained by Miss Emily Schweitzer, represent the first three Irish Setter U.D.T. title holders in the history of the breed.

from that country. Terry sired 71 litters from 55 dams; most of the extraordinary number of puppies, 259, came to excel in the field.

It was in 1923 also that Fred Lefferdink imported Sean of Boyne. Lefferdink's kennel was founded on Otto Pohl's stock, and this addition of the important Boyne stock put him in good standing in the breed.

A.A. Bell and Lewis H. Starkey appeared on the scene in the mid-1920's along with Dr. T.J. O'Connell and H.A. Wisher, of Philadelphia, who imported many fine field dogs.

The Milson Kennels were established in 1923 with Milson Peggy as the first dog of note. Sidney H. Sonn of Harrison, New York, was winning nicely through the decade under the kennel management of Harry Hartnell. In 1930 the Milson dogs were transferred to Mr. Hart-

Int. Ch. Higgins Red Pat, owned by W.W. Higgins of Caldwell, New Jersey. Photographed by Tauskey in 1930.

Miss Laura Delano and two of her Irish Setters. A prominent breeder and exhibitor, the late Miss Delano was well-known for her beautiful Irish Setters and Dachshunds.

nell, who went on to breed perhaps one of the greatest Irish Setters that ever lived, Ch. Milson O'Boy, who rates very prominent mention in this book.

Edwin M. Berolzheimer exhibited his "of the Cloisters" kennel suffix on both field and show dogs. He owned Elcova's McTybe, the first American Kennel Club Irish Setter field champion on record.

The Irish Setters in the late 1920's were also represented by dogs belonging to E.D. Levering, Warren K. Read, Jr. William Davis, L.C. Fauble, John Collins, P.I. Appleman, J.F. Walter, G.G. Jennings, J.P. Link, Earl Kreuger and Mrs. Cheever Porter, who did so much to bring the beautiful Irish Setter before the public.

In 1924 Hollis and Jo Wilson in Amherst, Wisconsin started their End O'Maine Kennels. The Wilsons produced an incredible line of winning Setters and also handled professionally some of the top show dogs in the country. In 1962, they gave up their kennel activities, and Hollis Wilson became a very much in demand dog show judge.

Maurice and Beryl Baker of Minneapolis started with their Hedgewood Kennels in 1925, based on the renowned Law strain. Just as Hollis Wilson did, Maurice Baker gave up the kennel to go into judging in later years, but not before having made a name for himself in the breed.

In 1926 John Colbert of San Francisco and his Shanagolden Kennels produced many fine dogs which influenced the breeding program of many of the kennels in the area—and sold for record prices!

In 1928 the John Frasers established their Cu Machree Kennels, based on the Braeland Farms Queen bitch, and went on to breed many show champions over the years; they brought much attention to the breed while campaigning their Ch. Thenderin Brian Tristan through his Best in Show winning career, and with Ch. Cu Machree Tim, another Best in Show Irish Setter owned by Mr. and Mrs. R.S. Meriam during the 1950's.

It was in the 1920's also that the famous William C. Thompson and his wife, Helen, began their Red Hills Kennels in Minneapolis. The Thompsons bred occasionally and worked the dogs in the field. Before he died, Will Thompson had become a reputable judge and had written the book *The Irish Setter in Word and Picture*.

THE 1930'S

The great dog Ch. Higgins Red Coat had a tremendous influence on the breed. His prepotency was evident in many of the kennels during the 1920's. Included in this group were the kennels of Jack Spear and Ward Garner, which were established in the 1930's.

It was in 1923 that William W. Higgens of West Virginia imported Higgins Paddy of Boyne, who was bred four times to a top bitch named Craigie Lea Mona; these two dogs produced six champions of great importance to the breed from 1924 to 1929.

Ch. Rex's Red Don, owned by Mr. and Mrs. W.R. Lubben of Brewster, New York. Photograph by Tauskey.

These six dogs, Higgins Red Pat, Higgins Red Coat, Sister A.C.F., Barney of Boyne, Rose of Sharon II and Patricia of Boyne have had a profound influence on the breed. Many fanciers during the 1920's believed Red Pat to be the best Irish Setter ever seen. But as fate would have it, it was Red Coat that became the sire of 30 champions.

Actually all of the quality offspring of Paddy and Mona dominated the show ring for the 1920's and 1930's. Higgins Red Pat won the Best in Show honors at the very first Morris and Essex show on May 28, 1927. He continued to win additional honors in following years, including winning the breed at Westminster for three years. Twenty bitches were bred to Red Pat before his death from cancer in 1932. These breedings accounted for 65 registered puppies, of which six became champions.

TYRONNE FARM

Jack and Evelyn Spear's Tyronne Farm Kennels in Tipton, Iowa started in 1934 with their purchase of Jordan Farms Nancy and Tyronne Farm Joan; their stud was Ch. Tyronne Farm Jerry, which they got from Maurice Baker. Jerry was a champion sired by Paddy out of the Bakers' Ch. Hedgewood Judy.

The Spears exhibited at the bench shows extensively over the years and were dedicated to the breed. Perhaps their most famous dog was Ch. Tyronne Farm Clancy. During his show ring career he racked up an impressive total of 19 Bests in Show, including the 1950 Morris and Essex classic over an entry of 2,263 dogs, and was top-winning Irish Setter for 1949.

CROSSHAVEN

Crosshaven has been the kennel name for Mr. and Mrs. Ward Gardner since they got into the breed in the 1930's. Over the years Mr.

Ch. Peggy Belle, an Irish Setter known several decades ago, owned by W.H. Crossman of New York City.

Ch. Milson Sonny, whelped April 10, 1927, and owned by the Milson
Kennels in Harrison, New York. The sire was Ch. Higgins Red Pat **ex**
Ch. Milson Peggy.

Ch. Jordan Farm John, owned by the Jordan Farm Kennels in Bolivar,
New York and photographed in 1934.

Gardner has owned and bred some 14 champions. He kept the great bitches to breed, and when he started he purchased the best bitch he could possibly afford from the late Ernest D. Levering. Levering was a man devoted to developing the dual-purpose Irish Setter, a concept with which Ward Gardner heartily agreed.

This first bitch, purchased in 1933, was sired by Ch. Higgins Red Coat out of an imported bitch. Ward showed her to her championship in straight wins. She was not only a top show winner but also a great bird dog and a great producer. Ward Gardner was already a field trial judge and all of his dogs were trained by a professional trainer according to the Lefferdink Force System, a procedure devised by

The renowned Ch. Crosshaven O'Hollywood Hills photographed on January 12, 1946. Whelped January 13, 1944 by Ward Gardner at his Crosshaven Kennels, Walla Walla, Washington. This beautiful Irish Setter figured prominently in the Irish Setter world during this important decade for the breed.

fadin

Ch. Sally O'Bryan of Crosshaven, a great bench and field dog and a top producer for Ward Gardner's Crosshaven Kennels in Walla Walla, Washington. Her show record included 2 Bests in Show, 8 Sporting Groups, and 28 Bests of Breed. While being shown in 1939, she was the top-winning Irish Setter bitch in the U.S.

breeder and field man Fred Lefferdink, who started in the breed in the 1930's.

This first bitch, Ch. Ruxton's Shannon of Bryne, was bred to Redwood Rocket, owned by Lewis Starkey, and sired by Red Coat out of a bitch named Ch. Redwood Rhoda. Rhoda was a Best in Show winner and had won Best of Breed at the Garden one year. Her remains are in the Peabody Museum as an excellent specimen of the breed.

From this breeding came a litter of 12; six became champions. Ward Gardner kept two bitches which went on to win championships and fame. One was his Ch. Sally O'Bryan of Crosshaven, and the other was Ch. Stardust of Crosshaven.

One of the most famous of the Irish Setters of yesteryear was Ward Gardner's great Ch. Faig-a-Belle of Crosshaven. Gardner's kennels were in Walla Walla, Washington.

The next litter was sired by another Red Coat son, Ch. Redwood Russet of Harvale, and this litter produced another famous dog of that day, Ch. Copper Coat of Crosshaven. This dog did a lot of show-winning on the Pacific Coast for owners Henry and Doris Frank. James McManns showed the Gardner dogs in California and Hollis Wilson showed them in the midwest.

Before their retirement Sally O'Bryan had won two Bests in Show and eight Groups and at the time was the top-winning Irish Setter bitch in the U.S. Stardust was the second biggest winning bitch and their dam, Shannon, was the top producing bitch of the year. Ward Gardner and his Irish Setter bitches won seven out of 20 national Irish Setter trophies!

After retirement Sally and Stardust were both bred to Ch. Redwood Russet of Harvale. This double-cross to Red Coat produced additional champions including Ch. Kleiglight O'Aragon, who won 21 Bests in Show and 55 Sporting Groups and 104 Bests of Breed. "Pete," owned by H. Jack Cooper, was also Best of Breed at Westminster on three different occasions. He sired 595 puppies in 131 litters from 94 bitches. Sally also produced Ch. Faig-A-Belle of Crosshaven. Gardner gave her to Elizabeth Cuthbertson of the famous Hollywood Hills Kennels and she was bred to Ch. Rufus of Hollywood Hills. The stud puppy from this litter Gardner gave back to Mrs. Cuthbertson; it was bred to Redwood Rory of Crosshaven, a dog Mr. Gardner had given to Lew Starkey. She became Ch. Crosshaven of Hollywood Hills and was the top-winning bitch in the U.S. for two years in succession.

Ch. Bryan of Tyron, sired by Ch. Kinvarra Craig ex Ch. Ruxton's Mollie O'Day, photographed several years ago by Percy Jones.

Faig-A-Belle produced Ch. Redstar of Hollywood Hills, acquired by Mrs. John C. McAteer of Bermuda. Ward Gardner picked the puppy out for Paula McAteer, and the dog had a brilliant show career in the ring and as a stud in New England.

Crosshaven Lone Eagle was the last of Ward Gardner's line, which was in the 1960's. Today Ward Gardner claims his greatest pleasure has been breeding five straight generations of champion bitches and his winning 12 Best Brace in Show awards. Today he is active in the dog fancy as a judge, past director of the ISCA, winner of the Man of the Year Award, and outside the dog fancy, past master of Masonic Lodge, honorary member of Phi Delta Theta, a 32nd degree Mason and a Shriner, past President of Chamber of Commerce, and was honored in the 1970's as founder of the Walla Walla Kennel Club in 1934. He was appointed to the Northwest Trial Board by the AKC and was invited to judge at the ISCA First National Specialty Show, among other honors—which are numerous.

HAPPY VALLEY

In the early 1930's Dr. A.A. Mitten got hold of some Setters for his kennel which included the imported Irish Setter Ch. Delaware Kate. This bitch was a champion in England, Ireland and the U.S. and was undefeated in the breed in this country. Lost in 1932 while whelping a

Dr. A.P. Munn of West Long Branch, New Jersey with one of his Irish Setters photographed in the mid-1930's.

78

Boerchan Blameless, owned by Mrs. George B. St. George. Photograph by Tauskey.

litter, it was considered by many to be a great loss to the breed, since she was said to be the top Irish Setter bitch up to that time.

It was also during the 1930's that the Honorable Mrs. Katharine St. George, U.S. Congresswoman from New York, and her daughter, Mrs. Allan A. Ryan, purchased several notable Irish Setters. They imported Ch. Red Sails of Salmagundi and Ch. Beorcham Blameless and owned Ch. Jordan Farm Lady and Ch. Headliner The Flaming Beauty.

The Milson Kennels, after the death of Mr. Sonn and under the careful operation of Harry Hartnett, produced Ch. Milson O'Boy and several of his famous sons, including Ch. Milson O'Boy II and Milson Top-Notcher. Top-Notcher was a multiple Best in Show winner and O'Boy II became the foundation stud at the Knightscroft Kennels.

KNIGHTSCROFT

About 1932 Joseph and Henrietta Knight, Jr., were given an Irish Setter. Louden Knight's Terry was specifically given to them to re-

Ch. Milson Top Notcher with owner Harry Hartnett of the Milson Kennels in Harrison, New York, receiving the Best in Show Award at a Trenton Kennel Club show. Capt. Lyman H. Burbank presents the award. The judge was William L. Smalley.

Ch. Milson Christopher Robin, owned by Dr. and Mrs. Richard A. Kast of Buffalo, New York.

A Tauskey photograph of Ch. Milson Top Notcher, owned by the Milson Kennels, Harrison, New York.

place a dog of another breed which had been their beloved pet. Terry became a good quail dog but was by no means a show quality Irishman. However, his intelligence and good behavior won the Knights over to the breed.

It was not long before the Knights acquired some good bitches from Fred Nielson of Rosecroft kennel fame. This was also the time the Knights devoted a great deal of time studying and observing the breed in action but—as Joseph Knight tells us—not getting very far in the show ring. This situation changed markedly once they bought Milson O'Boy II from the late Harry Hartnett, owner of the famous Milson Kennels.

Ch. Knightscroft Fermanagh wins Best of Breed over 60-odd Setters at the April 27, 1947 South Seaboard Irish Setter Specialty Show in Towson, Maryland. Dr. Jay Calhoon, judge. Best of Opposite Sex went to Annally's Claret. The late Pat Morgan, owner of the Annally Kennels, handled Claret. The late Charlie Canaday is at extreme left. Percy Jones photograph.

Ch. Knightscroft Symphony, Sporting Group winner at the 1949 West-minster Kennel Club show. He was owned by Helen Naylor.

American and Canadian Ch. Draherin Billy Boy, captured in a light moment at the Davison, Michigan home of Dr. R.D. Helferty. Billy Boy is the sire of Dr. Helferty's Bermuda, American and Canadian Ch. Kelly Shannon O'Deke. Billy Boy is co-owned by Dr. Helferty and Ruth Cordes.

One of the top Irish Setters of yesteryear. . . Ch. Redwood Russet of Harvale, photographed by Athos Nilsen.

A top-winning dog of a few decades back, Ch. Charles River Blazing Beauty. The sire was Ch. Red Sails of Salmagundi *ex* Wamsutta Susie Q. Brown photograph.

The Knights made this great dog a champion and by breeding him to several of their Rosecroft bitches began producing quality Irish Setters. One outstanding litter was from Milson O'Boy II out of Jordan Farm Scarlet O'Hara. This was the beginning. . . breedings started to "nick"—and for the next two decades, the 1940's through the 1960's, the Knightscroft Irish Setters made quite a place for themselves in Irish Setter history.

By actual count the Knights bred 37 champions. The first great one was Ch. Rosecroft Premier, given as a pup to Fred Nielson and later sold after an important win at the Garden to Mrs. Cheever Porter. He made a great show record for himself under the guidance of Harry Hartnett. His sire was Ch. Milson O'Boy *ex* Rosecroft Fern.

Another great Setter bearing the Knightscroft banner was Ch. Knightscroft Symphony, sold as a youngster to Miss Helen Naylor of Pennsylvania. Miss Naylor was later known in the fancy as Mrs. Wal-

Erin's Beau Brummel, photographed a few decades ago.

Knightscroft Fermanagh, Best in Show at the 1946 Irish Setter Club of America Specialty show held at Rye, New York. Joseph Knight, owner-handler. Percy Jones photo.

ter Stickel. When Symphony finished her career, she was heralded as the greatest winning bitch in Irish Setter history up to that time. Her sire was Ch. Knightscroft Erin Elan out of Ch. Knightscroft Aileen Adair.

Henrietta Knight had a special favorite of her own, the great dog Ch. Knightscroft Fermanagh. Sired by the celebrated Ch. Milson O'Boy, the dam was Jordan Farm Scarlett O'Hara, and he started out on his illustrious show ring career by going Best of Breed from the classes at the Irish Setter Specialty show in September, 1946. It wasn't long before he had amassed a total of 17 Bests of Breed. But tragedy struck down this most promising Irishman when he jumped off the tailgate of a moving station wagon and injured his back. In spite of all the loving care, his excellent gait was never the same.

Ch. Clondeen Girl of Knocknagree, owned by Miss Laura Delano of Rhinebeck, New York, and photographed in 1936.

Joseph Knight was especially fond of Ch. Knightscroft Aileen Adair, dam of the aforementioned Symphony and also dam of Ch. Knightscroft Erin Elan, Symphony's sire. Erin Elan was a very active dog, and Joseph Knight liked his fighting spirit. He loved people but wasn't fond of other dogs, and Joseph Knight tells us that more often than not when he showed him the ring turned out to be a real Donnybrook!

Henrietta Knight passed away after a long illness in the spring of 1963, and Joseph Knight had begun reducing the kennel gradually. Since then he has devoted his "dog time" to occasional judging assignments in 15 of the sporting breeds. We can all reflect on the glory that the Knightscroft dogs brought to the show ring and the credit they have brought to the breed. Knightscroft is a name to remember.

CALDENE

Dr. Jay W. Calhoon, of Uhrichsville, Ohio, was established in 1936 when he purchased Judy Legore Colquohoun from Dr. Clyde Leeper. Judy went on to become a champion in both the U.S. and Canada. Dr. Calhoon bred his bitches to many of the top sires of the day, and his special blending of the Milson and Jordan Farm strains was influential in the breed at the time.

When Harry Hartnett retired in 1944 the Milson dogs were transferred to Dr. Calhoon and produced many top dogs until the kennel was disbanded in 1952. Most of his stock went to the Knockross Kennels of Welrose L. Newhall of Coraopolis, Pennsylvania, and Dr. Calhoon concentrated on his judging from that time forward. Ch. Caldene Mick O'Boy was top stud at the kennel until 1960, when his son, Ch. Knockross O'Boy, took over. He sired many top winning dogs at that time including Knockross Ruby, one of the top-producing bitches in the breed.

KINVARRA

The Kinvarra Kennels were established in 1932 by Lee and Marjorie Schoen in Darien, Connecticut. They imported Borrowdale Yseult of Kinvarra, their favorite foundation bitch. They also started

Ch. Mollie O'Day, photographed in 1937 by William Brown for owner Jack Spear.

with Ch. Kinvarra Son of Red Coat, who went directly back to the Higgins Red Coat line. The Schoens imported many dogs and Mrs. Schoen was very active with the dogs in the field. Their homebred Ch. Kinvarra Kermit sired a total of 29 champions. The Kinvarra lines are behind many of the top kennels started in the 1930's; among the most prominent and still active today is the Tirvelda line.

TIRVELDA

E. Irving Eldredge established his Tirvelda Kennels in Middleburg, Virginia in 1935. By the mid-1970's, Tirvelda had produced 95 champions—and the end is not in sight. Ted Eldredge, as he is called by his friends, had been keen on Irish Setters from the time he was a small lad, and by 1937 his first litter came along to establish the Tirvelda prefix in the show world based on Kinvarra bloodlines. He takes pride in the fact that his Irish Setters run free on several acres of open fields, except for the bitches in heat or after dark, and the number of residents in the breed in the kennel runs between 10 and 15, so that all the dogs get personal attention and regard in the breeding program established so many years ago.

Ch. Tirvelda Nutbrown Sherry is the top-producing bitch in the history of the breed; Mr. Eldredge considers her to be "exceptional." Some of the other great dogs which have borne the Tirvelda name are Ch. Tirvelda Maidavale, Ch. Tirvelda Michaelson, Ch. Tirvelda Aran, Ch. Tirvelda Nor'wester, and many others. The current winner during the highly competitive 1970's is Ch. Tirvelda Distant Drummer. Drummer started his Special career in February 1975 by winning the Combined Setter Specialty Show in New York City at the age of three. Halfway through 1975 he had won his third Specialty and a Group at the Detroit show.

In the early years Mr. Eldredge also imported dogs from England bearing the Boyne and Ardagh lines to fill out his breeding program and to help establish this famous line beginning with Ch. Tirvelda Malva and Ch. Kinvarra Kermit in his first homebred litter. A variety of other important bloodlines were introduced over the years to guarantee the exceptionally fine dogs carrying the Tirvelda banner.

Today, Mr. Eldredge also enjoys judging all of the Sporting breeds.

CARRVALE

Dr. Herman J. Carr and his wife Martha of Palatine, Illinois were owners of the Carrvale Kennels. Dr. Carr died in 1962, but he had started raising Irish Setters in 1938 while still living at the internes' quarters at a Chicago hospital. Many champions carried the Carr-

Best in Show at the 1952 Central New York Kennel Club show was Ch. Tirvelda Aran, owned by E. Irving Eldredge and handled by Charley Meyer. This important win was under judge Miss Kathleen Staples. Standing left to right are Club president Fred F. Smith, Bench Show Chairman Arthur Emery and Miss Staples.

vale prefix over their years in the breed, and their Ch. Carrvales' Sergeant Terrence and Ch. Carrvale's Terry Terhune were top studs as well as Best in Show winners.

FLAMING BEAUTY

If ever there was a kennel name appropriate to the breed of dog it represented it was Jack and Ann Funk's Flaming Beauty title. Jack had been fascinated by Irish Setters since he was a small boy and in 1939 acquired Ginger The Flaming Beauty. There have been many champions at their kennel, but perhaps the most famous was Ameri-

American and Canadian Ch. Headline The Flaming Beauty, sire of 16 champions and winner of 5 Bests in Show. In 1962 Beauty was #1 Sporting Dog in the nation. Owned and shown by Jack Funk, Beauty was whelped in July, 1957 and was sired by Ch. Thenderin Brian Tristan **ex** Ch. Larrie of Tidewater.

Ch. Patrick The Flaming Beauty, from the kennels of Jack and Ann Funk. This photo was taken in 1948.

can and Canadian Ch. Headline The Flaming Beauty, which was Top Sporting Dog in 1962. When retired in 1963 he had 9 Bests in Show, 56 Best Sporting Dog Group wins and 103 Bests of Breed. Several of his get have been champions also. In the mid-1970's Jack still is active as a handler of many of the nation's top show dogs, and both he and Ann are very active in all phases of the dog fancy.

SEAFORTH

Seaforth was the name chosen for their kennel by Mr. and Mrs. George Brodie, Jr. in the 1940's. Their kennel (in North Easton, Massachusetts) has produced many fine champion Irish Setters, the most prominent of all being Ch. Seaforth's Dark Rex. Rex was the winner of many show awards and was the sire of 20 champions. It was his great quality, which he passed on to his get, that helped the quality in the Thenderin, Innisfail, Coppercountry, Webline, Draherin and other important bloodlines. Another famous show winner was Ch. Seaforth's Poetry of Motion. Other top dogs from their kennels were Ch. Seaforth's Feudist Knight, Ch. Seaforth's Rex McDonald, Ch. Seaforth's Faig-A-Belle, Ch. Seaforth's Echo of Shamus, Ch. Thenderin Nomad, Ch. Kinvarra Macaroon and Ch. Seaforth's Echo of Dark Rex.

Ch. Seaforth's Dark Rex, pictured winning Best of Breed at the Del Monte, California, Kennel Club show under the late judge Alva Rosenberg. Rex went on to win the Sporting Group this same day under judge Ernie Ferguson. It was his third Group in three weeks. Bred and owned by Mr. and Mrs. George Brodie, Jr., Seaforth Kennels, North Easton, Massachusetts.

Ch. Seaforth's Echo of Dark Rex captured on film by William P. Gilbert for owner Sid Marx of Ridge, New York.

Their first Irish Setter was a beautiful bitch named Ch. Seaforth's Red Velvet, obtained from the Charles River Kennels of John Downs in 1946. The Brodies' two greatest dogs, Dark Rex and Poetry, were out of Red Velvet and sired by another famous winner, Ch. Tyronne Farm Malone.

While the George Brodies are no longer breeding Irish Setters, their interest is still just as keen as it ever was and they now make a major contribution to the breed through their judging assignments. George Brodie judged Intersex Competition at the first Irish Setter Club of America's National Specialty in 1973.

WESTWIND

The idea and future plan for her Irish Setter kennel began almost on the first day Luz Holvenstot first held a puppy in her arms. Her father imported the first Brahma cattle from India to Colombia, South America, where she was born and spent her early childhood. All kinds of animals, both wild and tame, had always been a passion with Luz, and she graduated with a B.S. degree in animal husbandry from Iowa University. She has been a student of animals ever since.

She acquired her first Irish Setter from the famous Knightscroft Kennels in 1942. "Magic" was a daughter of the famous Ch. Milson O'Boy II *ex* Ch. Rosecroft Kitty Kelly. As her interest increased in the obedience aspect of the dog fancy she can now claim to have finished many Irish Setters to their titles. Soon she herself was holding training classes and doing private training as well.

In 1943 she moved on the field trials, and she has been running her Irish Setters ever since. Her breeding program places emphasis on sensible, alert, affectionate as well as intelligent dogs, bred to the Standard.

While continuing a serious breeding program, Luz never breeds more than three litters a year, with a close eye to quality rather than quantity. In 1946 she joined the Irish Setter Club of America and acquired her all-breed handler's license the following year.

Since establishing her kennel in the mid-1940's and after several decades of showing and handling many breeds of dogs, she turned in her license with an eye to judging the Setter breeds. Meanwhile, the Westwind Irish Setters continue to run in field trials. She was also a past columnist for *Popular Dogs* magazine and is a past director of the Irish Setter Club of America.

FLEETWOOD FARMS

In 1943 Hugh and Virginia Rumbaugh established their Fleetwood Farms Kennels of Irish Setters. Over the years there has been a most impressive list of outstanding dogs, including Ch. Fleetwood

Ch. Westwind Scarlet Tempest pictured winning under judge Doris Swain, handled by owner Luz Holvenstot, Westwind Kennels, Long Valley, New Jersey.

Farms Peg O'My Heart, top-winning Irish Setter bitch in 1951 and 1952; Ch. Fleetwood Farms Sixty Special, top-winning Irish Setter 1961 through 1963; Ch. Fleetwood Farms Grand Marshall and Ch. Fleetwood Farms Brougham.

But in the 1960's the Rumbaughs reached the pinnacle of success. Their Ch. Starheir Aaron Ardee, a great grandson of their Fleetwood Farms Peg O'My Heart, became the #1 Irish Setter in history by having won the most Bests in Show, Groups, Bests of Breed, and the number of most dogs defeated. Over 380 judges awarded "Chance" over 465 winning ribbons, representing the defeating of over 68,000 dogs of all breeds in the Phillips Rating System. Dick Cooper handled Chance to this tremendous record and has handled for the Rumbaughs for many decades. Chance has won many trophies and Irish Setter Club awards, has been a magazine cover-dog, has appeared on television and in dog food advertisements, and, of course, is much in demand as a stud. The Rumbaughs think he is the most perfect Irish Setter they have ever seen.

WOLFSCROFT

Dr. Wolfgang A. Casper started in Irish Setters in 1946. It was a good beginning, since his first dog was a Knightscroft bitch named Dixie Belle. An outcross with an English import produced the first litter to bear the chosen kennel name of Wolfscroft, which was registered with the American Kennel Club.

In 1949 Dr. Casper was co-founder of the Staten Island Companion Dog Training Club and to this day is an Honorary Life Member. In 1950 he reorganized the Eastern Irish Setter Association and was its president for 5 years. More than 25 years later he is still on the club's board of directors. He is also a board member of the Staten Island Kennel Club and its delegate to the American Kennel Club, as well as show chairman for the Combined Setter Club of America, a club he founded in 1960 and still serves. He is also a past board member and active in the Irish Setter Club of America, English Setter Association of America and associate member and past Board member of the Association of Obedience Clubs and Judges.

One of Dr. Casper's hobbies is photography and many of the glorious photographs of his dogs appear in this book and have appeared on the cover of the *New York Physician* magazine.

Born in Germany and a graduate of Berlin University School of Medicine, Dr. Casper came to New York in 1934 and now maintains his Wolfscroft Kennels on Staten Island, New York. He is a Senior Attending Dermatologist at St. Vincent's Hospital there, and Chief at Sea View Hospital as well.

Dr. Casper also considers modern art as one of his hobbies and states: "While modern art, especially painting, has become almost cubistic and static and unintelligible to most people, color photography offers a return to true nature with variations of color by virtue of

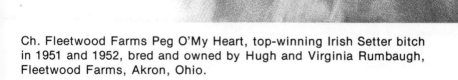

Ch. Fleetwood Farms Peg O'My Heart, top-winning Irish Setter bitch in 1951 and 1952, bred and owned by Hugh and Virginia Rumbaugh, Fleetwood Farms, Akron, Ohio.

A headstudy of Casper, owned by the Wolfscroft Kennels.

different color films and color filters, to be original and creative. My main hobby, however, remains m' dogs—Irish Setters—and there are six in my house. I train them for obedience; I show them and handle them in dog shows. I am an American Kennel Club approved judge for Sporting dogs, and belong to as many dog organizations as medical organizations."

Both Dr. Casper and his wife, who also is a physician, have always had an interest in dogs; Dr. Casper's father raised Great Danes, while Mrs. Casper's family had Miniature Pinschers, Dobermans, and German Shepherds. She is also a member of the Staten Island Kennel Club.

Dr. Casper claims that dogs have many of the same skin problems and allergies that people do, but our favorite story regarding Dr. Casper and his professional prowess concerns his Ch. Wolfscroft Amaranthus, C.D.X. It seems the dog came home one day with his left hind foot dangling, the tendons completely severed from a bad accident. Veterinarians gave up on the dog, but Dr. Casper took it upon himself to get a surgeon to repair the leg and the dog went on to win his championship as well as his obedience title.

We are also grateful that Dr. Casper's hobby of photographing his patient's skin problems before and after treatment extended into the dog fancy so that so many of the Wolfscroft Irish Setters captured on film can be shared with all of us in this book.

DRAHERIN

In 1946 Lucy Jane Myers first spotted Ch. Thenderin Brian Tristan and fell in love with Irish Setters. Within a matter of days after this first encounter she had purchased a four-month-old male from Jo and Hollis Wilson's End O'Maine Kennel. This dog was followed by 13-month-old Thenderin Elixir, C.D., a bitch which completed both her American and Canadian championships. She did well in the breeding department also, with nine champion offspring, including the Best in Show winner Ch. Draherin Echo of Elixir.

Obedience also captured her interest with the Irish Setters. Miss Myers owned and trained the first C.D.X. in the state of Minnesota, and she was active in field trials and still is today. Also many Best in Show winners have come from Draherin. American and Canadian Ch. Draherin Batchelor Boy was Canada's leading Best in Show dog for 1969; another, Canadian, American, and Bermudian Ch. Shannon's Erin, is a Best in Show winner in all three countries!

Other Draherin dogs of note are Ch. Draherin Windjammer and Draherin King's Ransom. Lucy Jane Myers has also been named to the Phillips System Hall of Fame for having placed five different dogs a total of six times on the Top Sire and Top Dam list compiled by Irene Phillips Khatoonian Schlintz. Draherin is a much respected name in all three phases of the dog fancy.

Best in Show at the 1953 Longshore-Southport Kennel Club show was Ch. Thenderin Brian Tristan, owned by Mr. and Mrs. James Fraser of Olmstead Falls, Ohio. Mrs. Paul Silvernail was the judge; Charley Meyer handled. Club president Taylor Coleman is shown presenting the trophy.

RED BARN

The Red Barn Kennels of William and Marion Neville was established in 1947 in Blauvelt, New York, with a bitch of the famous Knightscroft breeding. This first bitch won their affection, and very soon more Knightscroft and Boxley breeding came into the kennel to serve as their foundation stock. These included Ch. Kendare Red Dawn. Outcrosses to Ch. Red Star of Hollywood Hills, C.D.X., Ch. Tyronne Farm Malone II and Ch. Michael Bryan Duke of Sussex formed the nucleus of the kennel and they were well on their way to success in the breed.

In the next three decades nearly 50 champions bore the Red Barn prefix. The Nevilles claim this record is based on their quality stock

Ch. Red Barn Jezebelle pictured winning at the 1970 Windham County Kennel Club show. Jezebelle was bred and is owned by Mrs. Marion B. Neville, Red Barn Kennels, Blauvelt, New York.

and good stud dogs, which included Ch. Red Barn Crispin, Ch. Boxley April Blaze, Ch. Red Barn Royal Talisman and Ch. Red Barn Talleyrand to name a few. These top studs bred to bitches of great quality included their Ch. Boxley Holly Anne, dam of seven champions, as well as Ch. Knightscroft Primrose, Ch. Knightscroft Camellia, Ch. Boxley Bluebonnet, Ch. Red Barn Redwood, Ch. Red Barn Doretta, Ch. Red Barn Rosabelle, U.D.T. and Red Barn Noreen, all of which produced three champions each.

Many of the Red Barn Irish Setters have obedience titles, and the kennel boasts the most Bermuda champions, thanks to their good friend, Paula McAteer. Top show bitches include Ch. Red Barn Royal Holly, Ch. Red Barn Royal Charm and Ch. Red Barn Princess Caitlin.

When asked to sum up the aims and purpose of the Red Barn kennels, Marion Neville says: "Though I have always loved the competition of the show ring and hopefully transferred these 'good hands' of my youth in the horse show ring, I feel the goal of dog breeding is even more. To me the greatest delight will always be supplying the happy companion to the loving home. I would hope that this happy companion would also be sound, well-boned, typey, a dark-eyed, mahogany coated good mover."

Since the Red Barn Kennels are famous and reported to be one of the largest in the country, we also hope this is true. It is obviously the reason their record is so good and their dogs so beautiful.

DEVON

Frank and Dorothy Cory of Arlington Heights, Illinois owned the Devon Kennels, which were active in the 1940's. Their first two bitches, Wamsutta Dream Girl and Knightscroft Golden Glow, were both bred to Ward Gardner's Ch. Kleiglight of Aragon. In 1946 they obtained Ch. Charles River Color Sergeant from John Downs, and he won the November, 1947 Western Specialty show. It was at this show that Frank died tragically in the ring, but Dorothy went on showing the dog to a career which included 5 Bests in Show and 12 Sporting Group wins. Twelve years later his great-great-grandson, Ch. Conifer's Lance, repeated the Best in Show win Sergeant made at the 1949 Chicago International Show, to become the second Irish Setter to win this honor. On both occasions the dogs were handled by professional handler Dick Cooper, who is still very active in the handling of top show dogs. Sergeant sired 250 puppies, including 17 champions; he was a Top Sire for 1949 and 1950. His get also did well in field competition.

INNISFAIL

Nedra and Roy Jerome of Sepulveda, California whelped their first litter of Irish Setters in 1947 under their kennel prefix of Cu-Roi. They changed the Cu-Roi to Innisfail in 1952 with the arrival of their second litter sired by Ch. Seaforths Dark Rex *ex* Thenderin Cham-

Everett Gallico of the Wamsutta Kennels showing Warren K. Read, Jr.'s *eighteen*-year-old Irish Setter, Riley, just after he won the Veteran's Class at the 1938 Specialty Show of the Irish Setter Club of New England.

pagne. They referred to it as the art and music litter, and it produced three champions, one of which was Innisfail Color Scheme, C.D., which became the foundation of the Webline Kennels and a notable sire for them. Their Ch. Innisfail Best Regards became the foundation bitch for the Varagon Kennels of Val and Ray Gonsor, Granada Hills, California, and dam of Champions Flash Back of Varagon, Enchantment of Varagon and Legend of Varagon.

In 1959 new bloodlines were introduced with a puppy bitch sired by an Innisfail stud, Ch. Margevan Madcap of Innisfail, *ex* Ch. Bright Accent's Erin. The puppy grew up to be Ch. Glen Erin's Pride of In-

One of the great stars of yesteryear, Ch. End O'Maine McCabe. Photo Courtesy of the George Brodies.

nisfail, dam of the top-winning Ch. Innisfail Flashback's Design, multiple Best in Show winner and a top contender in the Phillips System ratings. Owned by Selma Stoll, M.D., "Gavin" was handled through his show career by Walt Shellenbarger.

BANSHEE

Ivan and Lenore Klapper of Gardiner, New York started their Banshee Kennels, based on Knightscroft and Red Barn lines in 1947. Perhaps their most outstanding bitch was Ch. Knightscroft Lady Vogue, C.D.; she was the dam of their Ch. Banshee Sharpshooter and Ch. Banshee Rebel Brigadier, C.D., and Granddam of Ch. Banshee Bushwhacker. Ivan served as president of the Irish Setter Club of America from 1961 through 1967, and the Klappers still maintain their keen interest in the breed.

THENDERIN

Thenderin really had its beginning in the 1940's when Joyce Holzman finished her obedience-trained Irish Setter, Ranger's Red Lass, to a C.D. title. In 1946 the family moved from Buffalo, New York to California, and Joyce purchased Ch. Red Ranger Pat and Ch. Kinvarra Portia, dam of 12 champions and foundation bitch for Thenderin Kennels. She was also chosen Best Brood Matron in 1948, 1949 and 1950. Unfortunately, she died whelping a litter of puppies sired by Ch. Red Star of Hollywood Hills. End O'Maine McCabe, which Joyce co-owned with Professor Orrin Evans, was another of her early greats. In 1953 Joyce married Athos Nilsen; both became professional handlers, and Athos Nilsen also gained fame as a dog photographer. Some of our great show dogs of yesteryear were captured on film by his artistry. In 25 years Thenderin has bred over 200 champions and was the recipient of the 1971 Irish Setter Club of America Breeders Award.

Thenderin dogs also have excelled in the field and obedience trials and have won many Bests in Show. In the old days, perhaps their best known dog was Ch. Thenderin Brian Tristan, whelped in 1948. Bred by the James Frasers, in the period from 1950 to 1954, he won 10 Bests in Show, 23 Best Sporting Group awards and 61 Bests of Breed—he won the Group at both Westminster and Chicago International in 1953. He also sired 30 champions.

HAGGINWOOD

No discussion of the important decade of the 1940's would be complete without the mention of Irene Phillips Khatoonian, now Mrs. Harold Schlintz. In 1943 she and her husband James H. Phillips established their Hagginwood Kennels in California. Until its finish in 1959 upon the death of James Phillips, there often were as many as 50 or 60 Irish Setters in residence at Hagginwood. During these 15 years their good eye accounted for 14 bench show champions, 4 with obedience titles as well, and many trained gun dogs.

Their Ch. Eric O'Hagginwood C.D. was trained as a gun dog also. Their Ch. Coppercoat of the Hills won a Best in Show in 1947 and was field-trained by Lee Baldock. Their Ch. Lady Kathleen O'Hagginwood was the dam of six bench show champions. Many others had obedience titles, and their Ch. Hagginwood Real McCoy went all the way to a C.D.X. title. In 1953 Ch. Lady Kathleen was winner of the Irish Setter Club of America Brood Bitch Award.

Ch. Coppercoat of the Hills pictured winning Best in Show at the 1948 San Joaquin Kennel Club show under judge Chris Shuttleworth. Handled by John Hickey for owners Mr. and Mrs. James Phillips of Sacramento, California; Mrs. Phillips is now Mrs. Harold Schlintz. The sire was Ch. Coppercoat of Crosshaven **ex** Serena.

American and Canadian Ch. Robin O'Dea wins the 1953 Irish Setter Club of Ohio Specialty Show under judge Irene Castle Phillips Khatoonian, now Mrs. Harold Schlintz. Handler is Edward W. McIvor for owner Fred J. Tetreau of Livonia, Michigan.

Irene is still active in the fancy as a columnist, Research Editor of *Kennel Review Magazine* (since 1970) and creator of the Phillips System, a rating system for the nation's top-winning show dogs which has been a top feature in *Popular Dogs* magazine from the 1950's up to now. She also created the Top Producers feature for *Popular Dogs* magazine and is listed in Who's Who of American Women and The National Registry of Prominent Americans. She is also the author of the book *Great Show Dogs of America*, based on the all-time winners according to her Phillips System ratings. In 1975 she married Harold Schlintz; the Schlintzes reside in Sacramento, California.

A head study portrait of classic beauty. . . Ch. Weblyn Mystic Mark, bred and owned by Mr. and Mrs. C.R. Webb, Webline Kennels, El Monte, California, breeders of three generations of champion Irish Setters. This magnificent photograph represents the artistry of famed dog photographer Joan Ludwig.

Ch. Webline Fame 'N Fortune is pictured winning the Sporting Group under judge Harold Schlintz at the 1970 Tucson Kennel Club show. Fortune was #9 Sporting Dog in 1970, #3 in 1971 and #9 Dog in the nation, all-breeds, in 1972. Whelped in 1967, he was sired by Ch. Webline Wizard of Macapa ex Ch. Webline Zamara. Handled by Tom Tobin for owners Mr. and Mrs. William Klussman.

THE 1950'S THROUGH TODAY

WEBLINE

Clayton and Madeline Webb started their kennel with the Weblyn prefix. It was used by the Webbs and Averil Rosslyn and later changed to Webline, though dogs of the day that achieved prominence in the breed carried both names.

In 1952 Dick Webb got Ch. Innisfail Color Scheme C.D. as a puppy from Nedra and Roy Jerome. This dog's show career was one that brought favorable attention to the breed as it hit the halfway mark of this century in the United States.

"Pat," as he was called at home, won the Irish Setter Club of Southern California Specialty Show three times and received special awards from the parent club. He sired ten litters from ten different bitches, and his get included champions from several countries as well as obedience dogs.

The Webline Kennels have received Breeder of the Year Awards for ten consecutive years, an honor it will be difficult for anyone else to duplicate. This achievement was accomplished while breeding no more than two litters a year! During the period from 1965 to 1973, Webline had the top-winning Irish Setters in the country, represented by Ch. Webline Rio Hondo, Ch. Webline Wizard of Macapa, Ch. Webline Golden Jubilee and Ch. Webline Fame N'Fortune. Each of these dogs won many Bests in Show and figured prominently in the Top Ten Sporting Dogs in the nation according to the Phillips System.

Today the Webline kennel is located in El Monte, California, where Dick is still serving the breed as a handler and agent for his own as well as his clients' dogs.

The William Klussmans of Woodland Hills, California owned Fame N'Fortune, handled for them through his brilliant show career by Tom Tobin. He was one of the top-winning Sporting Dogs in the nation in 1970 and is a Best in Show winner. He was the recipient of the Milson O'Boy trophy for having defeated 1,944 Irish Setter competitors within a one year period in the show ring.

CELOU

Louis Iacobucci's Celou Kennels came into being in the early 1950's when he obtained a Shawnlea bitch. The bitch was bred to a Charles River dog, and the litter produced Celou's Sheena MacRory, his foundation brood bitch. From Sheena we have six Celou champions, which account for two Best in Show wins for Louis. Louis became President of the Irish Setter Club of America in 1968 and was still in office in the mid-1970's. He was also winner of the Gaines Man of the Year award in 1973; he has been for many years president of the Providence, Rhode Island Kennel Club.

DUNGUAIRE

Arthur and Audrey Baines of East Longmeadow, Massachusetts imported their Ch. Brynmount Maydorwill Brandyson from England and campaigned him at the Eastern Seaboard shows throughout the 1950's. He was used at stud with American stock during this period and sired a total of eight champions. Most prominent of his get was Ch. Dunguaire Bryson, one of the top sporting dogs of 1956. Bryson won 9 Bests in Show, 34 Sporting Group Firsts and 97 Bests of Breed during his show ring career.

Ch. Kleighlight of Aaragon, owned by the Aaragon Kennels in Franklin Park, Illinois, wins Best in Show at a Mercer County Kennel Club show several years ago. Jack Cooper, handler. The judge was S.H. Beddow.

AARAGON

In Farmington, Michigan Charles and Alberta Benton were active in the obedience rings with their Aaragon dogs. In addition to their C.D.X. winner Timothy Shawn O'Dea, they bred a litter sired by Ch. General Beauregard *ex* Ch. Argo Lane's Countess of Cork; this litter included five champions.

It was also during the 1950's that the William Goldens of Pacific Palisades acquired Ch. Webline Golden Jubilee, C.D. But it was their Muldoon of Haleridge that obtained his C.D. title in 1957 and his U.D. the following year. Jubilee was preceded by another Webline Irish Setter, Ch. Webline Mi-Golden Flame, also a C.D. title holder. The Golden Irish Setters excel at both bench and field. In 1965 Walt Shellenbarge handled Jubilee to prominence as one of the top sporting dogs in the west.

SHANNON

It was in the early 1950's that one of the most significant kennel names appeared on the horizon, because in that year Charles and Betty Crawford of North Jackson, Ohio founded their Shannon Kennels.

After much preliminary research they purchased their first Irish Setter, Shamrock of Erin, from George Glassford. The Crawfords garnered their show ring experience with "Shamie"; when bred to Ch. Caldene Mick O'Boy, she produced two champions, Ch. Shamrock's Shawn of Erin and Ch. Shamrock's Red Rogue, C.D.

They next wished to purchase a stud of their own and purchased Knockross Nero from W.L. Newhall; Nero became their first champion. Soon after a new brood bitch was sought, but several years passed before their Knockross Ruby was purchased. They called her Shannon and eventually named their kennel after this magnificent bitch.

Ruby went on to become one of the top-producing dams in the history of the breed. She was the dam of 21 champions, in just four litters with several others pointed and producing champions of their own. Among Shannon's best-known progeny are American and Canadian Ch. Major O'Shannon and American, Canadian and Bermudian Ch. Shannon's Erin.

When Shannon was completing her championship Betty Crawford was also showing a dog named Irish Regardless. They completed their titles one week apart, and the decision was made to breed them to each other. The first litter, whelped in 1962, produced several top winners with the Shannon prefix including American and Canadian Ch. Shannon's Laird Shane, which finished in the Top Ten Setters in 1965 and 1966 and was Top Irish Setter and Top Sporting Dog in Canada in 1967.

The second litter, in 1964, also produced top winners including Lucy Jane Myers' Ch. Shannon's Erin, and Major O'Shannon, who was Top Irish Setter and Second Top Sporting Dog in the Nation in 1968. His record through 1970 included 209 Bests of Breed, 107 Group Firsts, and 33 Bests in Show. His show record remains unchallenged in the history of the breed.

KILLASHANDRA

Jane Morris of Hampton, New Jersey has been showing dogs since 1938 but got into the Irish Setter breed only in the early 1960's. Jane tries to keep Killashandra operations at no more than 24 dogs when her kennel is in operation so that the dogs receive individual attention. During the mid-1970's circumstances necessitated her selling her Ha'Penny Farm, and she put her papers and kennel photographs in storage so pictures of her dogs are not available for this book, un-

Ch. Hollybrook Serenade, with handler Patti Grant. The owner is Patricia P. Gallagher, Gala Glen Kennels, Melbourne, Florida. Serenade was Group First at the 1974 Pasadena Kennel Club show and won the Central California Specialty Show in 1973. Rarely defeated by other bitches, she is one of a few bitches to win a Group First in California.

fortunately. Especially missed is the photographic coverage given to her dogs in an article I wrote while editor of *Popular Dogs* magazine back in 1972.

GALA GLEN

Patricia Gallagher's Gala Glen Kennels came into being in 1960. Best known for her top-producing show bitches, she is justly proud of her Ch. Hollybrook Serenade, one of a few bitches ever to win a Group in California and one rarely defeated by other bitches when in competition. Winner of the 1973 Central California Specialty Show, this lovely bitch is also known for her excellent movement.

Over the years Gala Glen has produced other fine Irish Setters, such as Ch. Gala Glen September Dawn, Ch. Antrims Adonis of Gala

Glen, Ch. Gala Glen Bells A-Ringin, and Ch. Red Royal A Bit of Barney. In the obedience field Pat Gallagher finished Ch. Harmony Lane Sandpiper, C.D., highest-scoring dog in a trial at Daytona with a score of 199½, and also finished Ch. Red Devil of Chesachobe, C.D.X.

Pat Gallagher is also an Irish Setter judge; as a judge she expresses concern that too much emphasis is being put on coat and showmanship at the sacrifice of good movement.

BALLYCROY

Mrs. Fred (Constance) Vanacore, owner of the Ballycroy Irish Setter Kennels in Mendham, New Jersey, founded in 1960, is active in many phases of the dog fancy. In addition to raising and showing her dogs, she is known as a writer as well. Connie edits columns for the dog magazines and was the 1971 winner of the Gaines Dog Research Center editorial contest commemorating National Dog Week. The winning entry was taken from her commentary in the *Mendham Observer-Tribune*, for which she is dog columnist. On three separate occasions she has been honored by the Dog Writers Association of America for her columns also. She is an editorial consultant for the American Kennel Club *Gazette* and is an editor of the Irish Setter Club of America publication *Memo to Members*. She is active in other ways in the Eastern Irish Setter Association and the Irish Setter Club of America.

Her pride and joy, Ch. Ballycroys Northern Sunset, is also her top stud dog and is the result of the blending of two important strains in Irish Setters—the Knockross and Tirvelda lines. This homebred, as was his dam, Ballycroy's Rua Catlin, are the basis of her kennel breeding. Casey, as he is called at home, was one of a litter of 16, 14 of which survived; the litter contained several Irish Setters that went on to wins in the show ring. Casey is also the sire of two Best of Breed winners and a Specialty Show Best of Breed winner.

A vacation visit to Russia in 1972, a gift from her father, Mr. B. Boardman, is reported elsewhere in this book, and we are most grateful to Connie for this amazing insight into the breed in that country and for the valuable photographs reproduced in this book which let us see the type and quality of their dogs. We wish her great luck with Lara, the puppy bitch the Russian fanciers presented her with as a generous example of the feeling they had for their fellow Irish Setter fanciers.

SPORTMIRTH

Helen and Ed Treutel of Leonia, New Jersey started their Sportmirth Kennel back in the 1960's. With a very limited breeding program they still have managed to breed four Irish Setter champions, three Companion Dog title-holders, and one Irish Setter with a C.D.X. degree.

Red Coat of Tercor wins the Best Sporting Dog at the 1947 Westbury Kennel Association show under judge David Wagstaff. Harold Correll handling.

Their first bitch, American and Canadian Ch. Tirvelda Best Regards, C.D., won the annual Irish Setter Club of America Best Bitch Award two different years and completed her show ring career with over 100 Breed, Best Opposite and Group Placement wins. Her daughter Ch. Tirvelda Valentine also won the Irish Setter Club of America Best Bitch Award twice. During her show career she defeated nearly 3,000 other bitches and won 200 Bests of Breed, Bests of Opposite Sex and Group Placement wins.

Valentine's litter brother, Ch. Tirvelda Sportin' Life, C.D., finished with four majors and had 21 Bests of Breed and 11 Group Placements. Litter sister Tirvelda Taralee carries the C.D.X. title. Their homebred bitch Ch. Sportmirth Starbright finished her championship with three Specialty Show wins.

Ch. Tirvelda Nor'wester has been in residence with the Treutels for many years, though owned by Ted Eldredge, and is the sire of their Valentine, Sportin' Life and Starbright. His total is 15 champion get.

Helen Treutel was recording secretary of the Irish Setter Club of America for three years, while Ed has been president of the Eastern Irish Setter Association and the Palisades Kennel Club. At present (1975) he is first vice president of the ISCA and national show chairman as well. He is also to become a judge of Irish Setters.

GLENDEE

Thorne and Myra Harris and their Glendee Kennels became very active in the New Orleans area, in both bench and obedience rings. Glendee was known for Ch. Tyronne Farm Midnight, C.D.; Ch. Tyronne Farm Midday Flame, C.D., sired by the famous Ch. Wautoma dog owned by Mrs. Cheever Porter; Ch. Tyronne Farm Gloribee and Ch. Tyronne Farm Rex. Myra Harris also excelled as a handler and was a familiar face with winning Irish Setters over the years.

OTHER KENNELS ESTABLISHED BEFORE 1970

Names like Dr. William J. Fritz come to mind with his American and Canadian Ch. Michael Bryan Duke of Sussex dog handled by Horace Hollands years ago. Twice he placed in Westminster Group competition and had 11 Bests of Breed and 40 Group Firsts. He sired 11 champions, including one by Ch. Tirvelda Nutbrown Sherry which produced six bench show champions.

Virginia Hardin of the Runwild Kennels, prominent in obedience and field work, also showed and handled Irish Setters in the show ring. Long dedicated to the breed, Virginia Hardin is still active in the show ring and in the Irish Setter Club of America; she is particularly active in field work for the club.

Needless to say, before passing on to the 1970's mention must be made of the contribution made by the Bayberry Irish Setters. This

Ch. Michael Bryan Duke of Sussex, a top producer in 1965, 1966, 1967 and 1968; he was sire of 32 champions and was 2nd ranking Sporting Dog in the nation in 1962; owned by Dr. William Fritz. Sire was Thenderin Brian Tristan **ex** Ch. Merrilynn of Glenfield.

119

Ch. Tyronne Farm Rex, whelped February 6, 1959, by breeder Howard K. Mellang, was the sire of 12 champion offspring. Rex was also #3 ranking Sporting Dog in 1963. Handled here by Myra B. Harris, Rex was owned by Mrs. Cheever Porter of New York City.

kennel, owned by Mr. and Mrs. William C. Brooks, Jr. in Dalton, Georgia, holds a splendid record in the breed, based on the great bloodlines of the past. Many champions bearing their kennel prefix have made their mark in the history of the breed, including their champion sire and breed and group winner at Westminster, Ch. Bayberry Kincaide.

O'DEKE-LAKEVIEW

Robert D. Helferty, M.D. of Davison, Michigan got his kennel off to a flying start in the early 1970's. Within the first two years of its existence Dr. Helferty came up with a winner. . . not just any old winner, either, but one of the top dogs in the nation. His name is American, Canadian and Bermudian Ch. Kelly Shannon O'Deke. Bred by

Ch. Tuxedo Comanche Majorette pictured going Best of Winners on the way to her championship under judge Mrs. Marie Koontz. Handled by Denny Lafurie for owner R.D. Helferty, M.D. of Davison, Michigan. This win finished Majorette at this 1974 Lansing, Michigan show.

Ruth Cordes, Kelly was handled during his spectacular show career by Dick Cooper, Tom Glassford and Dennis Laturie, all Professional Handlers Association handlers whose expertise in the show ring brought out all the best in this great dog and superb showman.

Kelly was #7 Irish Setter in the nation in 1971, and #4 in 1972. And he didn't stop there. By 1973 he moved up to the #2 spot on the Phillips System charts. In 1973 he also won the honor of being #3 of all the Sporting Dogs in the country. His record boasts of 212 Bests of Breed, 13 All-breed Bests in Show (including a Best in Show in Bermuda), 8 Specialty Bests of Breed, 61 Sporting Group Firsts and 59 Sporting Group Seconds. He won the Irish Setter Club of America award for the most Specialty Bests in Show for 1972.

Officially retired in 1973, he was brought out again in 1974 in the Veterans Class at the Western Irish Setter Club Specialty Show in

Ch. Runwild Finnagan, whelped in November, 1960 and #6 Irish Setter in the breed in 1965. Sired by Ch. Carrvale's Terry Terhune **ex** Ch. Runwild Fiona, he was owned by Virginia Hardin of Runwild Kennels.

Chicago and not only won the Veterans Class but captured the Best of Breed win! He is currently retired once again and is at stud.

Dr. Helferty is also co-owner, with Ruth Cordes, of Kelly's father, the famous American and Canadian Ch. Draherin Billy Boy. He also has his sights set on the future career of another Billy Boy offspring, Ch. Tuxedo Comanche Majorette, sired by another great show dog, Ch. Major O'Shannon. Few "newcomers" to any breed can boast such early phenomenal success as Dr. Helferty, and we look forward to his further contribution to the world of Irish Setters in the show ring.

THE 1970'S

The beginning of the 1970's could well be called the years of the Setter, perhaps—to be more specific—called the years of the Irish Setter, for at this time the Setters dominated the Best in Show rings.

Top of the list, of course, was the record-holder for the breed, American and Canadian Ch. Major O'Shannon, owned by Albert M. Greenfield, the William Klussmans' Ch. Webline Fame N'Fortune and Dr. Selma Stoll's Ch. Innisfail Flashback's Design.

Further statistics on the nation's leading Irish Setters can be found in our chapter on the Phillips System Ratings. Beyond that it

Ch. Danalee Bright Legend is pictured winning at the 1973 Kern County Kennel Club show under judge Harold Schlintz. Whelped in 1967, his sire was Ch. Legend of Varagon, U.D.T. **ex** Stellaire's Red Velvet. Handled by Ray McGinnis for owners Dr. Robert Wendel and Diane L. McGinnis. Ludwig photo.

An Irish Setter beauty from yesteryear, Delaware Peggy of Happy Valley.

would be impossible to name all prominent contenders in the show ring during this decade when the Irish Setter has climbed all the way to the number three position in popularity. It is enough to say that many of them are represented in this book in photographs featuring their current top wins. But with rumor having it that there are over 7,000 Irish Setter Club members active in the breed today, it would be impossible to pay appropriate tribute to all of them. Therefore in compiling this book we have tried to feature the more prominent kennels, with the greatest records, and major winners to supplement the Phillips System ratings and give an adequate picture of the breed today.

We must also hope that a core of dedicated breeders and exhibitors in show, field and obedience will continue to hold the line on good breeding based on the Standard to preserve the Irish Setter from its dangerous over-popularity so that we will not lose the good groundwork and records achieved by our predecessors.

6. THE STORY OF CH. MILSON O'BOY

When a breed has been a popular winner around the show halls for over a century, a lot of good specimens of the breed must have come along in that time to help establish the dog in the fancy. It is always difficult to single out a single dog or even a couple to say they represented "the best," but we can tell when looking over the Phillips System how close the contenders are for the top ten. And at times the records for the twenty or even thirty are close in competition with those that do manage to get listed in the top ten.

But once in awhile there is a single dog in a particular breed that manages to capture the fancy so totally as an all-around representative of the breed that he manages to live on in the hearts and minds of everyone that ever laid eyes on him. Ch. Milson O'Boy was one of those dogs. A legend in his own time and a dog that lives on in the heart of his owner, Mrs. Cheever Porter, Ch. Milson O'Boy is still regarded as what an Irish Setter should be—and was!

All the good things that can be said about an ideal dog applied to O'Boy. He was a devoted and loving companion, he was a spectacular showman who commanded the immediate attention of the audience, and his conformation was the Standard personified! The product and result of a twenty-year breeding program, he—and his breeder/handler, Harry Hartnett, were to achieve fame both in and out of the show ring. Whelped on March 8, 1932, O'Boy was shown over a five-year period from 1933 to 1938 and during that time amassed a total of 103 Bests of Breed, 46 Best Sporting Groups, and 11 Bests in Show. This was quite a record in those days, and he was retired early in 1938 to be used at stud.

Perhaps O'Boy's greatest moment in the show ring came in 1935, when he won Best in Show at the Morris and Essex dog show. One hundred and twenty Irish Setters were present to compete, and after winning the Best of Breed award O'Boy went all the way to Best in Show over the total entry of 3,175 dogs under judge G.V. Glebe. That same year O'Boy won Best American-bred Dog in Show at the Westminster Kennel Club event.

Other honors were bestowed upon this marvelous dog as well. He was used to illustrate the Standard for the breed in the American Kennel Club *Complete Dog Book*, and he was deserving of this honor. Also, Dr. Jay W. Calhoon wrote a book which stands as a permanent memorial to the dog and relates much of the story of his life in and out of the show ring.

Ch. Milson O'Boy was also lauded as a prepotent sire. He sired 41 litters which accounted for a total of 163 puppies from the top-quality bitches of that era.

Mrs. Cheever Porter of New York City recognized the greatness of this flashing red dog and enjoyed every moment of his brilliant show career, and especially the years of his retirement. O'Boy died on June 29, 1945 after living thirteen happy years as a much admired and much loved and always to be remembered Irish Setter that even today is looked upon as near perfection in the breed.

The author remembers that when she was editor of *Popular Dogs* magazine, each June communication was received from Mrs. Porter placing her annual memorial advertisement in our Sporting Dog issue. It was a simple black-bordered box with just his illustrious name and birth and death dates. . .

Upon his death a lengthy obituary was printed in the *New York Sun* newspaper on July 20, 1945. It was written by Arthur Roland and praised O'Boy's accomplishments and noted the respect this great dog had earned in his lifetime. An obituary such as this one had not been printed since the death of the fabulous race horse, Man O'War. We publish this tribute to O'Boy in this chapter in its entirety.

For his greatness, and other reasons, the author chose Ch. Milson O'Boy as the dog to grace the frontispiece of this book.

CH. MILSON O'BOY PASSES ON
Irish Setter With Exceptional Crowd Appeal Dies in His Sleep
by Arthur Roland

"Ch. Milson O'Boy, one of the great show dogs of all times, is dead. The handsome Irish Setter passed away quietly in his sleep recently and now the only visible symbol of him is the stone that marks his resting place beside the other pets of his owner, Mrs. Cheever Porter, in the quiet beauty of the Hartsdale Canine Cemetery at Hartsdale, N.Y.

"It will be a long time, however, before O'Boy will be forgotten by those who saw him in the ring, for seldom has a dog had such crowd appeal as this Red Setter possessed. It is not better typified than by the incident which occurred at the Garden a few years ago. O'Boy was sitting on the bench beside his owner when a man in the blue overalls common to railroad workers approached and asked, 'Is that Milson O'Boy?'

"Informed that it was, he stood silent for a minute studying the dog and then explained, 'I'm sorry I came in looking like this but I haven't much time. I just got in on my run—I'm a fireman on the Pennsylvania—and I had to see him. I've cut his pictures out of the paper every time I've seen them and I've got them all up on the wall at home. I've never been around where he was being shown before, though, and I just had to see him.'

"There was almost an attitude of reverence in the way he put his hand and stroked the dog's head. He ran his hands over the silky coat and gently fondled the long ears. Then he looked at his watch, said, 'Well, I've got to be going. Thanks for letting me pet him,' and walked down the aisle glancing back to where O'Boy, apparently aware that he had been honored, stood slowly wagging his tail.

Ch. Milson O'Boy, pictured winning Best in Show at the 1935 Morris and Essex Kennel Club show. Bred by the Milson Kennels in Harrison, New York, and later owned by Mrs. Cheever Porter of New York City.

"That, of course, was just the appeal this dog had for one man. It was at the Garden however, that one of the most striking demonstrations of O'Boy's appeal to a crowd wa given. That was in the final of the 1936 show when the showy Irishman was representing the gun-dog group in the great sextette that came before the late C. Frederick Neilson O'Boy had captured the crowd when he won his group and they began rooting for him the minute he came into the ring for the Best in Show decision. Every time the judge looked in his direction there was applause and it grew deafening when the big fellow raced up and down the big arena keeping pace with the late Harry Hartnett, who handled him on all his ring appearances.

"When Neilson passed over O'Boy in favor of the smart little Sealyham, St. Marga ret's Surprise of Clairedale, the crowd made it very clear that it didn't like it at all. It was the first time in Westminster history that its Best in Show award had evoked such a hos tile demonstration. What the crowd did not know was that Neilson was one of O'Boy's admirers and that, in giving preference to the Sealyham, he was not following his heart but his responsibility to judge the dogs on comparative show standards as he saw them.

"Another great demonstration of the way this dog could capture the hearts of a crowd was given at the Morris and Essex of 1935. He certainly was a picture as he paced over the velvety turf on the polo field at Giralda Farms, against the evergreens and geraniums which bordered the judging platform and the bright summer clothes of the spectators. This time the gallery was bigger than at the Garden and its tribute to the great dog even more thunderous. When G.V. Glebe sent him to the center of the ring to receive the Best in Show trophy the crowd roared approval.

"What won the gallery every time O'Boy appeared in the ring was the fact that this dog made it perfectly clear that he knew what he was in there for. If ever a dog was trying every minute to win it was Ch. Milson O'Boy. He would never sleep with his collar on—to him that was the evidence that there was a show battle to be fought—and once the lead was around his neck it was all that Harry Hartnett could do to keep him quiet. He would race from the crate to the entrance of the ring and fidget around until it was time to go in. There was no relaxing for him until the contest was decided and he was back in the crate again. He would keep his eye as steadily on the judge as would his handler and there was no question but that he ate up the gallery tributes.

Al Smith an Admirer

"One of his great admirers was the late Al Smith. He followed O'Boy's show career and had a collection of photographs of him. As a matter of fact, the judging of Best in the Westchester Kennel Club show was delayed a bit one year because Al wanted his picture taken with O'Boy and was not content until the camera men had taken half a dozen shots. The one he liked best of them subsequently was framed and hung over his desk in the Empire State Building.

"For all his ring consciousness there was nothing of the prima donna about O'Boy. At home he was just a pet, devoted to his mistress, with whom he delighted to play special games that they had devised. Attached as he and his handler were to each other, these were pleasures he reserved for his owner. Harry used to say, 'He'll never play that way with me.'

"The son of Ch. Higgins Red Coat out of Milson's Miss Sonny, O'Boy was whelped on March 8, 1932. That made him more than thirteen years old at the time of his death, a ripe old age for a dog. Retired at the height of his career he had enjoyed a happy life as a pet, marred only by the death of his handler. There are few who saw him in his moment of greatest triumph who will ever forget him.

THE PEDIGREE OF CH. MILSON O'BOY

Higgins Paddy of Boyne

SIRE: **Ch. Higgins Red Coat**

Craigie Lea Mona

Ch. Terence of the Cloisters

DAM: **Milson Miss Sonny**

Milson Goldie

7. FIELD DOGS IN AMERICA

While it was the famous show and field dog Plunket and a field dog named Wrestler that were winning the first field trials abroad in the 1860's, it wasn't until 1870 that an Irish Setter (named Queen) won the first scheduled field trial in this country. The win was in Marin County, California and is not to be confused with the 1874 combination dog show and trial held by the Tennessee State Sportsmen's Association and written about elsewhere in this book as the first dog show in America.

Now just about a century later, we are amazed to see the increase in interest and entries since that first event with just four starters. The Brysons were very active with their field dogs and influential in the beginning years with their staging of the Tennessee event, but it was George W. Campbell, another avid dog man, whose Irish Setter named Tom was the first Irish Setter to win a Championship Stake in 1875.

While the Tennessee Sportsmen's Shows ended in 1878 after a five-year run, it can be said that these trials, held on the Belle Meade estate of General Harding, fostered the real beginnings of the serious trials in this country that were held from that time forward. The last of these memorable and significant Sportsmen's shows ended in a tie between an Irish Setter named Joe, Jr., a son of the famous Ch. Elcho, and Adam's Drake for the Championship Stake prize.

The first prairie chicken trial was held on September 4, 1877 at Hampton, Iowa. Two Irish Setters placed that year, and the following year the imported Irish Setter named Friend won the All-Age Stake. But there was no doubt about it: the Irish Setters generally were taking a second place to the English, or Llewellin, Setters in trial competition. The "Llewellin" name associated with English Setters can be attributed to the Englishman Purcel Llwellin, who was credited in England as having perfected the English Setter breed. Many of his dogs were imported to this country and worked remarkably well in the field and they therefore were associated with his name. This same Mr. Llewellin purchased the famous Plunket from the Rev. J.C. Macdona and later sold him to a buyer in America.

The English Setters and the Pointers were pretty much winning everything there was to be won in those early days. Breeding to specifications for field requirements, as the Llewellin dogs were, had not yet taken hold in the Irish Setter breeding program, and the Irish Setters obviously had a long way to go before they could be expected to triumph over the carefully bred Setters and Pointers which had such a substantial head start.

It wasn't until the fall of 1891, on November 23 to be precise, that the Irish Setter Club held its first trials (at High Point, North Carolina). Club president Dr. G.G. Davis and his contemporaries staged four annual field trials during the following years. The trials were resumed in 1907, when interest once again picked up on the Eastern seaboard. Interest in the midwest also was negligible during these early years of the 20th century, though the Western Irish Setter Club did record that a bitch named Hurrah won a Derby Stake as early as 1902. F.A. Johnson of Detroit was active in field work with his dogs, based on the Law strain, and Otto Pohl and his Donegal lines kept the Irish Setters in the running until he died in 1918.

THE 1920'S BRING NEW INTEREST

In the early 1920's many new names began to appear in field trial competition. Elias Vail, a professional trainer, began working dogs. G.O. Smith imported from Ireland a dog named Tipperary Eamon that went down in field trial history as the sire of 47 litters that produced in turn many other field trial winners. Dr. L.C. Adams began his Smada Kennels and became one of the first presidents of the Dayton, Ohio Pointer Club. Dr. Adams had already had Setters for thirty years. When Otto Pohl died in 1918 Dr. Adams obtained his Donegal lines, and after several breedings managed to come up with a field trial winner of note, Smada Byrd. Byrd was later sold to J. Horace Lytle, who did well with the dog until her death in 1935; Lytle wrote a book about their experiences in the field. Whelped in 1921, Byrd not only won in the field against strong competition but also whelped two litters during her lifetime.

California trials were beginning to catch on due largely to the interest of Dr. J.C. Negley and his Valley View Irish Setters. His dog Valley View Jiggs, bred to 46 bitches, produced over 200 registered Irish Setters. One of his get was Ch. Valley View Pat, one of the first Irish Setters to win in both the show ring and the field.

George and Lillian Gallus acquired their first Irish Setter in 1920 and trained it for duck hunting. It was only years later that they actually began to breed Irish Setters under their Glenfield Kennel name, based on Kinvarra and Aaragon bloodlines.

The dogs of Royal Ferris in Dallas, Texas continued to win during the second decade with imports. His dogs Red Hot, Tipperary Eamon's Ghost and Vernon's Sport did well for him. He also campaigned two bench champions, Ch. Bran of Boyne and Ch. Saccy Redall. In Tulsa, Oklahoma Ben Curtis came up with some good stock as a result of his imports. He was out with McKerry's Pat, McKerry Pat's Dusty, Red Law's Ghost and Linda Louise. He, like Royal Ferris, also owned a bench show champion (named Ch. Belle's Anniversary) and was quite well known at the time.

Other prominent names in the sport at this turning point in the field trial competition were J.D. Smith, J.A. Puryear, A.A. Scott, O.T. Graham, Dr. R.H. Washburn, Fred Sulzbach and Dr. Lloyd Thompson.

The Sulhamstead prefix belonging to Florence Nagle was first heard in field trial quarters as early as 1925; it was to continue being heard up through the 1960's. Ernest Levering's imports were first on the scene for Sulhamstead with his Sulhamstead Beppo D'Or and Trace D'Or. Les Blackwell ran Sulhamstead Major D'Or, and W.E. "Ned" LeGrande's imported Field Ch. Sulhamstead Norse D'Or for his Willow Winds Kennel. Norse amassed the greatest record of all, having placed in 41 stakes; he won the 1962 National Red Setter Championship Stake and was runner-up in the 1959 Middle Atlantic States Regional Shooting Dog Classic. As a sire he also did himself proud by producing 21 field trial winners. Starting in 1952 and for more than a dozen years thereafter, Willow Wind dogs were winners in more than 500 trials. All went back to Le Grandes original Sulhamstead stock, a record Florence Nagle can well be proud of.

THE 1930'S

In 1932 the American Kennel Club revised their trial rules and regulations. These new rules led to a considerable increase in entries at both the all-breed and specialty club trials. While the Irish Setter Club of America had once again resumed annual field trials in 1927, in 1934 the new rules and new popularity for the sport found the parent club holding two trials each year.

The first Irish Setter field trial champion under the new AKC rules was Elcova McTybe, a sire of seven future field trial winners. His championship in 1933 was followed by field trial Ch. Tipperary McKerry in 1934.

One of the strongest advocates of the field trial sport was a man named William Cary Duncan. Mr. Duncan loved the sport, loved the breed and was a great wit. For many years he was breed columnist for the American Kennel Club's magazine. For anyone truly interested in Irish Setters it would be worth a trip to the AKC library to read some of his early columns.

For instance, in his column in the December, 1936 issue William Duncan wrote about a field trial he had recently attended. His account gives a vivid picture of the way they went during those early days:

"The shades of night were falling fast when yours truly lined up the eight placed dogs to compete for the Cuneo Trophy. The winner was the Berolzheimer's Shawn McTybe of the Cloisters.

"The auto lights were shining when the cup was handed over. Taking everything into consideration sunset on Sunday marked the end of two perfect days. I can only say that there were ten or a dozen dogs in the 2 stakes good enough to trim the best we could muster 5 years ago."

Names of field trial judges appeared in his columns also, such as T. Carmody, E.G. Corey, G.R. Bares, S.J. McGowan, J.A. Reinhold, A.A. Browne, H.W. Davies, C.E. Doherty and A. Van A. Thomason.

Duncan faithfully reported the trials and the winners as well in his own inimitable style. Never afraid to offer an opinion, his clear evaluation and generous sense of humor made him a popular figure for many, many years.

Ruth and Frederick Kremer got into field trial runs in the 1930's and were still active in field work through the 1960's with the Autumn Hill Irish Setters. During their more than three decades in the sport their dogs won three *Sports Afield* magazine All-American Awards.

Other names became known during the 1930's. Field trials were being won by dogs owned by Patrick W. Hehir, J.H. Graham, H.A. Simms, Thomas Marshall (also a judge), Charles M. Coale, Alvin R. Bush, S.L. Taylor, Jack Spear, Mrs. Beatrice Everrett, W.J. Thayer, Bill Duncan, E.A. Smith, J.E. Hill and Earl Bond, to name several of the most active.

THE 1940'S

The early 1940's represented the World War II years, with the usual restrictions on importations, gas rationing, and the other limitations felt by all the dog fancy. But once America started to get back to normal, the desire to get back into the fields with the dogs came back with added interest and momentum, and by the 1950's the ranks were filled with Irish Setters.

The Marflow Kennels in Painesville, Ohio, were owned by Wolfram and Frieda Stumpf. In 1931 Swampland Sally marked the beginning of their kennel breeding program and in 1951 Wolfram Stumpf became active in the field. He is a charter member of the Irish Setter Club of Ohio, which was formed in 1947, and he is a judge for both field and bench shows.

THE 1950'S

The 1950's saw the formation of the National Red Setter Field Trial Club, which held its first semi-annual trial on April 13, 1952. The trials were held alternately in Delaware and Ohio. Among the members were A.E. Church, A.E. Bortz, Herm David, J.G. Cassidy, J.T.

Westwind Scarlet Magic on point. Bred, owned and trained by Luz Holvenstot, Westwind Kennels, Long Valley, New Jersey.

Clifton, John Van Alst, R.C. Baynard, W.E. Le Grande, Charles Winter, T.P. Ward, D.L. Martin and Robert and James Finn.

On October 17, 1953 the first National Red Setter Open Shooting Dog Championship Stake was run. Askew's Carolina Lady had her title withheld but she later became an American Kennel Club field champion and defeated more than 300 dogs in field competition, taking time out now and then to whelp! This she did with great success also. She was the dam of 15 field trial winners and granddam of many more, from just six litters.

Her son Field Ch. Ike Jack Kendrick was perhaps the most successful and best-known. He won 66 stakes and earned the title of the Irish Setter with the most wins in the field. He sired more than 40 field trial winners during his career at stud.

Herm David's dog The Dude sired seven field trial winners including Field Champion F'yn. Herm, who lived in Cleveland at the time, had the good fortune to see his first Irish Setter, Seamus Red Tuxedo, C.D., win first place in the Open Gun Dog Stake at the Irish Setter Club of Indiana trials back in 1950.

The Dude was a son of Field Ch. Askew's Carolina Lady, who placed in a great many field trial stakes. Herm has owned several

Irish Setters since then, including Sulhamstead Nat D'Or, from Florence Nagle's famous line.

Ralph Baynard's Double Jay won the 1955 and the 1957 Shooting Dog Championship Stakes and sired over a dozen field trial winners.

The David Hasingers from Philadelphia saw their Field Champion Valli Hi Lacey win at 20 field trial events, and a dog named Mr. O'Leary, owned by F.C. Bean, was a shooting dog champion that had a ten-year winning streak. Bean also owned Ch. Windyridge Tammy, who racked up 45 placements at trials.

Dr. James Wilson of Milltown, Wisconsin grew up with Irish Setters which were mostly field dogs. Jim, a veterinarian, and his wife Phyllis owned the Cherry Point Kennels. They had many field trial winners over the years as well as bench show winners. Perhaps they will always be best remembered as the breeders of American and Canadian Ch. Cherry Point Brask, one of the most famous show dogs in the history of the breed, campaigned by Mrs. Cheever Porter of New York City.

Edgar and Roberta McIvor of Plymouth, Michigan had the first dual champion in the breed. Dual Ch. Tyrone's Mahogany Mike, C.D.X. was also the first tri-title holder of *any breed* in American Kennel Club history! The McIvors, who used Ivor Glen as their kennel name, also owned Field Ch. Ivor Glen Devilera. From 1952 through 1960 Mike placed in two dozen stakes and sired four bench show champions and two field trial winners. The McIvors' interest quite obviously extended to the show ring as well and they had many champions over their years in the breed.

Lawrence and Eleanor Heist of the Red Arrow Kennels in Fontana, California also were proud owners of a triple crown dog. Their Bench and Field Trial Ch. Red Arrow Show Girl, U.D.T. also had a Mexican P.C. degree and was surely the winningest all-around Irish Setter in the history of the breed. Whelped in 1953, she was the first dog to hold all available titles. She was the dam of eight bench show champions, all of which were also obedience winners. Others earned Canadian championships as well. The Heists were involved in obedience work and were involved in the making of the Walt Disney film *Big Red*.

Dale and Irene Walker, owners of the O'Lannon Kennels in Menominee Falls, Wisconsin, were breeders and trainers of numerous obedience titlists and bench show champions from the early 1940's on. One of their O'Lannon line became the third triple crown winner in the breed. Dual Champion Titian Duke, C.D., whelped on October 24, 1956, was also the sire of a field and bench show champion and in 1958 was sold to M. Eberhardt of Pewaukee, Wisconsin. In the mid-1960's the Walkers came along with another dual champion, Mahoganys Titian Jingo. Jingo was Duke's son and himself sired seven field champions (three in one litter!) and one bench show champion. He

Dual Ch. Tyrone's Mahogany Mike, C.D.X., photographed in 1956. Owner is Mr. E.W. McIvor of Dearborn, Michigan.

had three points toward his Canadian championship when he was hit and killed by a car on September 7, 1967.

The fourth and fifth triple crown titlists were not too far behind Duke. The fourth was the Robert Frisches' Dual Ch. Molly Coddled Misty, C.D. The Frisches get the vote for the kennel with the most unusual kennel prefix in the breed. . . Molly Coddled. The Molly Coddled Irish Setters apparently weren't so mollycoddled that they couldn't be trained, since there were several other Molly Coddled Setters which were field trial winners. These included Molly Coddled Mayhem, Molly Coddled Maened, Molly Coddled Megapod and Molly Coddled GGD, also contenders for the title of dogs with the most unusual names. Not to mention the Heists' dog named Dirty Bird!

A close second for the unusual name award was the Baldpate Kennels of Ruth and Maurice Thrasher. They owned Sharoc's Colleen of Baldpate and three bench show champions, but somehow the name

Baldpate suggests a smooth-coated breed—perhaps a Mexican Hairless!

The fifth triple crown winner was Buck and LaVerne Stines' Dual Ch. County Cork's Red Knight, U.D. He placed in 18 field trials in California competition in the late 1940's at the Irish Setter Club of the Pacific trials. This club, formed in 1945, held its first field trials in 1949 and over the years has produced many fine field dogs.

The next triple crown winner to come along was also a California dog, Dual Ch. Merry Kerry Quite Contrary, C.D., owned by Michael and Katherine Gerdis of Long Beach.

Other owners' names from the mid-century period which appeared in the annals of field trial history were Irene (now Irene Schlintz) and Jim Phillips. Her famous Hagginwood Kennels in California are reviewed in the show chapter, but we would also like to mention here that her Best in Show-winning Ch. Coppercoat of the Hills was also trained for the field by Lee Baldock.

Ch. Ruxton's Shannon of Boyne and her daughter, future Ch. Sally O'Bryan of Crosshaven, getting her first lesson in field trial work at three months of age. Owner, Ward Gardner, Crosshaven Kennels, Walla Walla, Washington.

An Irish Setter belonging to the Joedan Farm Kennels "takes to the tree, in pursuit of game." This photograph was taken in 1934.

A litter of Irish Setter puppies being started on their early field training. This early field experience helps develop them physically and aids in later obedience and show training also. Bred and owned by Luz Holvenstot, Westwind Kennels, Long Valley, New Jersey.

Dual Ch. Elmcroft Mahogany Sue, excellent land or water retriever, though quite obviously an Irish Setter!

Ch. Verbu Missy Oogh, C.D.X. on point in the field. Missy has 7 points toward field trial championship. Bred and owned by Miss Emily Schweitzer, Verbu Kennels, Dundee, Illinois.

Also credited in the show chapter is the Draherin Kennels of Lucy Jane Myers of Duluth, Minnesota. Her bitch Lady's Colleen was the dam of at least a dozen field trial winners.

The William Cooks of the Flagstones Kennel in Portchester, New York made champions of several of their dogs, and Ch. Flagstones Flame, C.D., was also a field trial winner.

Kopper Key Kennels in Spencerport, New York were owned by Helen and Faunt Ekey, and it was the home of eight field champions during the Ekeys' active period in the breed.

Ballarrell was the kennel name of Charlotte and Burton Ballard, who were active in field work in and around Waukesha, Wisconsin. Their interests, however, were not strictly confined to the field; their Irish Setter Field Ch. Tam of Ballarrell, C.D. was shown in the show ring as well.

Sharon Clegg, who showed her very first Irish Setter, Raferty's Kathleen Magee, to a U.D. title, should also be mentioned here, since it was her Kate that whelped no fewer than eight field trial winners.

Elmer and Jane Homuth's Elmho Kennels in Fond du Lac, Wisconsin were active with both bench and field trial winners. Also active in the Wisconsin area were Marion and George Krauss with their field trial winners Mahogany Sputnik and Comets Katuri O'Colburn Acres. At Wind Lake, Wisconsin, Marcy and LeRoy Paluszynski finished Lady Bronze to a field championship.

Also in the midwest, in Gross Pointe, Michigan, Joan and Earl Morrison of the Sunnymoor Kennels finished a bench show champion named Red Rhapsody which bore their kennel prefix and had several field trial winners while active in the breed.

The Harold Hurds of Apache Acres Kennels in Utica, Michigan were interested in both field and obedience also. Perhaps the most outstanding of their field dogs was Ch. Argo Lane Bracelette, C.D. Their field trial winners Yankee Doodle Dandi and Ward Wilcharbo were also both C.D. dogs.

In Roseville, Michigan the Corray Kennels of Constance and Robert Ray had a hot prospect for the triple crown in their Ch. Duchess Derrycaine of Valmar, C.D. She was winning nicely in the

Ch. Westwind Scarlet Fandango and Ch. Westwind Scarlet Arabesque resting after their field work. Owned by Luz Holvenstot, Long Valley, New Jersey.

In the middle of Chicago city traffic at the premiere of the Disney film *Big Red*—the story of an Irish Setter—Ch. Verbu Missy Oogh, C.D.X. goes on point to show the skill of the breed when going on point; she remained steady amid the crowds and noise. Owned and trained by Emily Schweitzer, Verbu Kennels, Dundee, Illinois.

field also. They also owned Kelton of Hartsbourne Hei-Lo, C.D., and Kelton was a field dog too.

Other Michigan fanciers, Harold and Alida Nitz of Grand Rapids, bred litter brothers which became field trial winners. They were Ch. Indian Copper of Har-Nel, C.D. and Autumn Rusty of Har-Nel (Har-Nel being their kennel suffix).

In the 1960's field trials were still gaining in popularity. The Ernest Lewises of Pacific Palisades, California turned their interests to the Irish Setter and made quite a record for their County Clare Kennels. Their trainer and handler made several field champions for the Lewises, among which were Field Ch. Oxton's Shosaphine and Ch. Mighty Fawn. Fawn was a member of the 1965 Irish Setter *Sports Afield* Point Dog Team. Fawn was also a National Red Setter Shooting Dog Club champion, as was the Lewises' Ch. Country Clare's Shandy. There were others which distinguished themselves under the campaigning of Stanley Head. The Lewises also owned Ch. Innisfail Color Scheme, C.D.; this dog sired 25 champions during his lifetime.

Dan and Marion Pahy of Blairstown, New Jersey have had several field trial winners, among them their Kerry's Mavoureen O'Talisman, McGovern's Rusty O'Rourke, a bench show champion, and McGovern's Kerry O'Red and Kerry's Kathleen O'Red. The Pahys were competitors at the first Irish Setter Club of West New York trials in 1961 and are active in Irish Setter clubs in the New Jersey area also.

The spring of 1972 saw the winning of another triple crown award by Emily Schweitzer's Dual Ch. Duffin Miss Duffy, C.D. She was handled by Jake Huizenga.

Also Barbara Turner of Hingham, Massachusetts finished her Dual Ch. Donnington Crackerjack.

There have been and are numerous Irish Setter clubs which have organized since the 1920's, when field trials became of great interest to the sportsmen. More and more over the past one hundred years we have seen that the breeders and exhibitors alike are going toward the breeding of the all-around Irish Setter rather than the single-purpose dog.

Nothing could be more beneficial to the breed and its true purpose in the fancy. . . beautiful on the bench, alert and responsive in the obedience ring, and most important of all. . . doing what comes naturally in the field.

8. FIELD TRIALS TODAY

As our world grows smaller and smaller, so do our fields and forests—a natural result of the population explosion. Call it what you will, the situation has narrowed down the opportunities to work dogs in the field. Also, it is no longer necessary to hunt dogs to help supply the family with food for the table. Working dogs in the field or racking up a record at field trials has become a sport for wealthy people able to travel considerable distances with their dogs, or those who have simply chosen field trials as a family hobby and make almost a vacation out of it when they are able to take the time to travel.

In spite of restrictions, each year the American Kennel Club records a great many field trial events, and there are a surprising number of starters at these events. Sportsmen certainly have not lost their desire to work their dogs, even if it is only once in awhile.

The Irish Setter is—and always has been—the ideal bird dog. The hunter who wishes to be proud of the way his dog works as well as proud of the end results of his hunt will usually choose an Irish Setter for the task. Their great beauty, their spirit, and their successful conclusion at such an event place them second to no other breed. The rich red Irish Setter on perfect point in the field against a background of fall colors in lush surroundings is truly a beautiful sight.

Even though the Irish Setter looks beautiful prancing around a show ring and displays its remarkable intelligence going through his paces in the obedience ring, to see it working in the field, running free and successfully pointing when it has found the game, is perhaps the most beautiful picture of all!

At the end of 1974 the statistics for AKC licensed and member field trials clearly indicated the increasing interest in field trials. In 1974 the American Kennel Club stated that there were 386 field trials for the Pointing breeds, with over 30,000 starters. These figures show that Pointing breed trials doubled during the past decade. The number of starters at these trials increased by 118%.

Trials for Irish Setters only during 1974 were 9 with 536 starters, and 26 trials with one or more stakes open to other Pointing breeds, with 1,856 starters. There were 1,318 Irish Setter starters at Irish Set-

Canadian and American Ch. Red Barn Reflection pictured at 15 years of age when she participated in the Parade of Champions and Veterans Class at the 1972 Irish Setter Club of Canada Specialty show in Toronto. Flicka was owner-handled by Thomas G. Threlkeld of Halifax, Nova Scotia.

ter trials open to other pointing breeds. In 1974 there were 14 Irish Setters which attained the title of field champion, and four made amateur field champion, as compared to 1973 with 11 field champions and three amateurs.

While these American Kennel Club-published statistics clearly show that Brittany Spaniels and German Shorthaired Pointers represent 80% of all pointing breed starters (with over 20,000 starters), we also can see that the Irish Setter in the field is holding its own. If there is any doubt in anyone's mind as to the keen interest in field work, all you have to do is realize that during 1974 there were 55,890 Beagle starters—and 1974 was not their top year!!! Of course, Beagle trials have always been well attended and have maintained their incredible lead over the years, but the fact remains that all other field trials have increased by double or better in the past decade.

CHOOSING A FIELD DOG

The two vital points to bear in mind when buying a young dog for the field are the pedigree and the reputation of the kennel from which you purchase it. Many of the good and bad traits found in field dogs are definitely inheritable, so check the pedigree carefully before buying. Also check the performance record of the kennel. What is the ratio of field champions compared to the number of puppies actually started? How long have they been in the kennel business? Do they also train and work their dogs, or is the kennel operation just a breeding mill? Ask to see their record of wins. Above all, don't hesitate to ask to see some of the grown dogs work in the field.

There are advantages to buying young puppies, one being that you have a larger selection and can train the dog from start to finish yourself. Field dogs must be loyal creatures and must know just one master in the field, and bringing a dog up from a youngster offers this advantage.

BUYING THE OLDER FIELD DOG

Remember the old saying that you can't teach an old dog new tricks? Well, you can't break them of bad habits either, so if you are buying an older field dog be sure he doesn't have any bad habits! With the older dog be *sure* to see him work in the field and be sure he would fit in with what you may be working already. Ask the owner for a trial workout with the dog. Also ask other hunters their opinion of the dog's past performances. Make sure the temperament of the dog is sound and that he is still somewhat trainable and not completely set in his ways, since you may have a few more things you want to teach him. And make sure the price is right! Good field dogs can command a lot of money—as much as, perhaps even more in some cases—than show dogs. So ask for opinions and make comparisons with other dogs from other kennels as well as other prices on dogs

Head study of Ch. St. Cloud's Fermanagh III, owned by Mrs. Cheever Porter of New York City.

Ch. Candia Dandi, sire of five champions to date, owned by Thomas Stagg of Vineland, New Jersey.

from within the same kennel. Check out the pedigree once again before signing the final papers and the contract for purchase.

JOINING A FIELD TRIAL CLUB

Chances are that by the time you are considering buying your field dog that you will have become involved with someone else interested in the sport who is a member of a field trial club. If he is truly a friend, he will not only help you to join the club but also will advise you on where to go to purchase a satisfactory dog for use in the field. Membership in these clubs can be just as valuable to you as the breed club is to those who exhibit their dogs at bench shows. Club bulletins, the exchange of ideas at meetings, and the valuable information gained just by observing at one of these field trial events can be very helpful to newcomers in the field with so much to learn.

KINDS OF FIELD TRIALS

There are three kinds of field trial. A member field trial is one at which championship points are awarded by the club if it is a member of the American Kennel Club. A licensed field trial is one at which championship points may be awarded, though the club is not a member of the AKC but is licensed for this specific event. The third kind is called a sanctioned field trial and is a completely casual, informal trial with the dogs competing under regular rules but not for championship points. The club in this instance may or may not be a member of the AKC but will have obtained AKC sanction to hold the trial.

RIBBONS AND PRIZES

Clubs holding a licensed or member field trial shall offer five prizes in the form of ribbons or rosettes in the following colors at the regular stakes. First prize, blue; second, red; third, yellow; fourth, white and a special prize takes dark green. These ribbons are of regulation width and length and bear the name of the club, the trial date, and the facsimile of the seal of the American Kennel Club.

Ribbons and rosettes for sanctioned field trials, or in the nonregular stakes at licensed or member field trials, have different colors for winners. First prize is rose, second is brown, third is light green, fourth is gray and the special prize is a combination of any of these colors. However, the ribbons must bear the words AKC Sanctioned Field Trial but need not necessarily be of any certain size or design.

Money prizes, when offered, must be of a fixed amount or a percentage of the entry fee for each prize and shall be stated. Value for each prize must also be stated, and stud services are not permitted as prizes.

JUDGES

A field trial club may invite anyone who is in good standing with the American Kennel Club to judge at its trial. Those wishing to judge at trials, in other words, need not first obtain a license, but the AKC must be informed as to who exactly will be officiating. Advertised judges, however, who wish to judge at licensed or member field trials must first sign an agreement certifying that they have a thorough knowledge of the rules, regulations and procedures for the event and that they will judge in strict accord with them. As in all other dog events, the decisions of the judges are final in regard to the performances of the dogs, and the judges have full discretionary power to withhold awards for lack of merit.

ENTERING A FIELD TRIAL

The premium lists which announce the holding of a field trial by the club will give the name and address of the field trial secretary, who will receive all written entries. These premium lists contain the rules and regulations under which the show will be held and an entry form which you must fill out in order to enter your dog.

ELIGIBILITY FOR ENTRY

All dogs competing in a field trial must be individually registered with the AKC or a part of a registered litter. If whelped outside this country a foreign registry number must be obtained. There are variations on the rule as to time, etc., so if there is any doubt at the time of entry, it would be wise to check it out before entry deadline. Errors in entry forms are the responsibility of the owner. Don't arrive at your first trial and find that through a careless error or omission you are not able to compete!

Rules are strict about the health of the dogs competing also. Any dog that shows signs of infectious disease or has been exposed to another dog or dogs which are known to have infectious disease is ineligible and will be asked to leave the trial grounds. While a field trial committee may refuse your entry or ask that you leave, they cannot do so without cause and must file their complaint with the American Kennel Club. However, if you enter and attend, you must compete in all stakes in which you have entered, unless excused by the field trial committee at the trial after a consultation with the judge or judges.

CANCELLATIONS AND PROTESTATIONS

If wins are cancelled, the next dog is moved up and the original winner is not counted as having competed.

Any person who is a member of a member club of the AKC or who owns a dog entered in the field trial or who handles a dog competing in the trial may make a protest to the field trial committee either before or after the dog has been judged. All protests must be in writing, stating the specific nature of the protest and including the name and address of the person making the protest, as well as the violation of the rule or rules under which they are registering the protest. It is given then to the trial secretary along with a deposit of $10. The $10 is returned if the complaint is upheld. The club benefits if the protest is not upheld.

The field trial committee holds a meeting as soon as possible with all parties concerned being present and heard. A report of this meeting, with all other facts and written protests and deposits, is then sent to the American Kennel Club within seven days of the trial. There is such a thing as an appeal to the American Kennel Club requiring a $25 deposit which must be made within 30 days of the decision of the field trial committee. This deposit is also forfeited if the decision is upheld.

SPECIAL AWARD

At any licensed or member field trial the judges may make a "Judges' Award of Merit" in any stake to any unplaced dog for particularly excellent work. The name and registration number of each dog to which such an award is made shall be noted on the back page in the judges' book for the stake in which the award was made.

FIELD AND AMATEUR FIELD CHAMPIONS

Championship certificates are issued to owners of dogs which have completed all requirements for this title. A field champion may be designated as "dual champion" if it has also been recorded as a bench show champion, though no certificate is issued for this.

WHAT IS A FIELD CHAMPION?

At present a dog of one of the Pointing breeds (which includes the Irish Setter) will be recorded as a field champion after having won 10 points under the point rating schedule shown here in regular stakes in at least three licensed or member field trials, provided that 3 points have been won in one 3-point or better Open All Age, Open Gun Dog, Open Limited All-Age, or Open Limited Gun Dog Stake, that no more than 2 points each have been won in Open Puppy and Open Derby Stakes, and that no more than 4 of the 10 points have been won by placing first in Amateur stakes.

Championship points shall be credited only to dogs placed first in regular stakes. The number of points shall be based on the actual number of eligible starters in each stake according to the following schedule:

4 to 7 starters	1 point
8 to 12 starters	2 points
13 to 17 starters	3 points
18 to 24 starters	4 points
25 or more starters	5 points

SPECIALTY SHOWS

Rules for Pointing breed trials may find regular stakes offered as follows:

Open Puppy Stake for dogs six months of age and under fifteen months of age on the first advertised day of the trial.

Open Derby Stake for dogs six months of age and under two years of age on the first advertised day of the trial.

Gun Dog Stake (Open or Amateur) for dogs six months of age and over on the first advertised day of the trial.

All-Age Stake (Open or Amateur) for dogs six months of age and over on the first advertised day of the trial.

Limited Gun Dog Stake (Open or Amateur) for dogs six months of age and over on the first advertised day of the trial which have won first place in an Open Derby Stake or which have placed first, second, third or fourth in a Gun Dog Stake. A field trial-giving club may give an Amateur Limited Gun Dog Stake in which places that qualify a dog have been acquired in amateur stakes only.

Limited All-Age Stake (Open or Amateur) for dogs six months of age and over on the first advertised day of the trial which have won first place in an Open Derby Stake or which have placed in any All-Age Stake. A field trial-giving club may also give an Amateur Limited All-Age Stake in which places that qualify a dog have been acquired in amateur stakes only.

In an amateur stake at a licensed or member field trial all dogs must be owned and handled by persons who, in the judgment of the field trial committee, are qualified as amateurs.

WHAT CONSTITUTES AN AMATEUR OWNER OR HANDLER FOR THE POINTING BREED TRIALS?

An amateur owner of amateur handler is a person who, during the period of two years preceding the trial, has not accepted remuneration in any form for training or handling dogs in any form of dog activity, and who at no time in the past has for any period of two years or more operated as a professional trainer or handler of field trial dogs.

AN AMATEUR FIELD CHAMPIONSHIP

At present a dog of one of the Pointing breeds will be recorded an amateur field champion after having won 10 points under the point rating system schedule shown below in regular amateur stakes in at least three licensed or member field trials, provided that three points have been won by placing first in one three-point or better Amateur All-Age, Amateur Gun Dog, Amateur Limited All-Age or Amateur Limited Gun Dog Stake.

Amateur championship points shall be credited to dogs placed first through third in regular amateur stakes in accordance with the following schedule, based on the actual number of eligible starters in each stake:

	PLACEMENTS		
	1st	2nd	3rd
4 to 7 starters	1 point		
8 to 12 starters	2 points		
13 to 17 starters	3 points	1 point	
18 to 24 starters	4 points	2 points	
25 or more starters	5 points	3 points	1 point

Championship points from first placements in amateur stakes that are credited towards a field championship will also be credited towards an amateur field championship.

STANDARD PROCEDURE FOR POINTING BREED FIELD TRIALS

PROCEDURE 1. STANDARD OF PERFORMANCE

1-A PUPPY STAKES. Puppies must show desire to hunt, boldness, and initiative in covering ground and in searching likely cover. They should indicate the presence of game if the opportunity is presented. Puppies should show reasonable obedience to their handlers' commands, but should not be given additional credit for pointing staunchly. Each dog shall be judged on its actual performance as indicating its future as a high class Derby dog. Every premium list for a licensed or member trial shall state whether or not blanks are to be fired in a Puppy Stake. If the premium list states that blanks will be fired, every dog that makes game contact shall be fired over if the handler is within reasonable gun range. At least 15 minutes and not more than 30 minutes shall be allowed for each heat.

1-B DERBY STAKES. Derbies must show a keen desire to hunt, be bold and independent, have a fast, yet attractive, style of running, and demonstrate not only intelligence in seeking objectives but also the ability to find game. Derbies must point but no additional credit shall be given for steadiness to wing and shot. Should birds be flushed after a point by handler or dog within reasonable gun range from the handler, a shot must be fired. A lack of opportunity for firing over a Derby dog on point shall not constitute reason for non-placement when it has had game contact in acceptable Derby manner. Derbies must show reasonable obedience to their handlers' commands. Each dog is to be judged on its actual performance as indicating its future promise. At least 20 minutes and not more than 30 minutes shall be allowed for each heat.

1-C GUN DOG AND LIMITED GUN DOG STAKES. A Gun Dog must give a finished performance and must be under its handler's control at all times. It must handle kindly, with a minimum of noise and hacking by the handler. A Gun Dog must show a keen desire to hunt, must have a bold and attractive style of running, and must demonstrate not only intelligence in quartering and in seeking objectives but also the ability to find game. The dog must hunt for its handler at all times at a range suitable for a handler on foot, and should show or check in front of its handler frequently. It must cover adequate ground but never range out of sight for a length of time that would detract from its usefulness as a practical hunting dog. The dog must locate game, must point staunchly, and must be steady to wing and shot. Intelligent use of the wind and terrain in locating game, ac-

Ruxton's Heatherick's Gaiar, owned by Mrs. Ernest Levering.

curate nose, and style and intensity on point are essential. At least 30 minutes shall be allowed for each heat.

1-D ALL-AGE AND LIMITED ALL-AGE STAKES. An All-Age Dog must give a finished performance and must be under reasonable control of its handler. It must show a keen desire to hunt, must have a bold and attractive style of running, and must show independence in hunting. It must range well out in a forward moving pattern, seeking the most promising objectives, so as to locate any game on the course. Excessive line-casting and avoiding cover must be penalized. The dog must respond to handling but must demonstrate its independent judgement in hunting the course, and should not look to its handler for directions as to where to go. The dog must find game, must point staunchly, and must be steady to wing and shot. Intelligent use of the wind and terrain in locating game, accurate nose, and style and intensity on point are essential. At least 30 minutes shall be allowed for each heat.

1-E BACKING IN GUN DOG, ALL-AGE, LIMITED GUN DOG, AND LIMITED ALL-AGE STAKES. If a dog encounters its brace mate on point it should back on sight, preferably without caution from its handler. Failure of a dog to back when it sees its brace mate on point must be penalized, and a dog that steals its brace mate's point shall not be placed. A backing dog shall not be sent on by its handler until after it has demonstrated complete steadiness to wing and shot, unless directed by a judge in case of an unproductive find; nor until after the retrieve has been completed, if game is killed. A backing dog shall receive no less credit if its brace mate's point was unproductive.

1-F In a Gun Dog, All-Age, Limited Gun Dog, or Limited All-Age Stake held by a German Shorthaired Pointer, German Wirehaired Pointer, Vizsla, or Weimaraner Club, any dog placed 1st or 2nd must have demonstrated backing in addition to the basic requirements for hunting and pointing as described above. If a dog that is being considered for either 1st or 2nd placement has not had an opportunity to back, the judges must set up a brace or braces for this purpose after all braces in the stake have been run. The judges will then select a dog from among those that have run in the stake, and shall have it placed on point in an open location on a live planted bird. The dog to be tested for backing shall be cast off not less than 100 yards from the dog on point, and shall be permitted to hunt freely until it has established a back. It must back until it has demonstrated complete steadiness to wing and shot. In a Shoot-to-Kill stake the dog must back until the retrieve has been completed. A dog that backs when a back is set up in this manner shall receive the same credit as a dog that has demonstrated equal quality in backing during the normal course of running.

1-G No Gun Dog, All-Age, Limited Gun Dog, or Limited All-Age Stake shall be run in heats of more than 30 minutes at a licensed or member trial unless the running time is given in the premium list.

1-H In any stake in which birds are not shot, except in Puppy or Derby Stakes as specified in Procedures 1-A and 1-B, a blank cartridge (not a .22 cal. crimp) must be fired by the handler over any dog on point, after the game has been flushed. The handler must shoot within the time that would be required to kill a bird at natural shotgun range. Any deliberate delay in shooting must be severely penalized.

1-I A reasonable move of a dog to mark a bird flushed after a point is acceptable, but this shall not excuse a break or a delayed chase.

1-J Any club that anticipates an entry in a licensed or member field trial that might exceed the number of dogs that could be judged on the available running grounds during the available judging hours, should specify in its premium list that entries in any or all stakes will be limited and that entries will close when the limit or limits have been reached if this occurs before the specified closing time for entries. The limit shall be given in the premium list either as a specific number of dogs for the trial, or for each or any stake, or as the number of dogs that can be judged within the daylight hours that will be available on the date or dates of the trial.

PROCEDURE 2. JUDGES

2-A Each stake must be judged by two judges, except that the National Championship Stakes and the National Amateur Championship Stakes, as provided for in the Rules for Pointing Breed Trials, may be judged by three judges.

2-B The judges may place the dogs 1st, 2nd, 3rd, and 4th in each stake. They should withhold placement from any dog if its performance does not merit the crediting of any championship points.

The decisions of the judges shall be final with respect to the running and placement of the dogs, and in all questions concerning the merits of the dogs. They shall have full power to turn out of any stake any dog that does not reasonably obey its handler or that interferes with the work of its brace mate, and any handler who, in their opinion, willfully interferes with another handler or his dog.

2-C Any person who, during the running of a stake, strikes or otherwise abuses or mistreats a dog, or conducts himself in a manner prejudicial to the best interests of the sport, must be expelled from that stake by the judges who shall also report the matter to the field trial committee for possible action under Chapter 15, Section 2. A report of the incident and the action taken shall be sent promptly to The American Kennel Club by the field trial secretary.

2-D Any additional running of the dogs after the first series of heats has been completed, or after completion of any further series specified in the premium list, shall be entirely at the discretion of the judges. The judges shall determine the length and scope of any subsequent series, as well as the bracing of the dogs, conforming with any specific requirements for subsequent series that may be described in the premium list.

2-E If the two handlers with their dogs become separated while both are on course and under judgment, one judge shall accompany each handler; except that a judge should not follow a dog that cuts the specified course in order to reach the bird field.

2-F The judges may appoint an official observer at the bird field to report to them whether or not a dog had game contact before a judge reached the bird field. If an official observer is appointed, he should be identified to all participants.

PROCEDURE 3. FIELD TRIAL MARSHALS

3-A The field trial committee shall appoint one or more field trial Marshals. It shall be the duty of one Marshal to assist the judges and to carry out their instructions, including regulating and controlling the gallery, and seeing to it that the gallery is kept separate from and behind the judges, and that no one in the gallery talks to the judges while the dogs are down. Other Marshals shall see to it that braces are ready when called, and assist the field trial committee in all other matters necessary for the smooth and expeditious running of the trial.

3-B No person shall serve as Marshal assisting the judges in any stake in which he has entered or will handle a dog.

PROCEDURE 4. DRAWING AND BRACING

4-A The dogs shall generally be run in braces, and each dog in a brace must have a separate handler.

4-B If every dog entered in a stake at a licensed or member field trial has a different handler, the bracing of the dogs in that stake shall be established by a straight drawing and the braces shall then be run in the order drawn.

4-C If two or more dogs with the same handler are entered in a stake at a licensed or member field trial, such entries shall be segregated for the drawing for bracing so that no two dogs handled by the same person can be drawn for the same brace. The running order for all complete braces shall then be determined by a separate drawing after the bracing has been established. If, during the drawing for running order, any handler is drawn to handle in more than two consecutive braces in the same stake, and if there is a later brace to be drawn in which he has no entry, the next brace drawn in which that handler has no dog may be moved up to run following the second consecutive brace, so that the handler would not be required to run in more than two consecutive braces. However, this shall not apply if an alternate handler has been named.

4-D The bracing and running order established by either method shall not be changed under any circumstances; *except that*

(1) in the case of a scratch or absentee the brace mate of the absent dog shall be run with the dog from the next incomplete brace or, if there is no other known incomplete brace, with the bye dog or, if there is no bye dog and no knowledge that any subsequent brace will be incomplete may, at the discretion of the judges, be run alone in the running order drawn for its brace, or as the bye dog, and except further that

(2) if the foregoing procedure would result in the bracing together of two dogs handled by the same person, the two odd dogs shall be rebraced consecutively with the two dogs in the last brace in the stake in which that handler has no dog.

(3) Any new brace or braces so created must be run in the running order drawn for one of the two dogs in the brace, as the field trial committee may decide.

4-E If a bye dog remains after all the braces have been run, its brace mate shall be selected by the judges at their sole discretion from among the dogs that have run in that stake; or the judges may run such a bye dog without a brace mate. The judges alone shall decide whether or not any brace mate they select for such a bye dog shall be under judgment, and if under judgment, for what portion or portions of the heat, and their decision shall be publicly announced before the brace is started.

Ch. Kerry Boy of Knocknagree III, owned by Miss Laura Delano of the Knocknagree Kennels, Rhinebeck, New York.

PROCEDURE 5. COURSES AND BIRDS

5-A Stakes at licensed or member field trials may be run on any of the following types of courses, all of which must include sufficient acreage, adequate cover for birds, and suitable objectives:

(1) *Single Course With Bird Field* consisting of a back course and a bird field which has sufficient cover to hold birds and which is of adequate size to permit a dog to hunt naturally without excessive hacking. A bird field must not be less than 5 acres, and 10 acres is recommended. At a licensed or member trial no less than two birds must be released in the bird field for each brace in first series in all stakes except the Puppy Stake. Additional birds may be released either in the bird field or on the back course.

(2) *Single Course Without Bird Field* consisting entirely of a course without any specific bird field, on which birds are released in suitable places around the course. At a licensed or member trial no less than two birds must be released for each brace at a suitable place on the course in all stakes except the Puppy Stake.

(3) *Continuous Courses* consisting of a series of courses on which each brace starts where the last brace was picked up. On such a course it is assumed that there is adequate natural or released game.

(4) A stake may be run on Continuous Courses for first series, with a second series consisting of nothing but bird field work for the dogs selected by the judges, provided this is specified in the premium list.

5-B The same requirements for released birds that apply to other stakes at a licensed or member trial shall also apply to the Puppy Stake unless the premium list specifies that no birds will be released in the Puppy Stake.

5-C No released bird shall be removed from the course or from the bird field unless dead or crippled.

5-D Regular stakes at a licensed or member trial shall be run only on recognized game birds, and the birds should be strong, healthy, full-feathered and clean; except that in Puppy Stakes non-game birds may be used if specified in the premium list.

5-E Birds should, if possible, be released in natural cover rather than in artificially created cover. They should not be placed in holes nor in such cover as will impede their ability to fly or run. Hobbles are highly undesirable, and must never be used if there is adequate cover. If hobbles are used they must be of soft yarn which the birds themselves can remove, and must allow a minimum of three inches space between the birds' feet. Other artificial restraints may never be used. Birds may be rocked or dizzied but not to such an extent as to affect their ability to fly. Game stewards should wear gloves and should not hold birds against their bodies. Successive birds should not be released in or near the same spot.

A Percy Jones photograph of three beautiful Irish Setters.

5-F The premium list for a licensed or member trial shall specify the type of course and species of game to be released in each stake.

PROCEDURE 6. RUNNING AND HANDLING

6-A The duty of having a dog ready in place when required for judging rests solely with its handler or owner. All dogs should be ready on the grounds well in advance of the scheduled times for their braces so that the judges will not be held up in case of an absent brace. If a dog is not present at the place where it is to start within 5 minutes after it is called for by the judges to run in any series it must be disqualified. The judges are responsible for keeping the time.

6-B No more than one brace shall be run on a course or on any part of a course at the same time, irrespective of whether the dogs are in the same stake or in different stakes.

6-C In a stake on a single course with bird field the time of each heat shall include no more than 8 minutes in the bird field, except that in Puppy Stakes the time in the bird field shall not exceed 6 minutes. The time shall start when the first dog enters the bird field, except that a dog may be disqualified if it has cut the specified course in order to reach the bird field, in which case time starts when the second dog enters. Otherwise the judges, or the Marshal if instructed by the judges, shall see to it that both dogs in each brace are directed to the bird field at as nearly the same time as possible. If one dog has strayed or is otherwise held up on the course, the brace mate and its handler may ordinarily proceed on the course and enter the bird field unless otherwise directed by a judge.

6-D Time shall not be called when a dog is on point in the bird field unless so specified in the premium list. If time is called when a dog is on point in the bird field, its brace mate shall be stopped.

6-E In a Derby Stake, if the second dog is not on point or backing, its handler may, without penalty, hold or otherwise control the dog if there is any likelihood that it would interfere with the dog on point.

6-F A dog that is on point, roading, or obviously on game, when time is up, shall be allowed a reasonable time to complete its work.

6-G Judges must discourage and may penalize for continuous or excessive noise or loud vocalizing by handlers in any stake, and particularly in Gun Dog Stakes. Failure to heed the judges' instructions may result in disqualification.

6-H Any intimidation or blocking to restrain a dog from breaking wing or shot shall be severely penalized. In a Gun Dog, All-Age, Limited Gun Dog, or Limited All-Age Stake at a licensed or member field trial held by a German Shorthaired Pointer, German Wirehaired Pointer, Vizsla, or Weimaraner club, the handler is prohibited from controlling the dog by the collar at any time, and may not touch the dog in such a manner as to restrain or control it; except that he may tap the dog lightly on head or body to release it in any situation.

6-I A dog that works with a minimum of handling or commands must be given credit in a Gun Dog, All-Age, Limited Gun Dog or Limited All-Age Stake.

6-J A dog that is out of judgment for a continuous period of more than 5 minutes, or for more than 1/6 of the time specified for the heat if over 30 minutes, shall not be placed unless seen on point by a judge or unless, in the opinion of the judges, the dog's absence was due to unusual conditions.

6-K No person shall in any manner assist a handler in controlling his dog. The judges may disqualify a dog if a handler receives such assistance or if the dog receives direction of any kind from anyone except its handler.

6-L Any scouting shall be done only by a scout or scouts appointed by the judges and acting solely under the direction of one or both of the judges.

Lovely headstudy of Osborne's Stylish Marauder, photographed by Arthur J. Tefft.

6-M No dog shall be picked up during a heat except on direction or permission from a judge.

6-N All dogs started in a stake must remain on the grounds until the stake is completed unless excused by the judges or by the field trial committee.

6-O No one shall be permitted in the bird field at any time during the running of a stake; except for the judges, the official guns, the Marshal, and the handlers of the competing dogs while the dogs are in the bird field; and except for the game stewards to the extent necessary to release game.

6-P No person shall serve as an official gun or game steward in a stake in which he handles a dog or in which a dog owned by him is entered.

6-Q Promiscuous firing of guns or blank pistols on the field trial grounds is prohibited. The handler of a dog shall fire one blank and no more for each flush of one or more birds.

6-R There shall be no training of dogs anywhere on the course during the trial.

6-S The field trial committee and the judges shall not permit severe training, correcting, or disciplining of dogs on any part of the field trial grounds. The committee shall investigate any reports of such conduct or of any other conduct prejudicial to the best interests of pure-bred dogs, field trials, or the American Kennel Club. Any person who conducts himself in a manner prejudicial to the best interests of the sport shall be dealt with promptly, during the trial if possible, after the offender has been notified of the specific charges against him, and has been given an opportunity to be heard in his own defense, in accordance with Chapter 15, Section 2.

6-T The premium list for any licensed or member field trial must specify whether or not handling from horseback will be permitted in any or all stakes. If handling from horseback is permitted in any stake the club must have suitable horses available. Mounted and foot handlers are not to be segregated in the drawing.

The judges shall see to it that any mounted handler uses his horse only as a means of conveyance on the course and never as an active aid in handling. The handlers shall remain on the specified course in front of the judges and in the judges' line of travel, except as necessary to handle a dog that is seen on point. If one handler is mounted and the other is on foot, the judges shall set a reasonable pace to accommodate the foot handler. Mounted handlers must keep their horses at an ordinary walk at all times unless otherwise authorized by a judge.

A handler must always dismount before handling his dog on game and before firing. No handler's horse may be brought into the bird field.

A classic photograph of Higgins Red Coat.

PROCEDURE 7. SHOOT-TO-KILL STAKES

7-A The premium list must identify any Shoot-to-Kill Stake, and must specify, for each stake in which birds are to be shot, whether the shooting will be done by official guns or whether handlers will be required to shoot their own birds, and the shooting for all braces in the stake shall be done in the manner specified.

7-B The judges shall have complete authority over all shooting. They may require a change of official guns at any time, and may bar from further shooting in that trial any official gun or gunning handler who does not abide strictly by safe gunning rules.

7-C If the shooting is done by official guns, two qualified guns are required for each brace, one to accompany each handler. Provision must also be made for alternate or stand-by guns in case they should be required.

7-D When official guns are appointed they must be familiar with all of the requirements of this Procedure 7.

7-E One official gun must join each handler as he enters the bird field, or if a bird field is not used, at a designated place on the course. The official gun must always keep himself in the correct position for safety of dogs and persons.

7-F Game should be shot cleanly, in a sportsmanlike manner, in full flight, and at a distance that will give the dog a reasonable retrieve. An official gun represents the handler up to the time that game is shot, but must not interfere or assist in any manner with his work nor direct the work of the dog.

7-G Game flushed by a free running dog or birds that flush wild shall not be shot except on instructions from a judge. If a bird does not fly after an attempt to flush by a handler, it shall not be shot on the ground except on instructions from a judge.

7-H Official guns, and handlers acting as their own gunners, should wear game bags.

7-I Retrieving is required in all Shoot-to-Kill Stakes and counts as an important part of a dog's performance. After the shot the handler shall not command or signal the dog to retrieve until the dog's steadiness to wing and shot has been positively demonstrated. The dog must retrieve promptly and tenderly to hand. In a Shoot-to-Kill Derby Stake the dog must also retrieve, but steadiness to wing and shot and a finished retrieve are not required for placement.

If any dog that is being considered for 1st or 2nd place in a Shoot-to-Kill Stake has not had an opportunity to retrieve, the judges must set up a retrieve for the dog after all braces in the stake have been run. A live bird shall be planted and the dog set up on point. The handler shall flush the bird, and there shall be a back-up gunner.

ADDITIONAL RULES AND REGULATIONS

A booklet containing the complete rules and regulations for the field trial registrations and standard procedures may be obtained by writing to The American Kennel Club, 51 Madison Avenue, New York, New York 10010. There is no charge for a single copy; correspondence should be further indicated by marking the envelope to the attention of the Field Department.

9. THE IRISH SETTER IN OBEDIENCE

The first interest in obedience training for Irish Setters began in this country in the 1930's. Obedience training had been an immediate success in Europe, and in 1935 Mrs. Whitehous Walker came to this country from England and staged the first obedience class in Westchester County, New York. It was a rather meager start for what was to soon become an important and well-supported sport in the fancy—one for which the Irish Setter showed a natural aptitude.

In the spring of 1936, in Cleveland, Ohio the Western Reserve Kennel Club held the first obedience trial in the midwest, open to all breeds. The following month the Detroit Kennel Club also held an obedience trial, and at both of these events an Irish Setter, trained and shown by her amateur owner, Miss Emily Schweitzer, placed first. The bitch's name was American and Canadian Ch. Verbu Killeen Oogh. She went on to win her Companion Dog and Companion Dog Excellent degrees and was the first Irish Setter in the United States to accomplish this.

American and Canadian Ch. Verbu Norna Oogh was the breed's first Utility Dog Tracking title holder. Two of Norna's daughters, Verbu Susie Oogh and Verbu Noreen Oogh, were the second and third Irish Setters to earn U.D.T. titles after their names; they too were owned, trained and bred by Emily Schweitzer, certainly one of the first, most active, and most dedicated of obedience workers in our breed. She still is today, many years later.

It was Virginia Hardin, however, who owned and trained Verbu Christopher Oogh to his U.D. title. Miss Hardin, owner of the Runwild Kennels in Northbrook, Illinois, has trained and handled a number of breeds of dog and has been especially dedicated to the Irish Setters. She has owned a number of great ones and is also very much interested in field trials as well as obedience and showing. Christopher's half sister, Runwild Alannah, was also owned by Virginia and had a bench show championship as well as her C.D. Another of Virginia's top show winners in the early 1950's was Ch. Runwild Fin McCoul. Her Ch. Runwild Fiona was a top-producing bitch and field trial winner.

The Oxton name was famous in the early days of obedience also. The 1930's saw the names of Jake and Sally Huizenga appear on the California scene with their obedience dogs. In addition to field champions the Huizengas also took their Ch. Oxton Rex and Ch. Oxton's Irish Perfection to C.D.X. titles. As recently as 1972 Jake Huizenga was influential in the crowning of Dual Champion Duffin Miss Duff, C.D. Trained and handled by Jake, Miss Duffy is out of Emily Schweitzer's Verbu Miss Duffy.

Richard D. Jennings, a well-known judge of sporting dogs in the 1920's, registered his Hearthstone Kennel name in 1925; true to the "like father, like son" tradition, his son and daughter-in-law, Peter and Cynthia Jennings, carried on over the years in Connecticut. Peter bought Ch. Gay Holly O'Dandy in 1957 after a breeding to a champion Kinvarro bitch produced quality dogs bearing over six generations of the Hearthstone line.

The Argo Lane Kennels came into being when Joseph and Margaret Frydrych got their first Irish Setter back in 1943. This birthday present for Mr. Frydrych managed to endear the breed to them, and Canadian Ch. Jiggs Dandy of Galway was next, which started them in obedience competition. Jiggs was a Canadian C.D.X. title holder and an American C.D. winner. More than a dozen other Argo Lane dogs earned obedience titles, including Bench and Field Ch. Red Arrow Show Girl, U.D.T., winner of the coveted "Triple Crown" title. The name McCune was also prominent in obedience circles in the 1940's. The McCunes showed extensively from 1948 to the 1960's, and their best-known obedience dog was Canadian and American Ch. Phantom Brook's Burgundy, C.D.X.

The late 1940's also saw the winning ways of two other Irish Setter kennels in both the show and obedience rings, the Draherin Kennels of Lucy Jane Myers and the Red Barn Kennels of William and Marion Neville. Both kennels are still active today.

Lucy Jane's first Irish Setter, My Rusty Boy, C.D., was a birthday present in 1948, and her first bitch became an American and Canadian champion, the dam of eight champions in six litters and a C.D. title holder. Other Draherin Irish Setters are lauded in our chapter on the show ring.

The Nevilles' Red Barn Kennel in Blauvelt, New York produced Ch. Red Barn Rosabelle, U.D.T., the dam of three champions and obedience titlists. Also their Canadian and American Ch. Red Star of Hollywood Hills, C.D.X. has made a name for herself in all quarters. The Nevilles' show champions are also mentioned in our show chapter.

Arthur and Orpha Clemons have owned their Onesquethaw Kennels since 1949 and have produced nine obedience titlists, including Ch. Red Barn Primrose II, C.D.X., Riley's Ramsay MacDonald, U.D.T. and Riley's Norman Thomas, U.D. Dr. Ann and Dr. Wolfgang

Two great obedience and bench winners bred, owned and trained by Emily Schweitzer of Dundee, Illinois. On the left is American and Canadian Ch. Verbu Norna Oogh, U.D.T. and American and Canadian Ch. Verbu Peter Oogh, C.D.X. Norna was the first Irish Setter U.D.T. titlist in the history of the breed. Her daughters Susie and Noreen were the second and third to earn the title.

Int. Ch. Red Star of Hollywood Hills, C.D.X. pictured here as a young dog with his owner Mrs. Paula McAteer of Bermuda. Rusty was the sire of 30 champions and was the top stud dog in 1951, 1952, and again in 1955. Rusty was co-owned by John C. McAteer.

Casper got into Irish Setters in the 40's and finished Ch. Wolfscroft Amaranthus, C.D.X., and Ch. Wolfscroft Vanguard, U.D. over the years.

Roy and Doris Dafoe of the Challenger Kennels in Burlington, Ontario, Canada started with Red Barn bloodlines also, in the early 1950's, and three of their Challenger dogs have Canadian obedience titles. They are Bronze Knight, U.D., Irish Lancer, C.D.X. and Pride & Joy, C.D.

Lawrence and Eleanor Heist started their Red Arrow Kennels in Fontana, California in 1951, and were active in all phases of the dog field. There were 19 obedience title holders at their kennel, the most famous of which was American and Mexican Ch. Red Aye Scraps, American and Mexican U.D. title holder. Scraps was star of the Walt Disney motion picture *Big Red* and received the Patsy Award, given each year in the film capital for the best animal performance. They also owned Dual Ch. Red Arrow Show Girl, U.D.T. and Mexican P.C. (P.C. is the abbreviation for the Mexican obedience title *Perro Companero*); she further distinguished herself by whelping eight champion offspring, all of which also held obedience degrees, and four of which had Canadian championships.

The 1950's saw Kelly Fox of New York, owner of the Kilkara Kennels, showing his first Irish Setter, Ch. Kinvarra Lord Raglan, to a C.D. title in the middle 1950's. Treasure Trove was the name of Jack and Jean Terry's line, and their first obedience title holder was Crown Gold of Treasure Trove. A bitch of their breeding, Ch. Treasure Trove's Pirate Pearl, owned by Sam Lugonja, was a C.D. title holder also. A California veterinary student, Sharon Clegg, showed her Irish Setter, Raferty's Kathleen Magee, to a U.D. title. When the bitch was later bred to Ch. Patrick of Ide, she produced Ch. Shardmore Autumn Sheen, U.D. She earned the highest average score in Novice Class Obedience Tests of all Irish Setters in this country in 1959 with her score of 196.8. She further distinguished herself by whelping seven field trial winners and obedience titlists.

The 1960's saw George and Mary Givan of Detroit earn C.D. titles for two of their Argo Lane dogs, Champions Argo Lane Brian Adair, C.D. and Argo Lane Torpedo, C.D.

In the 1960's Raymond and Valerie Gonsor established their Varagon Kennels in Granada Hills, California. Their foundation bitch, Ch. Innisfail Best Regards, C.D.X., was a top worker and whelped many bench show champions.

Claire Andrews of the Kimberlin Kennels in Providence, Rhode Island got into Irish Setters while still in college and earned a U.D.T. title with her Lady Velvet of Hillcrest. Another U.D.T. dog of hers was Ch. Kimberlin Brian Boru, and some of her other Irish Setters are champions. Claire served as the first publicity chairman for the Irish Setter Club of America First National Specialty Show in 1973 and is still very active in the breed.

Ch. Delarda's Crimson Contessa, C.D., in action! This lovely photo shows the true beauty of the Irish Setter in motion. Owned by Madeline Blush of Baldwin, New York.

Helen and Madeline Bayless, of the Enilen Kennel prefix, reside in Woodland Hills, California and have owned five U.D.T. champions. Their Enilen Michael Terrence has a Mexican P.C. and a P.R. (*Perro Rastreador*) title as well. Their most recent title holder was their Enilen McCorkney's Garmhac, C.D.X. and Mexican P.C.

Other names prominent in the obedience rings over the years were Charles and Alberta Benton with their Timothy Shawn O'Dea, C.D.X., which was a field trial winner as well. Their Aaragon Kennel dogs did very well in the show rings also. Francis and Kathleen Byrne of Pacific Palisades, California took Thenderin Luimneach Siege all the way to a C.D.X. title, the Ralph Davises did the same with their Ch. Red Arrow Stardust, C.D.X., and Frank and Polly Glynn of Waukesha, Wisconsin put a U.D. title on their field trial winner, Lady of the Lodge. Of the Lodge was their kennel suffix. Lady earned the title in three trials in nine days with scores of 190 for each trial—something of a record at that time.

Ch. Oxton's Irish Perfection C.D.X., owned by Jake D. Huizenga, is a perfect example of an Irish Setter worthy of the double title, and further talented in the field. Sired by Ch. Oxton Rex, C.D.X. **ex** Queen of Ardkeen's Molly.

California was a popular area for obedience work, and the William Goldens of Pacific Palisades took their Muldoon of Haleridge all the way through the U.D. trials to a title in 1958. Allan C. and Dora Nelson of Upland, California finished their Ch. Red Arrow So Go to a C.D.X. title.

Mary Beth and Nicholas Helm operated their Yorkhill Kennels in St. Paul, Minnesota; their most well-known bitch was Ch. Yorkhills Red Rhapsody, C.D.X. Rhapsody was active in the field, on the bench and in breeding as well as in the obedience ring over a career which spanned a dozen years. Also in the midwest, in Plymouth, Michigan Edgar and Roberta McIvor finished their Dual Ch. Tyrone's Mahogany Mike to a C.D.X. title. And in Milwaukee, Wisconsin Arthur and Alice Norcross earned a C.D.X. title for their Mahogany Sue, while in Garden City, Michigan Ken and Shirley Opp finished Argo Lane's Gallant Lad to a C.D.X. title and to a Canadian C.D. degree.

Thomas and Norma Palmer finished Ch. Weblyn Westerner to a C.D.X. title and their American and Mexican Ch. Webline Winning Way to a C.D. title here and a Mexican P.C. title. They had other C.D. dogs as well. Ch. Dorwayne's Kristi Shannon, C.D.X. and several other obedience title holders were owned by the Wayne Pipers of Wisconsin.

There were of course other kennels which produced countless C.D. title holders over the years, but we regret a complete list cannot be included in this book. But we must certainly pay special tribute to Sam and Eleanor Dansin's triple crown winner in Field and Bench Champion O'Lannon Copper Penny, C.D.!

By 1960, just a quarter of a century after these first obedience trials, the American Kennel Club records revealed that 569 Irish Setters had been awarded their Companion Dog titles, 130 had earned their Companion Dog Excellent titles, 36 the Utility Dog title and 11 the Utility Dog Tracking title. It was also in 1960 that a bench and field champion dog named Dual Ch. Red Arrow Show Girl, U.D.T. became the first and ONLY dog of *any* breed to be awarded all three titles!

The most titled obedience Irish Setter, however, was American, Canadian and Mexican Ch. Legend of Varagon, U.D.T., P.R., P.U., Canadian C.D.X.! "Trifi" made history as the most titled Irish Setter in the world. He was a Group winner also and proved himself further as a stud by siring a Best in Show dog as well as numerous other American and Canadian offspring. This remarkable dog died in the mid-1970's at the age of 14; he was very proudly owned by Renee Taylor of California. She and Ronald Taylor have been active since the 1940's.

While our Irish Setters do not respond well to "blind obedience," they work well when their intelligence is respected and do well at obedience work. On the strength of the early and successful beginnings mentioned above, it is not hard to understand how our Irish Setters

Ch. Delarda's Crimson Contessa, C.D. in the show pose with her owner-handler, Madeline Blush of Baldwin, New York.

Mr. C.C. Stillman's Irish Setter puppies captured in this lithograph from the collection of Sid Marx.

have managed to make so many titles for themselves in the years which have followed.

MEXICAN TITLES

For those who are not entirely familiar with obedience titles in Mexico, a dog which earns the right to include P.C. after its name has completed the performance requirements for a *Perro Companero* title. The P.C. title is comparable to our Companion Dog degree. The letters P.R. after a dog's name indicate that the dog has earned a *Perro Rastreador* title. This is comparable to our Tracking Dog degree.

10. THE IRISH SETTER IN OTHER LANDS

THE IRISH SETTER IN CANADA

As the popularity of the Irish Setter continues to grow in Canada just as it has in the United States, it is interesting to note that the number of champions to be listed with the Canadian Kennel Club is rapidly approaching dogs in four numerals. Of the almost one thousand which have or are about to achieve their championships in their native Canada, we note that many of them are also champions in the United States.

This fact indicates not only that transportation in today's modern world provides the perfect opportunity for Canadians to venture south of their border to attend our dog shows but also that the quality of the Canadian Irish Setters is such that it allows for their dogs to compete on an international level and hold their own with all comers in the show rings. Of this the Canadians can be duly proud!

ARDEE

Special credit for the growth in popularity of Irish Setters in Canada is due a man named Harry Dean. There is no one other person in all of Canada who can be said to have done more for the breed than Harry Dean. Since 1934 Harry Dean has owned, bred or handled more than two dozen Canadian Irish Setter champions at his Ardee Kennels in Saskatoon, Saskatchewan. Five of his great working dogs attained their dual championships. There was Dual Ch. Ardee's Irish Ace, offspring of his Dual Ch. Moanruad Ambassador. Ambassador was a son of field champions; his sire was Field Ch. Admiral of Rye, and his dam was Field Ch. New Square Red Lassie. In fact, there were a total of eight field trial champions in Ambassador's immediate pedigree. Other dual champions were Glenderry's Amber Prince, Elmcroft Mahogany Sue and Lady Amber of Ardee.

While Harry Dean's chief interest was the field, he was also active in the show ring, and many Canadian champions bear the Ardee name and have helped establish the breed in Canada over the years. Harry Dean spared no time or expense to improve his stock by importing dogs to maintain the quality he desired. The aforementioned Dual Ch. Moanruad Ambassador was imported from Ireland and not only worked well for him in the field but also sired seven Canadian champions and many field trial winners. He imported his Field Ch. Bird Comet of Ardee, Willowview Gamester and Lady Claire from the United States, as well as bench show Ch. End O'Maine Billboard, a well-known dog in his time. Other prominent Ardee show dogs were Ch. Lady Gadeland of Ardee, Ch. Red Echo of Ardee, Ch. Elmcroft Red Ace, Ch. Bird Dixie of Ardee and Ch. Red Ace of Ardee III. Harry Dean has also made a contribution to the breed as a field trial judge.

At the turn of the century, however, Canada was known for its St. Lambert Kennels, owned by Samuel Coulson of Montreal and David Ward of Toronto. Many of the St. Lambert bitches were bred during the first decade of the 20th century to America's early imported Shan Law lines, tops in quality at the time. F.A. Walsh of Winnipeg, Manitoba imported a dog named Cushbawn Desmond from England during this period also. In 1920 Dr. John D. DeRonde, owner of the Palmerston Kennels in New York, imported Tyronne Larry from E.C. Howard of Montreal. Larry became a champion in both countries and sired over 140 puppies of both show and field quality.

COLNBROOK

Relatively new to the breed is David E. Powell of Vancouver, British Columbia. He has been interested in Irish Setters since the mid-1960's and has bred 23 champions to date. Three of them have been Group winners, and one has gone on to win a Best in Show. This he accomplished by breeding his stock, which stemmed from the Cherry Point line, to the well-known lines in the United States, Bayberry, Innisfail, etc., among them. He has been a leading breeder in Canada since the beginning of the 1970's, based on the accomplishments of the Irish Setters bred according to this plan.

David Powell's dogs are campaigned not only in Canada but also in the United States and Bermuda as well. His Canadian and Bermudian Ch. Colnbrook Zodiac is one of his favorites and has a show ring record of five Bests in Show, 22 Group Firsts, 40 Bests of Breed, and many Group placings to his credit. Zodiac also finished up 1974 by being named Top Irish Setter and Top Sporting Dog in Canada. Zodiac's sire was Blazer, also out of Colnbrook Delight, and he was whelped in April, 1970 also. Both of these dogs were campaigned through the first half of the 1970's so their ring careers can in no way be considered complete.

THE HONSBERGERS

Jean and Kenneth Honsberger were active at one time in obedience and bench shows with their Kenten lines. They owned Canadian Ch. Prince Rory of Kenten, C.D. and Canadian Ch. Toni of Kenten and had their home base in Ontario.

Canadian and Bermudian Ch. Colnbrook Zodiac pictured winning one of his 5 Bests in Show. Owned by David E. Powell of Vancouver, British Columbia, Canada.

DAFOE

Doris and Roy Dafoe of Burlington, Ontario became interested in obedience work with Irish Setters in 1950. Their Challenger kennel name was based on their Red Barn lines and finished their Canadian and American Ch. Red Barn Red Stardust, Canadian Champion Price Rory of Kent, C.D., and Canadian Ch. Argo Lane Beryllium before getting into more serious obedience work in Canada. Two of the Challenger dogs went beyond the C.D. titles; Bronze Knight was a U.D. title holder, and Irish Lancer was a C.D.X. dog.

A lovely headstudy of Canadian Ch. Colnbrook's Annabelle, owned by David E. Powell of Vancouver, Canada. This lovely Canadian bitch has been shown in three countries and has 4 Bests of Breed and 24 Best of Opposite Sex wins to her show ring credits.

WILDAIR

Since 1940 Gertrude W. Drew has managed to finish well over a dozen Irish Setter champions from her Wildair Kennels in Toronto, Ontario. In addition to those bearing the Wildair prefex she finished Ch. Ace Flyer of Aaragon.

KILLANE

Two of the outstanding dogs of John and Muriel Royston's Killane Kennels in Ontario were American and Canadian Ch. Argo Lane's Rising Star and American and Canadian Champion Killane Rogue. While these two dogs in no way complete the kennel, the Roystons also are proud of eight other Killane Irish Setters which have earned their championships at the Canadian shows, and there are more champions in the making.

CONIFER

C.W. and Mrs. Morehen, owners of the Conifer Kennels in Ontario, own American and Canadian Ch. Conifer's Guarda Siochana in addition to several other Canadian champions bearing the Conifer

Ch. Lady Haliburton, owned by H.M. McLeod of Halifax, Nova Scotia, photographed several years ago.

name. Bev Rivett of Ontario owns Canadian and American Ch. Conifer's Guarda-Siochana purchased from the Morehens as well as Canadian Ch. Conifer's Prince O'Shannon.

BAYKNOLL

Even though it is estimated that almost a quarter of the Canadian champions also pick up their American titles, there are of course many prominent breeders and exhibitors who do not venture out of their own country. D.J. and B. Knoll of the Bayknoll Kennels in Alberta have finished a minimum of six Canadian champions.

THRELWYN

Perhaps the most outstanding example of Canadian success in the breed in modern times is that achieved by the Thomas G. Threlkelds. They believe in showing in both countries and in blending bloodlines from the top dogs in the breed, and they have gone to the top by winning the title of top dog in all breeds.

The Thomas G. Threlkelds registered their Threlwyn kennel prefix in 1955 and maintained their kennel at Halifax, Nova Scotia. They were famous for having campaigned four famous Irish Setters over the years. One of these, and perhaps the best known, was American and Canadian Ch. Draherin Bachelor Boy. Jeffrey was born June 14, 1966, sired by Draherin County Leitrim *ex* Glen Cree High Time. He started his American career in March, 1968, handled by Ken Murray. His championship was earned by July, 1968, and he won the Golden Leash award from the Irish Setter Club of America for that same year. In April, 1969 he began his Canadian championship career and took Best in Show at the first show. He finished for the Canadian title in four shows with two Bests in Show.

Jeffrey is the Canadian all-time Best in Show winner, all breeds, and has defeated more dogs than any other dog in the history of the Canadian Kennel Club to achieve his record of 65 all breed Bests in Show, two Specialties, 195 Group Firsts and a total of 235 Group placings; he was Best of Breed 245 times. Jeffrey was shown 263 times under 106 different Canadian and American judges. He was winner of the Irish Setter Club of Canada award in 1969 and every following year through 1973. He was also winner of the Ralston Purina award for six consecutive years and was Top Winning Irish Setter for 1969 through 1973, No. 2 Sporting dog in 1969 and 1970, and No. 1 Sporting Dog for 1971, 1972 and 1973. He was retired in June, 1974.

Another of the Threlkelds' top dogs was Canadian and American Ch. Ton-Leigh's Patrick Sean. Pat was whelped June 15, 1955 and was by Ch. Redstar Talent Scout out of Red Barn Margot. Pat completed his American championship under the handling of Anne Hone Rogers with four majors. He finished his Canadian championship in four shows with all Best of Breed wins and placements in the Group. Pat won the Irish Setter Club of Canada Best of Breed award in 1958.

15-year-old Flicka (Can. and Am. Ch. Red Barn Reflection), after her show career was over, attended 215 dog shows "for exhibition only" as her kennel mate's "manager." Her kennel mate Can. and Am. Ch. Draherin Bachelor Boy, Canada's Top Winning Dog for many years, all-breeds! Proud owner is Thomas Threlkeld, Halifax, Nova Scotia.

Mike, or Ch. Hollywood Hills Honor, was another of their greats. Whelped in July, 1955, his sire was Ch. Margevan's Real McCoy *ex* Hollywood Hills Patricia. A consistent Sporting Group winner, he once won 16 Groups in 16 shows. Pat also was a Best in Show winner and won the Irish Setter Club of Canada Best of Breed trophy for 1959, 1960 and 1961.

Canadian and American Ch. Red Barn Reflection was a lovely bitch known best as Flicka. She completed her American championship from May to November in 1959 before she had reached two years of age. In 1959 she won four annual trophies from the Irish Setter Club of New England. She completed her Canadian title in seven consecutive shows, undefeated in the classes. At that time she was the only Irish Setter bitch to have won a Best in Show, a feat she accomplished a total of three times. In 37 times shown in Canada, she won 32 Bests of Breed and 10 Group Firsts, and she won the Irish Setter Club of Canada Best of Breed trophy in 1962. She was born November 11, 1957; her sire was Ch. Red Barn Royal Talisman *ex* Ch. Red Barn Royal Polly.

As this book was being written I received the information above and the photographs of the above mentioned dogs from Mrs. Thomas G. Threlkeld. In the accompanying letter she informed me that Tom had died in his sleep the night before the 1975 Combined Setter Specialty Show at the Statler-Hilton Hotel in New York City just before the Westminster Kennel Club show. She informed me that since Tom had wanted to be included in this book that she was sending me this material which he had gathered just before his death. The author is most grateful.

IRISH SETTERS IN BERMUDA

Beyond any doubt it is Mrs. Paula McAteer who can be said to be the guiding force behind Irish Setters in Bermuda.

Paula first came into prominence in the breed in the early 1950's with her International Champion Red Star of Hollywood Hills, C.D.X. This magnificent dog was top stud dog in 1951, 1952 and again in 1955; he sired 30 champions. One of the early C.D.X. obedience title holders, this dog did much to endear the breed to Paula and John McAteer, who have owned a succession of glorious Irish Setters over the years.

Ch. Ravenhurst Salty was another of their favorites, as was Ch. Redlog Strawberry Blonde, C.D.X., Bermudian Ch. Red Barn Apache and many others.

Paula is also most active in the Bermuda Kennel Club, serving as its president in the mid-70's; she also handles for other Irish Setter owners to round out her participation at the shows. In 1974 she handled Frances Robinson's Bermudian Ch. Red Barn Sean of Killarney to a Best of Breed, Group Second, and Best Local Dog in Show under judge Robert Waters. The McAteers and their daughter Karolynn are

Mrs. Paula McAteer and another of her winning Irish Setters going Best in Show under judge Marie Meyer at a Bermuda Kennel Club show. Bermuda News Bureau photograph.

also active with their horses in Bermuda, and we can think of no more beautiful sight than the McAteers, their horses, and their beautiful Irish Setters riding along the pink sand beaches of beautiful Bermuda!

IRISH SETTERS IN RUSSIA

One of the requirements in Russia for the Irish Setter to attain a bench show championship is that the dog also excel in the field. Since there is no widely sold commercial dog food in Russia, the dogs are fed on meat, of course, along with cereals and other so-called "human food." Though reported to be somewhat smaller than our dogs, and also bearing less feathering and angulation, the Irish Setters of the Russian dog shows are substantial in build with good hindquarters, though with rather less angulation than we like to see in the breed.

In 1972 it was the great good fortune of Mrs. Fred Vanacore, owner of the Ballycroy Kennels in Mendham, New Jersey to be invited by her father on a vacation trip to the Soviet Union. Constance Vanacore had been corresponding since 1969 with Mrs. Tatiana Krom, a leading Irish Setter judge and geneticist for the Moscow Hunting Society. Mrs. Krom and her husband and an interpreter friend met Connie on her arrival in Moscow and took her to see the Russian Irish Setters in the Moscow area. Connie was impressed with what she saw. . . dark coats, almond eyes, good bone and nice level planes to their heads. Connie felt some were a bit wider than our dogs are and stated, "They give an overall impression of being truer to pictures of our Setters of forty years ago than to what we are breeding today."

The dogs are exhibited completely untrimmed, with feet and even whiskers as they grow naturally.

Dogs in Russia are bred on a small scale and on a controlled basis. Top price for an Irish Setter is around $35.00. In order to own an Irish Setter you must also be a hunter—registered with the Hunting Society—and in order to qualify to show an Irish Setter at a bench show your dog must be hunted in the field. Annual field trials are held so that these dogs may qualify for this important part of their achievement in competition. Therefore, most dog owners own one or two dogs so that their dogs can qualify.

Veterinary care is free, and fancy dog collars are worn which bear the medals and insignia the dogs win in their competitions. Bronze, silver and gold medals are awarded instead of ribbons. Owners must travel great distances to the field reserves for these competitions, in which the dogs hunt several kinds of game, such as quail, snipe, partridge, wood-grouse, land rails, and a bird common to the Soviet Union called a black cock. This also holds true for the English and Gordon Setters in Russia as well as their Pointers.

1972 in Moscow, Russia. Connie Vanacore and Russian Irish Setter fanciers in that country pose with their dogs to have this photograph taken at a leading Russian dog show. Mrs. Vanacore made this trip and was given the "red carpet treatment" as a result of correspondence begun in 1969 with Mrs. Tatiana Krom, an Irish Setter judge and geneticist.

A bench and field champion bitch photographed in Moscow, Russia in 1972 by Connie Vanacore while vacationing in that country. Size and substance of this bitch seem somewhat more sparse than on dogs in other countries, and the feathering is not profuse, but Mrs. Vanacore states that the Russian Irish Setters are sturdy and have strong hindquarters.

Russia acknowledges both local and national champions, and these regional titles can be won many times, though there is usually only one regional show per year. Every few years there is a show called an All National, and the national champion from this show is the top winning dog. Dogs are rated excellent, very good, good, fair, poor or unacceptable, depending on both performance and conformation.

Russia held its first dog show in 1923, and shows have survived all regimes and political changes, though they are on a smaller scale than in other countries. As it is elsewhere in the world, the dedicated core of devoted breeders managed to preserve the important bloodlines during the various wars and invasions. While the first Irish Setters went to Russia in the 1880's directly from Ireland, many of the Russian Irish Setters were lost during the 1917 revolution. By 1920, however, there was a distinct effort underway once again to bring the Irish Setter back to its preferred place in the fancy, and in plenty of time for that first dog show in 1923 under the new Soviet regime, in spite of the devastation of their civil war and World War I. After World War II they imported dogs to introduce new strains from the English and German lines, and it is acknowledged that the Muscovite strain based on their importations has produced the best hunting and show stock to be found in the Soviet Union.

Mrs. Krom, with whom Mrs. Vanacore has maintained her interesting correspondence regarding the breed, is the person who each November plots the breeding charts for all the eligible dogs and bitches in the Moscow area, choosing the pairs of dogs and bitches she believes to be genetically compatible to produce a true dual hunting-show Irish Setter litter. She was also the woman who alerted the Irish Setter breeders in Moscow to Connie's visit and greeted her at the plane upon her arrival. The afternoon ended with a visit for ice cream and champagne at the apartment of Mrs. Nevstrueva, another Irish Setter fancier in Moscow, where the conversation quite naturally continued to center around the subject of dogs.

The highlight of Connie's trip, however, was when upon her departure several of the Irish Setter fanciers gathered with her at the airport once again and presented her with a flight bag containing a 4½-week-old Irish Setter puppy bitch, named Lara, said to be the pick of the litters in Moscow at the time!

11. THE IRISH SETTER AND THE PHILLIPS SYSTEM

In the mid-1950's Mrs. John Phillips, already famous for her Hagginwood Irish Setter Kennels and as a judge of many breeds of dogs, devised a point system based on show records published in the *American Kennel Gazette* to measure the successes of the nation's show dogs.

As in all sports, competition and enthusiasm in the dog fancy runs high, and Irene Phillips—now Mrs. Harold Schlintz—came up with a simple, yet certainly the most fair, method of measuring wins for this competition, which over the years has provided many thrills for dog lovers interested in the good sportsmanship so essential to a competitive sport.

The Phillips System which Mrs. Phillips compiled herself during the early years was sold as an annual feature to *Popular Dogs* magazine, whose editor at that time, Mrs. Alice Wagner, did much to make it the most important measure of success for a show dog. Later, when I took over as editor of *Popular Dogs* in 1967, I carried on and did the compiling of the figures as well. For the five years I was tallying the finals for the Phillips System it was a constant source of enjoyment for me to watch the leading dogs in this country climb to the top. Because I knew that so many others felt the same way, and since Irish Setters are really Irene's breed, I asked Irene Schlintz to allow me to include the Irish Setter statistics in this book so that they would become a matter of permanent record. She kindly obliged and we publish them herewith.

THE PHILLIPS SYSTEM: WHAT IT IS AND HOW IT WORKS

The Phillips System was designed to measure with fairness the difference between a dog show win scored over many dogs and one scored over just a few dogs. For example, a Best in Show won over 1,000 dogs should obviously have more significance than a Best in

Show scored over 200 dogs. The Phillips System acknowledges this difference by awarding points in accordance with the number of dogs over which the win was scored. Points are awarded for Best in Show or Group Placings only. Bests of Breed do not count.

The Best in Show dog earns a point for each dog in actual competition. (Absentees or obedience dogs are not counted.) First in each of the six Groups earns a point for each dog in each of the six Groups. The dog which places second in the Group earns a point for each dog in the Group less the total dogs in the breed which were First. Third in the Group earns a point for each dog in the Group less the total of the breeds which were First and Second. And Fourth in the Group earns a point for each dog in the Group less the total of the breeds which were First, Second and Third.

Source for the count are the official records for each dog show as published each month in *American Kennel Gazette* magazine, official publication for the American Kennel Club. An individual card is kept on each and every dog which places in the Group or wins Best in Show during the entire year; the figures are tallied for publication at the end of each 12-month period. *Popular Dogs* publishes this tally annually and, of late, has been publishing it on a quarterly basis, since interest has run so high for this now well-established rating system.

In the beginning only a few of the top dogs were published, but starting in 1966 the phrase "Top Ten" in each breed was established; figures published included the total points, number of Bests in Show, and all four of the Group Placings. It is extremely interesting to note, as the years pass, the total points accrued by each of the top dogs. It is proof positive of the amazing increase in the number of entries at the dog shows, to the extent that from the mid-1950's when the system was first presented to the mid-1970's it was recorded that the #1 dog in the nation amassed over 50,000 points to win the title of top show dog in the nation!

EXPLANATION OF THE CHARTS

The following listings of top show winners are arranged so that the numerical columns reflect, from left to right, the total points, number of Best In Show wins, Group Firsts, Group Seconds, Group Thirds, and Group Fourths.

TOP SHOW WINNERS

1960 Top Ten
1. Ch. Shawnlea Fanfare   3,425   2   5   4   6   3
#9 Sporting Group

1961 Top Ten
1. Ch. Conifer's Lance   4,693   5   8   0   2   0
#3 Sporting Group

1962 Top Ten
1. Am. and Can. Ch. Headliner The   6,912   5   40   11   4   1
Flaming Beauty
#3 Dog in the Nation—All Breeds
#1 Sporting Group

2. Ch. Michael Bryan Duke of Sussex   6,402   8   32   11   5   0
#2 Sporting Group

1963 Top Ten
1. Ch. Tyronne Farm Rex   6,591   0   14   10   10   4
#3 Sporting Group

2. Ch. End O'Maine Reddy Go   4,679   3   26   4   3   1
#6 Sporting Group

1964 Top Ten
1. Ch. Cherry Point Brask   7,443   2   18   16   10   8
#4 Sporting Group

1965 Top Ten
1. Ch. Webline Golden Jubilee   6,947   2   20   5   2   1
#2 Sporting Group

2. Blayneywood Country Squire   5,989   5   22   5   1   3
#3 Sporting Group

3. Ch. Runwild Finnagain   3,769   3   10   6   3   3

1966 Top Ten
1. Ch. Webline Rio Hondo   14,163   9   20   14   7   6
#2 Sporting Group

2. Ch. Webline Golden Jubilee   10,637   7   22   10   1   1
#3 Sporting Group

3. Ch. Blayneywood Country   10,252   9   33   8   1   0
#4 Sporting Group

4. Ch. Webline Wizard of Macapa #7 Sporting Group	7,713	3	13	3	2	0
5. Ch. Tirvelda Nor'Wester A 1973 Top Producer has 17 Chmps.	2,964					
6. Ch. Shawen's Cavalier	2,190					
7. Ch. Argo Lanes Rixans Squire	1,453					
8. Ch. Shannons Laird Shane	1,442					
9. Ch. Cherry Point Ambush	1,273					
10. Ch. End O'Maine Pat Hand	763					

1967 Top Ten

1. Ch. Webline Rio Hondo #3 Sporting Group	11,320	3	28	16	9	7
2. Ch. Webline Wizard of Macapa #6 Sporting Group	5,476	0	12	13	4	0
3. Ch. Webline Golden Jubilee	3,472	1	14	11	3	3
4. Ch. Runwild Finnagain	2,333	0	4	7	9	3
5. Ch. Garden State Renos Blaze	1,941	0	4	5	4	5
6. Ch. Argo Lanes Rixans Squire	1,605	0	7	4	2	1
7. Ch. Shannons Laird Shane	1,127	0	1	5	2	1
8. Ch. Donamar Bold Echo of Varagon	927	0	2	1	2	0
9. Ch. Tirvelda Nor'Wester	703	0	1	3	1	0
10. Ch. Tirvelda Bridget Susieann	694	0	1	3	3	3

1968 Top Ten

1. Ch. Major O'Shannon #2 Sporting Group	13,543	10	30	7	8	5
2. Ch. Webline Rio Hondo #5 Sporting Group	8,040	2	16	13	8	10
3. Ch. Webline Wizard of Macapa #7 Sporting Group	7,324	1	7	20	6	2
4. Ch. Shannon's Erin	1,681	1	4	0	1	1
5. Ch. Glendee's Bourbon on the Rocks	1,663	1	11	5	2	1
6. Ch. Mahogany's Socair Buacaill, CD	1,587	2	3	1	0	0
7. Ch. Tirvelda Bridget Susieann	1,550	1	6	5	3	4
8. Ch. Webline Golden Jubilee, CD	1,395	1	6	1	5	1
9. Ch. Cherry Point Shanahan	1,366	0	2	4	3	5
10. Ch. Celous Michael Macrory	1,050	1	2	0	2	1

1969 Top Ten
1. Ch. Major O'Shannon #2 Sporting Group	19,079	10	41	18	5	3
2. Ch. Shannon's Erin #5 Sporting Group	8,665	2	11	10	4	0
3. Ch. Webline Fame and Fortune	4,127	1	5	4	8	1
4. Ch. Jo Ett's Marvelda Blazer	2,634	0	11	1	4	1
5. Ch. Mohogany Socair Buacaill, CD	2,630	0	11	1	1	2
6. Ch. Tirvelda Middle Brother	2,144	0	6	4	3	3
7. Ch. Glendees Bourbon on the Rocks	1,666	1	3	2	3	4
8. Glendees Duke of Sherwood	1,385	1	3	1	5	0
9. Ch. Innisfail Flashbacks Design	1,157	1	5	0	1	0
10. Ch. Heritage Counterspy	1,103	0	2	0	3	3

1970 Top Ten
1. Ch. Major O'Shannon #2 Sporting Group	20,784	10	35	20	8	1
2. Innisfail Flashbacks Design #8 Sporting Group	9,129	3	15	10	3	1
3. Webline Fame N Fortune #9 Sporting Group	8,670	1	15	9	7	4
4. Tirvelda Middle Brother	6,813	4	16	6	0	3
5. Ch. Mohogany Socair Buacaill, CD	2,504	2	2	0	0	0
6. Ch. Danalee Bright Legend	2,424	0	3	2	4	6
7. Ch. Glendees Bourbon on the Rocks	2,269	2	8	6	4	0
8. Ch. Squire Sean of Essex	1,589	1	2	3	2	0
9. Ch. Jubilee Farms Gaucho	1,488	1	1	2	5	1
10. Ch. Rox-San Danny Boy	1,421	1	3	1	0	0

1971 Top Ten
1. Ch. Webline Fame N Fortune #3 Sporting Group	18,850	8	25	9	5	1
2. Ch. Starheir's Aaron Ardee #5 Sporting Group	15,707	9	21	17	9	2
3. Ch. Innisfail Flashbacks Design #6 Sporting Group	10,863	3	15	6	4	1
4. Ch. Kelly Shannon O'Deke	5,552	0	7	23	7	2
5. Ch. Bayberry Tobago	1,643	0	2	4	2	0

6. Ch. Danalee Bright Legend	1,400	0	1	1	4	3
7. Ch. Bronze Blaze of Tamarask	1,395	0	3	2	3	1
8. Ch. Tirvelda Valentine	1,289	0	1	2	3	1
9. Ch. Tirvelda Middle Brother	1,263	0	5	1	2	0
10. Ch. Donamar Bold Conquistodore	1,184	0	3	6	2	1

1972 Top Ten

1. Ch. Starheir's Aaron Ardee #7 Dog in Nation—All Breeds #2 Sporting Group	23,068	12	31	18	1	3
2. Ch. Webline Fame N Fortune #9 Dog in Nation—All Breeds #3 Sporting Group	20,096	5	17	17	9	0
3. Ch. Kelly Shannon O'Deke #7 Sporting Group	10,219	4	15	14	7	5
4. Ch. Danalee Bright Legend	8,025	1	7	11	8	7
5. Ch. Tirvelda Red Baron of Dunholm	3,840	3	7	2	3	0
6. Ch. Innisfail Flashbacks Design	3,632	1	2	2	1	2
7. Ch. Bronze Blaze of Tamarisk	1,676	0	2	3	3	5
8. Ch. Che Mars Mr. Kelly	1,378	0	1	6	0	0
9. Ch. Bayberry Sonnet	1,199	0	1	3	3	2
10. Ch. Jubilee Farms Gaucho	1,130	0	0	2	5	1

1973 Top Ten

1. Ch. Starheir's Aaron Ardee #2 Sporting Group	24,902	14	48	17	2	2
2. Ch. Kelly Shannon O'Deke #3 Sporting Group	18,280	5	19	6	4	1
3. Ch. Kimberlin Kyrie	4,402	0	8	8	3	1
4. Ch. Che Mars Mr. Kelly	4,315	1	10	9	0	2
5. Ch. Tirvelda Red Baron of Dunholm	3,370	1	9	9	2	2
6. Ch. Glenavan Hallelulia, CD	2,768	0	1	4	4	2
7. Ch. Spiretop Firestorm	2,193	0	4	5	2	1
8. Ch. Danalee Bright Legend	1,877	0	0	4	2	0
9. Ch. Webline Free 'N Easy	1,580	0	1	1	5	2
10. Ch. Bayberry Tobago	1,519	0	1	3	0	3

Hugh Rumbaugh and two of his dogs in a perfect woodland setting.

1974 Top Ten						
1. Ch. Kincora Blazing Banner #5 Sporting Group	13,781	8	21	12	9	6
2. Ch. Thenderin William Muldoon	7,375	1	15	3	4	1
3. Ch. Glenavan Sensation	5,415	1	9	10	8	2
4. Ch. Draherin King's Ransom	4,368	1	6	6	1	1
5. Ch. Pauls Patrick O'Flanagan	4,282	0	8	7	4	4
6. Ch. Starheirs Aaron Ardee	3,318	1	2	3	0	1
7. Ch. Shannon's Odyssey	2,869	1	2	3	3	1
8. Ch. Tirvelda Red Baron of Dunholm	2,859	2	6	5	2	0
9. Ch. Windjammers Nautilus	2,092	1	2	2	1	2
10. Ch. McKendress Bold Venture	1,554	1	1	2	1	1

Another of Mrs. Schlintz's innovations is her compilation of each year's top sires and dams. This category requires that each dam produce three or more champion offspring within any given year and that each sire produce five or more. *Popular Dogs* listed every sire and dam that qualified and also the top ten dogs from all six Groups. In this book, however, Irene has listed all eligible Irish Setters since she began her special feature, called the Honor Roll.

TOP PRODUCERS NOT AMONG TOP TEN GROUP WINNERS

TOP PRODUCING SIRES

CH. DRAHERIN AUBURN ARTISTRY (SA-146975); 2/28/62; 1966*
Ch. Innisfail Color Scheme, CD x Ch. Draherin Echo
Breeder: Owner, Miss Lucy Jane Myers   Handler: Owner
Champion Offspring: 13**. Sire of a second generation top producer.

CH. DRAHERIN COUNTRY LEITRIM (SA-199784); 5/20/63; 1971
Ch. Draherin Auburn Artistry x Yorkhill's Country Kerry II, CD
Breeder: Owner, Miss Lucy Jane Myers   Handler: Owner
Champion Offspring: 22. A second generation top producer.

CH. DRAHERIN IRISH REGARDLESS (SA-861186); 4/10/57; 1967,
    1969
Ch. Tyronne Farm Malone II x Ch. Thenderin Elixer, CD
Breeder: Owner, Miss Lucy Jane Myers   Handler: Owner
Champion Offspring: 24. Sire of a top producer.

KNOCKROSS O'BOY (S-786189); 4/9/55; 1967
Ch. Caldene Mick O'Boy x Ch. Sharoc Coquette
Breeder: Owner, Dr. W.L. Newhall
Champion Offspring: 36

*Year dog was a top producer.
**Total number of champions as of March 1, 1975.

CH. THENDERIN WIND RULER (SA-524031); 8/10/63; 1971
Ch. Thenderin Chaparal Cayenne x Ch. Thenderin Odessey
Breeder: Barbara Jean & Justin D. Call   Handler: Owner, Joyce
    Nilsen
Champion Offspring: 11

CH. TIRVELDA EARL OF HAREWOOD (SA-170811); 9/3/62; 1973
Ch. Michael Bryan Duke of Sussex x Ch. Tirvelda Nutbrown Sherry
Breeder: Irving Eldredge   Handler: Michael Leathers
    Owners: Mr. & Mrs. David Wilson
Champion Offspring: 16. A second generation top producer.

CH. TIRVELDA MICHAELSON (SA-190588; 9/3/62; 1972, 1973, 1974
Ch. Michael Bryan Duke of Sussex x Ch. Tirvelda Nutbrown Sherry
Breeder: Owners, Mr. & Mrs. Irving Eldredge   Handler: Owner
Champion Offspring: 29. A second generation top producer.

CH. TIRVELDA NOR'WESTER (SA-178572); 9/3/62; 1973
Ch. Michael Bryan Duke of Sussex x Tirvelda Nutbrown Sherry
Breeder: Owner, Irving Eldredge
Champion Offspring: 17

CH. TITIAN INTREPID (S-969633); 1966
Knightscroft Lord Fergus x Red Barn Belle Starr
Owners: Mr. & Mrs. Joe Jennings
Champion Offspring: 12

CH. WEBLINE MYSTIC MARK (S-945913); 8/29/58; 1971
Ch. Innisfail Color Scheme, CD x Ch. Knightscroft Erin McCuhl
Breeder: Weblyn Kennels   Handler: Owners, Mr. & Mrs. C.R.
    Webb.
Champion Offspring: 24. Sire of a top producer

TOP PRODUCING DAMS

CH. ARGO LANE'S TIPPITY WICKET 1965
Ch. Esquire of Maple Ridge x Kilkenny's Queen Noreen, CD
Champion Offspring: 5

CH. CELOU'S TRACEY MACRORY 11/17/66; 1966, 1967
Ch. Conifer's Lance x Ch. Celou's Sheena Macrory
Champion Offspring: 10

CH. CHERRY POINT GROUSE 3/13/61; 1969
Ch. Yorkhill Achilles x Ch. End O'Maine Morning Bird
Champion Offspring: 4

BEST
LOCAL DOG
IN SHOW
PHOTO BY G. FENDLER

BEST
IN SHOW

This typical field trial photograph features one of Phil Bomhoff's Irish Setters "doing what comes naturally!" Mr. Bomhoff works his dogs near the Fairfield, New Jersey area where he resides.

Opposite, above:
Bermuda Ch. Red Barn Sean of Killarney pictured winning Best of Breed, 2nd in the Group and Best Local Dog in Show at the 1974 Bermuda Kennel Club Show under judge Robert Waters. Sean was also winner of the Novice Class at the first Irish Setter National Specialty show at Valley Forge, Pennsylvania in 1973. He is owned by Miss Frances E. Robinson and handled by Paula McAteer.

Opposite, below:
Canadian and American Ch. Draherin Bachelor Boy pictured winning Best in Show under American judge Dr. Frank Booth at the 1971 St. John show in Canada, owner-handled by Thomas G. Threlkeld of Halifax, Nova Scotia.

CH. DRAHERIN ANNIE LAURIE 2/28/62; 1969, 1971, 1974
Ch. Innisfail Color Scheme, CD x Ch. Draherin Echo of Elixir
Champion Offspring: 13

CH. DRAHERIN HOPE 6/13/63; 1969
Ch. Weblyn Mystic Mark x Ch. Draherin Echo of Elixir
Champion Offspring: 9. Dam of a top producer

CH. KNOCKROSS RUBY 3/7/58; 1966, 1967, 1969
Knockross O'Boy x Knockross Milo
Champion Offspring: 21. Dam of 3 top producers.

CH. KNOCKROSS SUSIE 1968
Knockross O'Boy x Knockross Suzanne
Champion Offspring: 5

CH. RED BARN REDWOOD 8/15/60; 1969
Ch. Boxley April Blaze x Can. Ch. Red Barn Reflection
Champion Offspring: 3

CH. SEERAT'S BERRY GAY RHU 1967
Red Barn Owoor x Neerb's Colleen Rhu
Champion Offspring: 7

CH. SHAMIE 6/26/62; 1969
Ch. Draherin Irish Regardless x Ch. Knockross Ruby
Champion Offspring: 5

CH. SHAMROCK HEATHER 1965, 1968
Ch. Shamrock Clancy O'Reilly x Shamrock Fancy
Champion Offspring: 9

CH. THENDERIN MISPICE 1967
Ch. Thenderin High N'Handsome x Ch. Innisfail Mona Lisa
Champion Offspring: 8

CH. TIRVELDA NUTBROWN SHERRY 9/9/60; 1965, 1966, 1967, 1968, 1969
Ch. Kinvarra Malone x Hartsbourne Sallyanna of Tirvelda
Champion Offspring: 23. Dam of 4 top producers.

CH. TYRONNE FARM GLORIBEE 2/5/61; 1968, 1969
Ch. End O'Maine Red Cloud x Tyronne Farm Victoria
Champion Offspring: 12. Dam of a top producer.

Ch. Webline Wizard of Macapa, bred and owned by Mr. and Mrs. C.R. Webb, was the sire of 17 champions. Sired by Ch. Webline Mystic Mark **ex** Webline Luminous Lass, the Wizard was #7 Sporting Dog in the U.S. in 1966, #6 Sporting Dog in 1967 and #7 Sporting Dog in 1968. He had 4 Bests in Show to his credit as well.

CH. WEBLYN MADRIGAL 8/28/58; 1969
Ch. Innis fail Color Scheme, CD *x* Ch. Knightscroft Erin McCuhl
Champion Offspring: 11. Dam of a top producer.

CH. SHANNON'S SHARON (SA-159825); 1970
Ch. Draherin Irish Regardless *x* Ch. Knockross Ruby
Champion Offspring: 5

CH. WEBLINE ZAMARA (SA-31502); 1969
Ch. Innisfail Color Scheme, CD *x* Ch. Thenderin Valentine, CD
Champion Offspring: 6

The winner! Ch. Tirvelda Middle Brother poses proudly in front of the trophy wall at the home of his owner, Helen Olivio of Long Island, New York. Brother was one of three top show dogs owned and campaigned by Mrs. Olivio. Sal Miceli photograph.

Opposite:
Nobility of expression is personified in this endearing study of Dajo's Crimson Rose, owned by Dajos Kennels of Puyallup, Washington.

CH. KIMBERLIN CARA (SA-360438); 1971
Celou's Lex Macrory x Ch. Shawnlea's Gayla
Champion Offspring: 4

CH. CANDIA FAWN (SA-288317); 1971
Ch. Muckamoor's Marty McCuhl x Draherin Echo's Hope
Champion Offspring: 5

CH. MISS WAGG'S TO RICHES (SA-483363); 1971
Can. & Mex. Ch. Scarlet Flash of Varagon x Kelly Sue Nolan
Champion Offspring: 3

CH. WEBLINE REGALIA (SA-246398; 1971
Ch. Draherin Auburn Artistry x Ch. Weblyn Madrigal
Champion Offspring: 3

CH. TIRVELDA BRIDGET SUSIE ANN (SA-233259); 1973
Ch. End O'Maine Jack High ex Ch. Hartsbourne Sallyanne of Tir-
velda.
Champion Offspring: 6

CH. WILSON FARM COUNTRY FARM 1973
Ch. Draherin Irish Regardless x Ch. Wilson Farm Partridge
Champion Offspring: 6

TIRVELDA QUEEN MAB 1974
Champion Offspring: 3

Records of the top producers was started with the March, 1965 issue
of *The American Kennel Gazette—Pure-Bred Dogs* and ends with the
February issue 1975.

12. IRISH SETTER CLUBS AROUND THE WORLD

IRISH SETTERS CLUBS IN IRELAND

The Irish Red Setter Club was established in 1885 in Dublin. Perhaps no other happening up to that time did so much to announce to the world that the Irish Red Setter was now a breed unto itself! Its zooming popularity in its homeland and abroad left no doubt that the breed had "arrived" and was a favorite with dog people and that its future was secure in the fancy.

There was also a Dublin Canine Association which held a dog show in 1872, and an Irish Kennel Association was founded 25 years later. In 1908 these two organizations combined and became the Irish Kennel Club, authorized by the English Kennel Club (not to be confused with the British group known as the Kennel Club).

In 1909 it was proposed that all dog clubs be formed into one; a central body to foster purebred dogs, put on shows, and to carry out the powers delegated by the English Kennel Club. World War I put all such plans into the future, however.

After the cessation of hostilities, the Irish fanciers found they were reluctant to acknowledge authority administered by the English Kennel Club and simply continued to put on their own shows. At a public meeting in January, 1922, a breed council was formed by the various clubs and on February 3, 1922 the first meeting of the Executive Council of the Irish Kennel Club was held, with the late Honorable Justice H. Hanna, K.C. as first Chairman.

The club was determined to establish a kennel club which would be a model administrative body, entirely democratic, ensuring equal opportunity to all dog fanciers, providing completely impartial decisions without fear or favor and completely non-political and non-sectarian. There was formidable opposition to the establishment of an Irish governing body from a minority who represented the "Old Guard"; they feared they might be black-listed for participating in unrecognized shows not held under a license from the Kennel Club, London.

Gala Glen's Kerry Lynn, Irish Setter owned by Barbara Parks, Lindale Kennels, Dillard, Georgia.

American and Canadian Ch. Draherin Billy Boy, pictured winning the Sporting Group under judge Haskell Schuffman at the October, 1971 Metra Kennel Club in Toronto, Canada. Handler Carol Hollands handled for co-owners Dr. R.D. Helferty and Ruth Cordes. Billy Boy is the sire of Dr. Helferty's great American, Canadian and Bermudian Ch. Kelly Shannon O'Deke.

A meeting was called on January 20, 1922 with twelve members being present to draw up a constitution covering rules for putting on bench shows and field trials. These rules are pretty much followed even today, since Judge Hanna was a strong administrator and set the club on a course which has been its strength throughout its history.

Judge Hanna created guidelines, precedents, rules and regulations, proposed amendments to the constitution, and attended practically every meeting during his fifteen-year reign. After an initial rebuff, he also successfully negotiated a reciprocal agreement with the Kennel Club, London, which is what so many of the members wanted. He was the designer of the club's Green Star point system for championships as well.

The Green Star system of points was introduced about 1925. To obtain a championship a dog must obtain 16 points. The value of points is determined by the number of dogs representing the breed at each show, and not the number entered. An index figure is assessed every year in regard to each breed and the number of registrations recorded for it.

The Green Star Committee consists of three persons appointed by the Executive Committee of the Irish Kennel Club. It is necessary for all of the gundog breeds, as well as a few other breeds, to also earn a Field Trial Certificate in order to qualify for a championship. However, it should be noted that other dogs with lesser qualifications may become Bench Winners of Yearly Champions.

Immediately upon its establishment, the Irish Kennel Club was recognized by Norway and Germany. The American Kennel Club raised an objection on the grounds that the name "Irish Kennel Club" was misleading because it did not represent the whole of Ireland. But late in 1925 the AKC agreed to accept their pedigree certificates, which is what the Irish Kennel Club was seeking.

Up until 1925 the Kennel Club in London also had declined to recognize the Irish Kennel Club and refused to cooperate with it in any way. Perhaps the Irish Kennel Club's acceptance and recognition by the American Kennel Club influenced the London organization to some degree, for the Irish Kennel Club has since become recognized universally.

Their first dog show was held in Dublin on March 17, 1922. They held six shows that year with entries numbering in the hundreds; today the Irish Kennel Club shows take entries numbering in the thousands.

Each April the Irish Kennel Club holds its annual meeting to report the work of the previous calendar year, submitted by the Secretary along with the audited accounts. The club is housed at Fottrell House in Dublin, at #4 Harcourt Street.

IRISH SPECIALTY CLUBS

Specialty clubs which looked after the welfare of the Irish Red Setter included the Irish Setter Association, created in 1908 by Mrs. Ingle Bepler; the Northern Irish Setter Club; the Irish Setter Club in Scotland; the Red Club in France, founded in 1906; and the Irish Setter Breeders Club in England. In Ireland there was also the Belfast and District Irish Setter Club, Ulster Irish Red Setter Club and the Pointer and Setter Society.

THE IRISH SETTER CLUB OF AMERICA

The Irish Setter Club of America, Inc., the parent club for the breed in the United States, was founded in 1891. The purpose of the club was to promote the breeding of pure Irish Setters; to develop and bring to perfection their natural high qualities for field use; to define and publish a description of their type; to urge the adoption of said type upon competitors at field trials, bench shows, and obedience trials, breeders and others, as the standard by which Irish Setters should be judged, and to encourage the competition of Irish Setters at such places.

In the beginning the ISCA was a show-giving club, but with the tremendous increase in registrations in the breed the club did away with dog shows (until 1973, when the first national Specialty show was held) and functioned mainly as the center of activity for all its member clubs all over the nation. The parent club grants permission for the local clubs to hold their regional Specialties and grants approval for the judges, makes research grants to various universities and foundations, and publishes a monthly "Memo To Members" paper with news of interest to Irish Setter owners and breeders. The ISCA also compiles the stud books and lists of bench and field champions and obedience titled Irish Setters.

The ISCA sends a delegate to the American Kennel Club meetings in New York City each month to act as liaison between the AKC and its members. Numerous annual prizes and trophies are awarded for accomplishment within the breed each year, booklets on various subjects are composed and distributed, and club jewelry bearing the ISCA insignia is also available. Other plans to benefit the dogs and the club members are always being considered.

In 1971 the Irish Setter Club of America established a totally independent American Irish Setter Foundation. The purpose was to encourage research into the various health problems especially afflicting the Irish Setter breed. Mrs. W. Barry Neville is the club librarian who screens any and all material to be included in a proposed Irish Setter Club of America library which hopefully will be housed at the American Kennel Club.

The author, Joan McDonald Brearley, captured with a favorite Irish Setter during a moment of mutual admiration. Photo by Sal Miceli.

JOINING AN IRISH SETTER CLUB

Anyone new to the breed who wishes to do his very best for his dog should certainly plan on joining an Irish Setter Club. These clubs keep you informed on what is happening in the breed and can often offer sage advice through their members, which might help the newcomer avoid many of the pitfalls along the trail to successful breeding and exhibiting.

Since there are many regional clubs in addition to the parent club, it would be best for anyone interested to write directly to the American Kennel Club, 51 Madison Avenue, New York, New York, 10010 to secure the name of the Corresponding Secretary for the Irish Setter Club of America, Inc., who will upon request give you the name and address of the person to contact for the nearest regional club. But by all means, join an Irish Setter Club whether your dog is to be just a pet to love and enjoy at home, or whether you intend to get involved in field, show or obedience competition.

IRISH SETTER CLUB OF AMERICA PRESIDENTS, 1891-1975

1891-1892	William H. Child
1893-1894	W.L. Washington
1895-1918	Dr. G.G. Davis
1919-1920	Joseph S. Wall
1921-1922	Dr. C.A. Gale
1923-1927	Dr. J.D. DeRonde
1928-1929	Walter Arnold
1930	Mrs. E.A. Sturdee
1931-1933	W. Cary Duncan
1934-1935	Walter C. Ellis
1936-1937	John E. Cuneo
1938	Walter C. Ellis
1939	Dr. G.S. Currier
1940-1946	John C. Neff
1947-1949	J.P. Knight, Jr.
1950-1952	Lee M. Schoen
1953-1960	L.O. Gatchell
1961-1967	Ivan Klapper
1968—	Louis Iacobucci

THE IRISH SETTER CLUB OF AMERICA'S FIRST NATIONAL SPECIALTY SHOW

Friday, August 10, 1973 was the date of the Irish Setter Club of America's first National Specialty Show, at the Valley Forge Military Academy grounds in Wayne, Pennsylvania. 522 Irish Setters, accounting for 779 entries, competed from all over the United States, Canada and Bermuda. Claire Andrews, Publicity Chairperson for this special event, announced that it represented the largest gathering of Irish Setters ever to be held in this country. Five judges from four states and England officiated at the show in three rings starting on August 10 with the sweepstakes judging, junior handling classes, and dog entries. Saturday, August 11 judging commenced with classes for the bitches, obedience, non-regular classes and the Best of Breed competition. 91 entries followed in the Parade of Champions event.

This most successful "first" adventure of the parent club was followed by the Annual Awards dinner dance on that Saturday night and preceded by a Foundation meeting Friday evening with W.J. Rasbridge, prominent Irish Setter fancier and judge in his native England, speaking on progressive retinal atrophy (PRA).

Based on the popular success of the First National a Second National Specialty was held in Pontiac, Michigan on June 13-16 the

Hugh Rumbaugh and his beloved Ch. Starheir's Aaron Ardee. This charming photograph of the owner of Fleetwood Farms in Akron, Ohio and his beautiful dog appeared in a local newspaper along with the story of Ardee's fabulous show career.

Winner at Westminster, 1975! Owner-handler Sid Marx shows his Irish Setter Dunlavrie M'Lady Sharon to Winners Bitch under judge Mrs. Tom Stevenson. Sharon is co-owned with Mrs. Florence Clark.

Opposite, above:
Ch. Dajo's Red Jacket pictured winning at a recent show under judge Frank Burch, on the way to his championship. This lovely son of American and Canadian Ch. Dajo's Sir Guy is co-owned by Dale Jones and Tommie Lou Porter, Puyallup, Washington.

Opposite, below:
Mother and son Irish Setters owned and photographed by Dr. Wolfgang A. Casper of the Wolfscroft Kennels, Staten Island, New York. This beautiful photograph typifies the classic beauty of the Irish Setters.

following year, and once again included the Irish Setter Club of America annual meeting, a symposium and dinner dance. Show Chairperson for both Specialties was Edward F. Treutel of Leonia, New Jersey.

Since the First National Specialty Show in 1973, subsequent Specialties have been held on an annual basis in other parts of the country.

KENNEL CLUBS THE WORLD OVER

Kennel clubs from which information can be obtained regarding Irish Setter activities and groups in other countries are:

THE CANADIAN KENNEL CLUB
111 Eglinton Avenue East
Toronto, Ontario
CANADA

AUSTRALIAN NATIONAL KENNEL CLUB
Royal Show Grounds
Ascot Vale, Victoria
AUSTRALIA

KENNEL CLUB
1 Clargers Street
Piccadilly, London, W.1
ENGLAND

NEW ZEALAND KENNEL CLUB
Post Office Box 523
Wellington 1
NEW ZEALAND

And, of course, the Irish Kennel Club and the American Kennel Club mentioned earlier in this chapter. Other clubs dealing with all breeds of gun-dogs also exist in which Irish Setters are welcome. These include the North of Scotland Gun-Dog Association and the Scottish Field Trial Association and the Yorkshire (England) and Ulster (Northern Ireland) Gun-dog clubs.

13. THE STANDARD FOR THE BREED

GENERAL APPEARANCE — The Irish Setter is an active, aristocratic bird-dog, rich red in color, substantial yet elegant in build. Standing over two feet tall at the shoulder, the dog has a straight, fine, glossy coat, longer on ears, chest, tail, and back of legs. Afield he is a swift-moving hunter; at home, a sweet-natured, trainable companion. His is a rollicking personality.

HEAD — Long and lean, its length at least double the width between the ears. The brow is raised, showing a distinct stop midway between the tip of nose and the well-defined occiput (rear point of skull). Thus the nearly level line from occiput to brow is set a little above, and parallel to, the straight and equal line from eye to nose. The skull is oval when viewed from above or front; very slightly domed when viewed in profile. Beauty of head is emphasized by delicate chiseling along the muzzle, around and below the eyes, and along the cheeks. Muzzle moderately deep, nostrils wide, jaws of nearly equal length. Upper lips fairly square but not pendulous, the underline of the jaws being almost parallel with the top line of the muzzle. The teeth meet in a scissors bite in which the upper incisors fit closely over the lower, or they may meet evenly. *Nose*—Black or chocolate.

EYES — Somewhat almond-shaped, of medium size, placed rather well apart; neither deep-set nor bulging. Color, dark to medium brown. Expression soft yet alert. *Ears*—Set well back and low, not above level of eye. Leather thin, hanging in a neat fold close to the head, and nearly long enough to reach the nose.

NECK — Moderately long, strong but not thick, and slightly arched; free from throatiness, and fitting smoothly into the shoulders.

BODY — Sufficiently long to permit a straight and free stride. Shoulder blades long, wide, sloping well back, fairly close together at the top, and joined in front to long upper arms angled to bring the elbows slightly rearward along the brisket. Chest deep, reaching approximately to the elbows; rather narrow in front. Ribs well sprung. Loins

Another show. . . another triumph for American, Canadian and Bermudian Ch. Kelly Shannon O'Deke as they pose for this informal photograph after one of Shannon's Best in Show wins. The handler is Tom Glassford; owner, Dr. R.D. Helferty of Davison, Michigan.

A lady and her dog. . . Helen Olivio of Long Island, New York, poses with one of her three top-winning Irish Setter champions in the living room of her home. Sal Miceli photograph.

of moderate length, muscular and slightly arched. Top line of body from withers to tail slopes slightly downward without sharp drop at the croup. Hindquarters should be wide and powerful with broad, well-developed thighs. *Legs and Feet*—All legs sturdy, with plenty of bone, and strong, nearly straight pastern. Feet rather small, very firm, toes arched and close. Forelegs straight and sinewy, the elbows moving freely. Hind legs long and muscular from hip to hock, short and nearly perpendicular from hock to ground; well angulated at stifle and hock joints, which, like the elbows, incline neither in nor out. *Tail*—Strong at root, tapering to fine point, about long enough to reach the hock. Carriage straight or curving slightly upward, nearly level with the back.

COAT — Short and fine on head, forelegs, and tips of ears; on all other parts, of moderate length and flat. Feathering long and silky on ears; on back of forelegs and thighs long and fine, with a pleasing fringe of hair on belly and brisket extending onto the chest. Feet well feathered between the toes. Fringe on tail moderately long and tapering. All coat and feathering as straight and free as possible from curl or wave.

COLOR — Mahogany or rich chestnut red, with no trace of black. A small amount of white on chest, throat, or toes, or a narrow centered streak on skull, is not to be penalized.

SIZE — There is no disqualification as to size. The make and fit of all parts and their overall balance in the animal are rated more important. Twenty-seven inches at the withers and a show weight of about 70 pounds is considered ideal for a dog; the bitch 25 inches, 60 pounds. Variance beyond an inch up or down to be discouraged.

GAIT — At the trot the gait is big, very lively, graceful, and efficient. The head is held high. The hindquarters drive smoothly and with great power. The forelegs reach well ahead as if to pull in the ground, without giving the appearance of a hackney gait. The dog runs as he stands: straight. Seen from the front or rear, the forelegs, as well as the hind legs below the hock joint, move perpendicularly to the ground, with some tendency toward a single track as speed increases. But a crossing or weaving of the legs, front or back, is objectionable.

BALANCE — At his best the lines of the Irish Setter so satisfy in overall balance that artists have termed him the most beautiful of all dogs. The correct specimen always exhibits balance whether standing or in motion. Each part of the dog flows and fits smoothly into its neighboring parts without calling attention to itself.

Ch. Bayberry Sonnet pictured winning Best of Breed at the 1974 Staten Island Kennel Club show under judge Arlene Thompson. Handled by owner Sid Marx of Ridge, New York.

Judge Irene Khatoonian Schlintz awards Sporting Group First to Ch. Major O'Shannon at a Genesee County Kennel Club show. Handled by Tom Glassford for owner Albert Greenfield, Jr., Major was #10 dog in the nation, all-breeds, in 1968 and #2 Sporting Group, #8 all-breeds in 1969 and #7 all-breeds in 1970, according to the Phillips System. Sire was Ch. Draherin Irish Regardless **ex** Ch. Knockross Ruby.

Ch. Starheir's Aaron Ardee, the #1 winning Irish Setter in the history of the breed! Aaron has won more Bests in Show, Groups and Bests of Breed than any other Irish Setter. Over 380 judges awarded him more than 465 top placement ribbons during his show career, which also established a record with his defeating over 68,000 other dogs of all breeds to win his top position in the Phillips System. He is pictured above winning a February, 1974 Best in Show at Louisville under judge Vincent Perry. Handled by Dick Cooper for owners Hugh and Virginia Rumbaugh, Fleetwood Farms, Akron, Ohio.

THE IRISH STANDARD FOR THE BREED

The Irish Red Setter Club was established in 1885 and in 1886 set up the following Standard of Points for the breed:

HEAD — Should be long and lean, and not coarse at the ears. The skull oval (from ear to ear), having plenty of brain room, and with well-defined occipital protuberance. Brows raised, showing stop. The muzzle moderately deep, and fairly square at end. From the stop to the point of the nose should be long, the nostrils wide, and the jaws of nearly equal length, flews not to be pendulous. The colour of the nose dark mahogany, or dark walnut, or black, and that of the eyes (which ought not to be too large) dark hazel or dark brown. The ears are to be of moderate size, fine in texture, set on low, well back, and hanging in a neat fold close to the head.

NECK — Should be moderately long, very muscular, but not too thick, slightly arched, free from all tendency to throatiness.

BODY — Should be proportionate—shoulders fine at the points, deep and sloping well back. The chest as deep as possible, rather narrow in front. The ribs well sprung, leaving plenty of lung room. Loins muscular, and slightly arched. The hindquarters wide and powerful.

LEGS AND FEET — The hind legs from hip to hock should be long and muscular; from hock to heel short and strong. The stifle and hock joints well bent, and not inclined either in or out. The forelegs should be straight and sinewy, having plenty of bone, with elbows free, well let down, and, like the hocks, not inclined either in or out. The fee small, very firm, toes strong, close together and arched.

TAIL — Should be of moderate length, proportionate to the size of the body, set on rather low, strong at root and tapering to a fine point; to be carried as nearly as possible on a level with or below the back.

THE COAT — On the head, front of the legs and tips of the ears should be short and fine, but on all other parts of the body and legs it ought to be of moderate length, flat, and as free as possible from curl or wave.

FEATHERING — The feather on the upper portion of the ears should be long and silky; on the back of fore and hind legs should be long and fine; a fair amount of hair on the belly, forming a nice fringe, which may extend on chest and throat. Feet to be well feathered between the toes. Tail to have a nice fringe of moderately long hair, decreasing in length as it approaches the point. All feathering to be as straight and as flat as possible.

COLOUR AND MARKINGS — The colour should be a rich golden chestnut, with no trace whatever of black; white on chest, throat or toes, or a small star on the forehead, or a narrow streak or blaze on the nose or face not to disqualify.

So read the early Standard. . . an interesting comparison to that we adhere to today. Obviously the narrow streak of white on the forehead or nose makes reference to the Palmerston Strip mentioned earlier in the chapter on the early history of the breed, which became a mark of distinction at the time.

Judges used a Scale of Points when judging the Red Setters and such points were allocated as follows:

Head	10	Forelegs and Feet	10
Eyes	6	Tail	4
Ears	4	Coat and Feather	10
Neck	4	Colour	8
Body	10	Size, style	
Hind-Legs and Feet	10	General Appearance	24

TOTAL — 100 POINTS

We do not judge in this country according to a point system with our Irish Setters, but after interpreting the two Standards it is interesting to note the point distribution in the early days as compared to our emphasis on the breed's strong points.

This Standard was written after a meeting of the Club which included J.K. Millner, J. Hamilton, J.M. Barry, W. Despard, L.F. Perrin, C. Moore, D. Sullivan, J.F. Dillon and Major J.J. Giltrap, one of its officers. When Mrs. Ingle Bepler started the rival club in 1908, the Irish Setter Association in England, the latter association adopted this same Standard. However, in 1930 in Dublin the Standard was revised to include an opening statement requirement which reads: "Style. Must be racy, full of quality, and kindly in expression." There were several other word and sentence changes, all of which brought the Standard up to reading as it appears in the beginning of this chapter. This Standard is the same one the parent club of Ireland has supplied to the Irish Kennel Club for affiliation in the 1970's.

Westwind Scarlet Dark Gem in perfect show stance with Leslie Hovenstot handling. Bred and owned by the Westwind Kennels, Long Valley, New Jersey.

Beautiful Irish Setter puppies bred and owned by the Westwind Kennels, Long Valley, New Jersey. The sire was Ch. Barrewynne Highland Lancer **ex** Westwind Scarlet Magic.

"The Old Timers" at Dr. Wolfgang Casper's Wolfscroft Kennels. . . Ch. Wolfscroft My Wild Irish Rose and her son Ch. Wolfscroft Vanguard, C.D.X. and U.D. are shown in this heart-warming photograph taken by Dr. Casper.

Best in Show at the first (November 19, 1950) Kennel Club of Santiago, Chile kennel club show was the Irish Setter Ballyknock Red Kerry, imported to Chile from the United States by H. Gerald Smith, Economic Counselor of the American Embassy in Santiago. Left to right: Mr. Smith, Dr. Spender Talbois and Mr. Thomas W. Burgin, the judge brought from Argentina, and the Honorable Claude G. Bowers, American Ambassador to Chile. The show drew 250 entries.

14. A CENTURY OF IRISH SETTERS

From the scant cross-breedings and imports during the first years of the Irish Setter in the United States we must admit that the breed has come a long way during its first hundred years. While "You've come a long way, Baby," may be a rather contrived advertising slogan of the 1970's, it can be said to apply to our breed, which has certainly accomplished great strides in the dog fancy since the first champion was recorded in 1876. In fact, as we pass the one hundred year mark in the breed we find that the Irish Setter is not only the number three breed in popularity in the United States, but there even is considerable speculation that they may go higher. . . perhaps to the number one spot.

AKC REGISTRATIONS

By 1975 the Irish Setter was indeed enjoying the number three position for the greatest number of registrations with the American Kennel Club. Always a popular breed in this country because of its great beauty, the Irish Setter started the year 1975 with the announcement of a record 61,549 registrations during the previous year. This impressive figure represented an increase over the previous year, which had reached over 54 thousand. This was more than ten thousand over the 1972 total of 43,707 according to the AKC tally.

Just a decade earlier the Irish Setter was not even listed among the nation's top ten favorites, but the number ten dog that year boasted registrations of only slightly over 13½ thousand; the Irish Setter was in the number 25 position, with total registrations of 4,015.

WESTMINSTER WINNERS

Just a century after the first Irish Setter completed its championship we find that entries at the shows are up considerably. Since the first Westminster show in 1877 Irish Setter entries have fluctuated over the years, because of requirements laid down by the show-giving clubs, etc. We are also happy to report that the Best of Breed award now is a traditional sterling silver medal bearing the Westminster Kennel Club insignia, surely a safer award than the pistols and rifles

American, Canadian and Bermudian Ch. Kelly Shannon O'Deke, photographed in October, 1973 at the peak of his sensational career. Shannon's record includes 13 all-breed Bests in Show, 8 Specialty wins, 61 Sporting Groups and 212 Bests of Breed. He was #3 Sporting Dog in the nation in 1973 and an Irish Setter Club of America award winner in 1972, in addition to his other honors. Bred by Ruth Cordes and owned by Dr. R.D. Helferty of Davison, Michigan.

Opposite:
Mother and puppies depicted in a pose of endearment that is just a small part of the charm of the Irish Setter. Owned by Red Barn Kennels, Blauvelt, New York.

which were at times awarded in the early days by the original Westminster Bench Show Committee comprised of William M. Tileston, C. DuBois Wagstaff, H. Walter Webb, Dr. W.S. Webb, Louis B. Wright and E.H. Dixson.

Oddly enough, at this most prestigious of all American dog shows, and in spite of the astounding rise in popularity in the breed, an Irish Setter has never yet won Best in Show at the Garden event. And only once, in 1935, has one (Mrs. Cheever Porter's Ch. Milson O'Boy) managed to capture the Best American-bred Dog in Show award.

OTHER DOG SHOWS

Irish Setter show entries are always high at the outdoor shows where these (and other) large dogs can really move out and show themselves to advantage. Also they do well at shows where there is an Irish Setter Specialty event which brings fanciers from farther distances to compete. The number of starters at the field trials is most impressive. Field trials perhaps show our Irish Setters at their very best doing what comes naturally to them in the great outdoors.

THE DANGERS IN POPULARITY

While we all glory in the admiration of our favorite breed, such an alarming increase in popularity can prove highly detrimental to a breed since it leads to and clearly indicates over-breeding during years when the canine population explosion is proving to be a very serious problem. Each year millions of unwanted animals must be destroyed because of not being purchased or placed in good homes, and the end result often leads them to experimental laboratories, wild packs, humane societies or death in some other form.

Only planned, top-quality breeding on a small scale should be undertaken if we are to save the breed from the ravages of over-breeding. Integrity on the part of breeders and education of the public are as important to the breed today as they were a hundred years ago when the dedicated breeders were trying to establish and perpetuate the valuable bloodlines that have made the breed what it is today. We must all work toward the betterment of dogs and their lot, but always with an eye on that all-important Standard.

This isn't always easy to do, since the Irish Setter's great beauty and remarkable friendly personality endear it to an ever-increasing number of fanciers.

IRISH SETTER TEMPERAMENT

While the Irish Setter is basically an outdoor sporting dog bred to excel in the field, we well know they have also distinguished themselves in the show ring. However, anyone who has ever owned an

Irish Setter and has included it as a member of his family will be quick to tell you that as companion and pet there is no better dog.

While their outdoor and hunting heritage means that they must be granted a great deal of opportunity to run and exercise, Irish Setters also adapt themselves very well to living in the house as a part of the family life. Their seemingly endless energy is part of their charm but can be controlled when the time comes to join the folks inside the house for everyday living.

One of the Irish Setter's most desirable characteristics is its desire to please; they are in no way to be considered as "a one-man dog." The Irish Setter relates easily to every member of the family, from the youngest to the oldest. It's loyalty cannot be questioned, and its patience with children is almost not to be believed.

The Irish Setter can in no way be called a "barker." It is one of the few breeds which does not bark without cause and therefore can be depended upon in most cases to be a rather responsible guard dog for the home. Big in size, he is not easily intimidated so does not feel obligated to pick fights with either people or other dogs. Its great dignity and appealing good looks help set it apart from other breeds also. There is no better companion when it comes to temperament, beauty or loyalty than the Irish Setter. As a show and field dog it holds its own against any breed.

IRISH SETTERS AND FAMOUS PEOPLE

Quite naturally the resplendent beauty of the Irish Setter has down through the centuries attracted the rich and the famous among dog lovers.

In times past they were the constant and favored companions and hunting dogs of lords and ladies and the aristocracy of many nations, including their native Ireland. The wealthy of the United States indulged in breeding the very best show dogs and field trial contenders and delighted in showing them off in their early expensive automobiles. Movie stars such as Janet Gaynor were photographed with their tawny Irish Setters for the movie magazines and posed willingly with these beautiful dogs at the famous California shows! Mary Pickford owned one of Dr. J.D. DeRonde's Palmerston Kennel Irish Setters.

Even today stars like Rock Hudson can be seen in the fan magazines and publicity pictures with his Irish Setter, Jill. The December 3, 1974 issue of the *New York Times* featured a page one photograph of Golda Meir, former Premier of Israel, in the garden of her home in Ramat Aviv, a Tel Aviv suburb, with her Irish Setter. Countless other political figures, sportsmen and movie stars have also fallen under the Irish Setter charm.

Unquestionably in recent times, however, the most prominent Irish Setter owner has been ex-President Richard M. Nixon. . . no

"On point," is Ch. Wolfscroft Amaranthus, C.D.X., owned and pho
graphed by Dr. Wolfgang A. Casper of Staten Island, New York. T
remarkable "Randy" finished both his championship and obedier
title after a complete recovery following an accident in which
almost completely severed his left hind leg. When veterinarians g
up, Dr. Casper himself undertook the stitching of the receding te
dons while Randy was under anesthesia for more than an hour. Af
three weeks the cast was removed and Dr. Casper taught him to w
once more. In addition to finishing his ring and obedience titles, y
can see from the above photograph that Randy is still very much
home in the field also.

Opposite:
Dual Ch. Duffin Miss Duffy, C.D., owned by Miss Emily Schw
Verbu Kennels, Dundee, Illinois, and trained in the field by Jake
zenga of the Oxton Kennels in Salinas, California. Miss Duffy i
tured here being awarded a prize by Louis Iacobucci, President
Irish Setter Club of America.

matter what your politics may be, there is no denying that he did put the Irish Setter breed in the public eye!

In his early days as President, Nixon was given an Irish Setter, Tirvelda King Timahoe, which joined Trisha Nixon's Yorkie, Pasha, and Julie's Miniature Poodle, Vicki. This lovely Irish Setter was soon photographed with almost every other important dignitary on the Washington scene as they met with Nixon in the Oval Office in the White House, disembarking from *Air Force I* after a cross-country flight, or walking the beach at San Clemente with Nixon and his friend Bebe Rebozo. And it is safe to say that the "King" certainly survived his stay in the White House better than the "President!"

King Timahoe was not the only Irish Setter making news when he arrived at the White House to become a member of the first family. Back in Bloomsbury, New Jersey his sire, Ch. Tirvelda Rustic Duke, turned up in town at the home of Richard Long after more than five months of being lost. Twenty pounds lighter, and more than 90 miles from home, Rusty seemed no worse for the wear.

After many false alarms, with people all claiming to have located the lost dog after newspaper and radio reports about him, Jane Morris, owner of the Killashandra Kennels in Hampton, New Jersey, called the Longs and went over to their home and identified the dog. Miss Morris was a friend of Rusty's owners, Mr. and Mrs. William F. Franks, Jr. of York, Pennsylvania. She called the Franks and told them she had found Rusty and a joyful and very emotional reunion followed.

However, Mr. Long wanted further proof that the Franks were actually the owners, since he had received calls from other people that the dog might be theirs. The Franks told Mr. Long that Rusty could be identified by a single white hair on his right shoulder. Everyone present looked for it but none could find it. The Franks were frantic, and it was only after they all drove to the Franks' veterinarian's office and put Rusty under a bright light that the hair could be seen, and Mr. Long released the dog to them.

The Franks said that Rusty was tired and just watched them all throughout the procedure, and slept all the way home. But when they reached the driveway of their home, he sat up, and when let out of the car he headed straight for kennel #1—his very own kennel.

Mr. Long, who admitted to becoming emotionally involved with the dog during his stay with him, had to be content with the $100 reward given him by the Franks—or buy his own Irish Setter!

AN IRISH SETTER "ON CAMPUS"

The campus was that of Yale University and the owner was Professor William Lyon Phelps. The Irish Setter was "Rufus H. Phelps," who over the years at the college at his master's side had a sniffing

Old time movie star Janet Gaynor is pictured romping on the beach in front of her home at Santa Monica, California in this photograph, which was featured in an October, 1929 issue of *Kennel Review* magazine.

acquaintance with literary giants such as George Bernard Shaw, John Galsworthy, Hugh Walpole, John Masefield, Joseph Conrad and others. Rufus was a popular figure on campus and is reported to have had his own personal charge account at the local butcher shop. His death at 14 years of age was recorded world-wide in the newspaper as "The most literary dog in the world."

IRISH SETTER ON TELEVISION

When speaking of Irish Setters and famous people we must mention a famous television personality and his Irish Setter. Merv Griffin, on one of his 1974 television programs, invited Doris Day and Jacqueline Suzanne to talk about their work with the California humane societies and the agencies' adoption services.

One of the dogs which Doris brought along to the show was a purebred Irish Setter available for adoption, and it went home with the host of the show—Merv Griffin. In the months that followed the

Judge Irene Khatoonian Schlintz declares Winners Bitch to be Thenderin Winter Wind at the 1973 First Annual National Specialty Show of the Irish Setter Club of America; owner-handled by Joyce Nilsen. Club President Louis Iacobucci presents the trophy. Ashbey photograph.

Opposite:
Dun Laoghai're M'Lady Sharon, owned by Mr. and Mrs. Andrew Clark of St. James, Long Island and photographed by Sal Miceli.

dog would make frequent appearances on the show with Merv, and he frankly admits that the dog goes with him just about everywhere. . . including flights in Merv's private plane between his television studio and his home up the California coast.

THE IRISH SETTER IN THE MOVIES

When Walt Disney did something he did it big. . . be it a Disneyland or a motion picture. In the 1960's Walt Disney decided to make a Technicolor motion picture titled *Big Red* with an Irish Setter as the star. There was a gala premiere at the Chicago Theatre in Illinois, and Emily Schweitzer's glorious Ch. Verbu Missy Oogh, C.D.X. was invited to appear at the opening.

At the height of mid-day traffic on Strate Street in front of the theatre, Missy performed all her obedience title requirements to perfection, including clearing the high jump with the greatest of ease. As

American and Mexican Ch. Candy K's Katy Dunn, one of the top show and foundation bitches at Dolores and Dale Hughes Candy Kennels in El Cajon, California. Handled by Dale Hughes.

a finale to her demonstration of trained obedience perfection, Missy displayed her keen ability to work in the field when she was set free in an arrangement of artificial flowers and weeds in a large fenced in area in which there had been planted a live, but dizzied, pheasant. True to her form, Missy went on point after finding the bird and remained steady as flash bulbs flashed and cameras clicked away at the ringside. The crowd was delighted with her performance.

Equally proud of their Irish Setter was Lawrence and Eleanor Heist of the Red Arrow Kennels in Fontana, California. It was their dog, the famous American and Mexican Ch. Red Aye Scraps, American and Mexican U.D., that was actually the star of the motion picture. Scraps was trained for the leading role in the movie by William Koehler and later won the movie industry's Patsy Award, given each year to the best animal actor in the movies!

Winner of the 1962 motion picture Patsy Award was the Irish Setter which portrayed Big Red in the Walt Disney movie of the same name. Owned by Larry Heist, Big Red poses here with his trophy while being photographed by C. Lydon Lippincott.

One of the top-winning Irish Setters during the 1960's, Ch. Webline
Wizard of Macapa is pictured here winning Best in Show at an Orange
Empire Kennel Club show under judge Helen Walsh. Wizard was one
of the Top Ten Sporting Dogs in the country and was bred and owned
by Mr. and Mrs. C.R. Webb, Webline Kennels, El Monte, California.
He was handled to this wonderful win by Dick Webb. Camar photo.

Opposite, above:
American and Canadian Ch. Dajo's Sir Guy, pictured winning Best of
Breed at the Ventura Kennel Club show in July, 1974, under judge Clifton Hulsey. Sir Guy is stud dog for Dale and Ruth Jones of the Dajos
Kennel in Puyallup, Washington. Guy finished for his championship in
one weekend with three 5-point major wins and included a Group First
and a Group Fourth as well.

Opposite, below:
Ch. Ballycroy's Northern Sunset, owned by Constance Vanacore, BIS
at the Old Dominion Kennel Club show on September 30, 1973. Photo
by Ashbey.

BEST DOG
IN SHOW

Arwyn Vagabond (Blue), owned by Mr. and Mrs. T. Holden in England.

Scraps's stand-in for the role was another Red Arrow Kennel dog, Ch. Red Arrow Smooth Sailing, also prominent in dog show circles and also bred by the Heists.

James and Evelyn Hale of the Haleridge Kennels in Malibu, California also had a significant part in the production of this movie glorifying the Irish Setter. Over 60 of the Hales' Irish Setter puppies were used over the ten-month period of filming the whelping scenes in the picture. Also, Big Red's mother, Molly, was portrayed by the Hales' bitch Haleridge Princess Cenna.

During the filming of the whelping scenes owner Jimmy Hale would encourage the mother to lick the puppies, adding realism to the scene, by smearing the puppies with dog food! In spite of the devious methods used to attain realism, the movie did much to endear the Irish Setter to the American public.

THE IRISH SETTER IN THE LEGITIMATE THEATRE

George and Lillian Gallus of Detroit had two of their Irish Setters appear in a Shakespearean classic at the Cass Theatre in that city in 1960. The production was "*A Midsummer Night's Dream,*" in which Ch. Michael Bryan Duke of Sussex and Ch. Merri's Rita of Glenfield took part. These two Irish Setters "trod the boards" and the ring mats as well during their illustrious careers.

A publicity still of a boy and an Irish Setter used in Walt Disney's film *Big Red*.

Ch. Tirvelda Valentine, two-time winner of the Irish Setter Club of America Best Bitch award, defeating nearly 3,000 bitches and taking 200 Breed, Best Opposite and Group Placing wins. Valentine is the daughter of American and Canadian Ch. Tirvelda Best Regards, C.D., herself the winner of the I.S.C.A. Best Bitch award two times. Valentine is owned by Mr. and Mrs. Edward F. Truetel of Leonia, New Jersey.

Opposite, above:
First place winners in the Bred by Exhibitor classes at the 1973 Irish Setter Club of America National Specialty show were the bitch Derrinraw's Royal Erin, owned by Ellen Reilly, and the dog Derrinraw's Sir Michael, owned by Judy Esteban. Irene Khatoonian Schlintz judged the bitches and Ward Gardner the dogs, and the two winners were litter brother and sister!

Opposite, below:
American, Canadian and Bermudian Ch. Kelly Shannon O'Deke pictured winning one of his 13 Bests in Show, this one under judge A. Treen at the 1973 Lexington Kennel Club show. Tom Glassford handles for owner Dr. R.D. Helferty, Davison, Michigan.

LEXINGTON KENNEL CLUB
BEST IN SHOW

THE IRISH SETTER IN LITERATURE

While delving into the lively arts, let us not forget the Irish Setters immortalized in the printed word. There have been a few books dealing with their lives and accomplishments. Judge and dog writer J. Horace Lytle of Dayton, Ohio had purchased and trained Smada Byrd; as a result of his deep affection for the dog he wrote a book about Irish Setters' remarkable rapport in the field and as companions. The book was published in 1924 and titled *Breaking A Bird Dog*.

In 1927 Dr. Lloyd Thompson also put pen to paper to write a tribute to one of his Irish Setters as the hero of the story and titled it *King of Mapledale*.

And in 1934 Miss Marie Louise Welch wrote a book about the courage, affection and intelligence of the Irish Setter based on one of her own dogs. She called her work *Your Friend and Mine*.

THE IRISH SETTER AS A RACING DOG

While many of the early Irish Setters were mis-used as racing dogs and cart-pulling dogs in somewhat of a side show fashion, there have been honest attempts over the years to race these dogs not so much against each other as against racing dogs of other breeds.

By the 1970's there were five racing clubs on the West Coast which concentrated on racing and in which Irish Setters competed. A Tim Fitzpatrick of Murphy, California, races his team of Irish Setters in sled dog races and has done rather well, finishing as high as second place at times.

Generally, the Irish Setter does not do well racing or as a sled team in the snow against breeds like the Huskies and the Malamutes or the cross-bred Northern dogs. But on sand and in the warmer climates, such as Arizona and California, they do much better and are capable of greater speed. Their long legs and lighter conformation, which obviously aids them on sand, offers no advantage in the snow. They feel the cold more quickly, and their leaner legs offer less resistance to snow. In the desert the shorter hair and long legs give them a distinct advantage.

THE TARGHEE HOUND

The Targhee Hound is a deliberate cross between the Irish Setter and the Greyhound bred specifically for racing and racing purposes only. This combination seems to "nick" for this sport and they are frequent winners. A Targhee hound has also been described as a cross between a male Staghound and a female Irish Setter. During the 1960's the Targhee hounds held an impressive lead over all other racing breeds, or combinations of racing breeds, in West Coast competition.

Best and Best American Bred in Show several years ago at a Lackawanna Kennel Club show was Ch. End O'Maine Luckalone, owned by Floyd Jeffords of Miami Springs, Florida and handled by Charley Meyer. William F. Gilroy was the judge. Walter Fletcher, club president, presents the trophy.

Ch. Westwind Scarlet Cascade pictured winning at a field trial in 1973 with breeder-owner-handler Luz Holvenstot, Westwind Kennels, Long Valley, New Jersey. Bushman photo.

Opposite, above:
Ch. Delarda's Blithe Spirit, C.D., pictured winning at the 1973 Westchester Kennel Club show under judge Joe Tacker. Owner-handled by Madeline Blush of Baldwin, New York. Ashbey photograph.

Opposite, below:
Ch. Bayberry Brandy's Courage pictured winning a Best of Winners award on the way to championship. Brandy is co-owned by Suzanne Narkin and Sid Marx, pictured handling at this 1974 show. Gilbert photo.

248

BEST OF OPPOSITE

ASHBEY PHOTO

BEST OF WINNERS

GILBERT PHOTO

In an attempt to make the Targhee hound an even faster racing dog, one breeder tried a breeding of a Targhee/Husky combination. The name given this cross was Chilcoot Huskies. In their first attempt at racing in 1970 they won two out of five races. But somehow the sport of racing Irish Setters, or sled teams of them, simply has not caught on enough to be considered an important or popular sport.

LITTER RECORDS

While in this day and age the emphasis is on small quality litters, in view of the population explosion, etc., the large breeds of dogs do every once in a while come up with record births for single litters.

The largest Irish Setter litter we know of consisted of 23 puppies, whelped in 1925 in Waukegan, Illinois. Perhaps the top-producing sire in the breed was Ch. Pat Law, owned by Walter McRoberts. Out of 82 puppies in six litters, the get consisted of litters of 15, 18, three of 13 and one of ten.

Ch. Garden State Reno's Blaze pictured winning Best of Breed at the 1963 Alexandria, Virginia dog show. Owner-handled by Helen Olivio of New York.

15. BUYING YOUR IRISH SETTER PUPPY

There are several paths that will lead you to a litter of puppies where you can find the puppy of your choice. Write to the parent club and ask for the names and addresses of members who have puppies for sale. The addresses of breed clubs can be obtained by writing the American Kennel Club, 51 Madison Avenue, New York, N.Y. 10010. They keep an accurate, up-to-date list of reputable breeders from whom you can seek information on obtaining a good healthy puppy. You might also check listings in the classified ads of major newspapers. The various dog magazines also carry listings and usually a column each month which features information and news on the breed.

It is to your advantage to attend a few dog shows in the area where purebred dogs of just about every breed are being exhibited in the show ring. Even if you do not wish to buy a show dog, you should be familiar with what the better specimens look like so that you may at least get a decent looking representative of the breed for your money. You will learn a lot by observing the dogs in action in the show ring, or in a public place where their personalities come to the fore. The dog show catalogue will list the dogs and their owners with local kennel names and breeders whom you can visit to see the types and colors they are breeding and winning with at the shows. Exhibitors at these shows are usually delighted to talk to people about their dogs and the specific characteristics of their particular breed.

Once you have chosen your breed above all others because you admire its exceptional beauty, intelligence and personality, and because you feel the breed will fit in with your family's way of life, it is wise to do a little research on it. The American Kennel Club library, your local library, bookshops, and the breed clubs can usually supply you with a list of reading matter or written material on the breed, past and present. Then, once you have drenched yourself in the breed's illustrious history and have definitely decided that this is the breed for you, it is time to start writing letters and making phone calls to set up appointments to see litters of puppies.

A word of caution here: don't let your choice of a kennel be determined by its nearness to your home, and then buy the first cute puppy

Ch. Thenderin Nomad posed informally in the stance that made him a big winner.

Opposite, above:
Ch. Thenderin Xclusive Edition pictured winning Best of Opposite Sex over 55 bitches at the 1974 Atlanta Kennel Club show. "The Queen" is a Best of Breed winner and has Group Placements to her credit; she was Brood Bitch winner at the 1975 New York Combined Setter Specialty Show. She is pictured here with Neal Koontz. Co-owners are Jane Zaderecki and Ann Savin, Westbury, Long Island, New York.

Opposite, below:
Another Best in Show award for the fabulous American, Canadian and Bermudian Ch. Kelly Shannon O'Deke. This win was under judge Mrs. Helen Walsh in March, 1973 at the Western Pennsylvania Kennel Club show. Handler, Tom Glassford. Owner, Dr. R.D. Helferty of Davison, Michigan. Gilbert photograph.

Ch. Laurel Ridge Star Rocket was Best in Show at the 1954 Willimantic Kennel Club show under judge A.J. Brock. Handled by Art Baines for owner Merritt M. Swartz of Canton, Massachusetts. Photo by Gunderson.

that races up to you or licks the end of your nose. All puppies are cute, and naturally you will have a preference among those you see. But don't let preferences sway you into buying the wrong puppy.

If you are buying your dog as a family pet, a preference might not be a serious offense. But if you have had, say, an age preference since you first considered this breed, you would be wise to stick to it. If you are buying a show dog, all physical features must meet with the Standard for the breed. In considering your purchase you must think clearly, choose carefully, and make the very best possible choice. You will, of course, learn to love whichever puppy you finally decide upon, but a case of "love at first sight" can be disappointing and expensive later on if a show career was your primary objective.

To get the broadest possible concept of what is for sale and the current market prices, it is recommended that you visit as many kennels and private breeders as you can. With today's reasonably safe, inexpensive and rapid non-stop flights on the major airlines, it is possible to secure dogs from far-off places at nominal additional charges, allowing you to buy the valuable bloodlines of your choice if you have a thought toward a breeding program in the future.

While it is always safest to actually *see* the dog you are buying, there are enough reputable breeders and kennels to be found for you to buy a dog with a minimum of risk once you have made up your mind what you want, and when you have decided whether you will buy in your own country or import to satisfy your concept of the breed Standard. If you are going to breed dogs, breeding Standard type can be a moral obligation, and your concern should be with buying the best bloodlines and individual animals obtainable, in spite of cost or distance.

It is customary for the purchaser to pay the shipping charges, and the airlines are most willing to supply flight information and prices upon request. Rental on the shipping crate, if the owner does not provide one for the dog, is nominal. While unfortunate incidents have occurred on the airlines in the transporting of animals by air, the major airlines are making improvements in safety measures and have reached the point of reasonable safety and cost. Barring unforeseen circumstances, the safe arrival of a dog you might buy can pretty much be assured if both seller and purchaser adhere to and follow up on even the most minute details from both ends.

Best Team in Show, the Irish Setters owned by Miss Laura Delano, at the 1951 International Kennel Club of Chicago under judge Harry T. Peters. Frasie photo.

Ch. Seaforth's Dark Rex captured in all his blazing red glory in this painting by Nedra Jerome of the Innisfail Kennels. Dark Rex was one of the top dogs at George and Barbara Brodie's Seaforth Kennels in North Easton, Massachusetts.

THE PUPPY YOU BUY

Let us assume you want to enjoy all the cute antics of a young puppy and decide to buy a six-to-eight-week-old puppy. This is about the age when a puppy is weaned, wormed and ready to go out into the world with a responsible new owner. It is better not to buy a puppy under six weeks of age; it simply is not yet ready to leave the mother or the security of the other puppies. At eight to twelve weeks of age you will be able to notice much about the appearance and the behavior. Puppies, as they are recalled in our fondest childhood memories, are gay and active and bouncy, as well they should be! The normal puppy should be interested, alert, and curious, especially about a stranger. If a puppy acts a little reserved or distant, however, such

Best of Breed at the 1954 Irish Setter Club of Ohio Specialty was Ch. Caldene Mick O'Boy, handled by Mabel Pyle. The judge was A.L. Jones, and the owner is W.L. Newhall of Coreopolis, Pennsylvania. Norton of Kent photo.

Future American and Canadian Ch. Verbu Lea Oogh, C.D., pictured here at 10 weeks of age. Owned, bred and trained by Miss Emily Schweitzer, Verbu Kennels, Dundee, Illinois.

act need not be misconstrued as shyness or fear. It merely indicates he hasn't made up his mind whether he likes you as yet! By the same token, he should not be fearful or terrified by a stranger—and especially should not show any fear of his owner!

In direct contrast, the puppy should not be ridiculously over-active either. The puppy that frantically bounds around the room and is never still is not especially desirable. And beware of the "spinners"! Spinners are the puppies or dogs that have become neurotic from being kept in cramped quarters or in crates and behave in an emotionally unstable manner when let loose in adequate space. When let out they run in circles and seemingly "go wild." Puppies with this kind of traumatic background seldom ever regain full composure or adjust to the big outside world. The puppy which has had the proper exercise and appropriate living quarters will have a normal, though spirited, outlook on life and will do his utmost to win you over without having to go into a tailspin.

Best in Show at the 1955 Ladies Dog Club in Massachusetts was Mr. Merritt M. Swartz's Ch. Laurel Ridge Star Rocket, under judge Mrs. Francis V. Crane. Handler is Hollis Wilson. Shafer photo.

If the general behavior and appearance of the dog thus far appeal to you, it is time for you to observe him more closely for additional physical requirements. First of all, you cannot expect to find in the puppy all the coat he will bear upon maturity. That will come with time and good food, and will be additionally enhanced by the many wonderful grooming aids which can be found on the market today. Needless to say, the healthy puppy's coat should have a nice shine to it, and the more dense at this age, the better the coat will be when the dog reaches adulthood.

Look for clear, dark, sparkling eyes, free of discharge. Dark eye rims and lids are indications of good pigmentation, which is important in a breeding program, and even for generally pleasing good looks.

When the time comes to select your puppy, take an experienced breeder along with you if this is possible. If it is not possible, take the Standard for the breed with you. Try to interpret the Standard as best you can by making comparisons between the puppies you see.

Check the bite completely and carefully. While the first set of teeth can be misleading, even the placement of teeth at this young age can be a fairly accurate indication of what the bite will be in the grown dog. The gums should be a good healthy pink in color, and the

259

teeth should be clear, clean and white. Any brown cast to them could mean a past case of distemper and would assuredly count against the dog in the show ring and against the dog's general appearance at maturity.

Puppies take anything and everything into their mouths to chew on while they are teething, and a lot of infectious diseases are transmitted this way. The aforementioned distemper is one, and the brown teeth as a result of this disease never clear. The puppy's breath should not be sour or even unpleasant or strong. Any acrid odor could indicate a poor mixture of food, or low quality of meat, especially if it is being fed raw. Many breeders have compared the breath of a healthy puppy to that of fresh toast, or as being vaguely like garlic. At any rate, a puppy should never be fed just table scraps, but should have a well-balanced diet containing a good dry puppy chow and a good grade of fresh meat. Poor meat and too much cereal or fillers tend to make the puppy too fat. We like puppies to be in good flesh, but not fat from the wrong kind of food.

It goes without saying that we want to find clean puppies. The breeder or owners who shows you a dirty puppy is one from whom to

Westwind Scarlet Blaze photographed in 1946. Owner is Luz Holvenstot, Westwind Kennels, Long Valley, New Jersey.

Best in Show at the 1950 Morris and Essex Kennel Club show was Ch. Tyronne Farm Clancy. Judge was Hugh A. Lewis, and the owner-handler is Jack A. Spear of Tipton, Iowa. The late Mrs. M. Hartley Dodge, Club president, presents one of the trophies.

steer away! Look closely at the skin. Rub the fur the wrong way or against the grain; make sure it is not spotted with insect bites or red, blotchy sores or dry scales. The vent area around the tail should not show evidences of diarrhea or inflammation. By the same token, the puppy's fur should not be matted with dry excrement or smell of urine.

True enough, you can wipe dirty eyes, clean dirty ears and give the puppy a bath when you get it home, but these things are all indications of how the puppy has been cared for during the important formative first months of its life, and can vitally influence its future health and development. There are many reputable breeders raising healthy puppies that have been reared in proper places and under the proper conditions in clean housing, so why take a chance on a series of veterinary bills and a questionable constitution?

MALE OR FEMALE?

The choice of sex in your puppy is also something that must be given serious thought before you buy. For the pet owner, the sex that would best suit the family life you enjoy would be the paramount

International Ch. Verbu Nornan Oogh, U.D. Nornan lived from 1934 to 1946 and was owned by the Schweitzers.

Four-month-old puppies bred at the Westwind Kennels of Luz Holven-stot several years ago.

choice to consider. For the breeder or exhibitor, there are other vital considerations. If you are looking for a stud to establish a kennel, it is essential that you select a dog with both testicles evident, even at a tender age, and verified by a veterinarian before the sale is finalized if there is any doubt.

The visibility of only one testicle, known as monorchidism, automatically disqualifies the dog from the show ring or from a breeding program, though monorchids are capable of siring. Additionally, it must be noted that monorchids frequently sire dogs with the same deficiency, and to introduce this into a bloodline knowingly is an unwritten sin in the fancy. Also, a monorchid can sire dogs that are completely sterile. Such dogs are referred to as cryptorchids and have no testicles.

If you want the dog to be a member of the family, the best selection would probably be a female. You can always go out for stud service if you should decide to breed. You can choose the bloodlines doing the most winning because they should be bred true to type, and you will not have to foot the bill for the financing of a show career. You can always keep a male from your first litter that will bear your own "kennel name" if you have decided to proceed in the kennel "business."

Ch. Thenderin Brian Tristan wins Best in Show at the 1953 Butler County Kennel Club show under judge William E. Henry with his handler Charley Meyer. Owned by Mr. and Mrs. James R. Fraser of Olmstead Falls, Ohio.

An additional consideration in the male versus female decision for the private owners is that with males there might be the problem of leg-lifting and with females there is the inconvenience while they are in season. However, this need not be the problem it used to be—pet shops sell "pants" for both sexes, which help to control the situation.

THE PLANNED PARENTHOOD BEHIND YOUR PUPPY

Never be afraid to ask pertinent questions about the puppy, as well as questions about the sire and dam. Feel free to ask the breeder if you might see the dam, the purpose of your visit to determine her general health and her appearance as a representative of the breed. Ask also to see the sire if the breeder is the owner. Ask what the puppy has been fed and should be fed after weaning. Ask to see the pedigree, and inquire if the litter or the individual puppies have been registered with the American Kennel Club, how many of the temporary and/or permanent inoculations the puppy has had, when and if the puppy has been wormed and whether it has had any illness, disease or infection.

You need not ask if the puppy is housebroken. . . it won't mean much. He may have gotten the idea as to where "the place" is where he lives now, but he will need new training to learn where "the place" is in his new home! And you can't really expect too much from puppies at this age anyway. Housebreaking is entirely up to the new owner. We know puppies always eliminate when they first awaken and sometimes dribble when they get excited. If friends and relatives are coming over to see the new puppy, make sure he is walked just before he greets them at the front door. This will help.

The normal time period for puppies around three months of age to eliminate is about every two or three hours. As the time draws near, either take the puppy out or indicate the newspapers for the same purpose. Housebreaking is never easy, but anticipation is about 90 per cent of solving the problem. The schools that offer to housebreak your dog are virtually useless. Here again the puppy will learn the "place" at the schoolhouse, but coming home he will need special training for the new location.

A reputable breeder will welcome any and all questions you might ask and will voluntarily offer additional information, if only to

Charley Meyer and his Irish Setter Ch. Oakley Downader, photographed several years ago.

Ch. Seaforth's Red Velvet, a bitch of great quality and type which passed on to her offspring all of her outstanding qualities. Red Velvet was the top foundation bitch at George and Barbara Brodie's Seaforth Kennels, North Easton, Massachusetts.

brag about the tedious and loving care he has given the litter. He will also sell a puppy on a 24-hour veterinary approval. This means you have a full day to get the puppy to a veterinarian of your choice to get his opinion on the general health of the puppy before you make a final decision. There should also be veterinary certificates and full particulars on the dates and types of inoculations the puppy has been given up to that time.

PUPPIES AND WORMS

Let us give further attention to the unhappy and very unpleasant subject of worms. Generally speaking, most all puppies—even those raised in clean quarters—come into contact with worms early in life. The worms can be passed down from the mother before birth or picked up during the puppies' first encounters with the earth or their kennel facilities. To say that you must not buy a puppy because of an infestation of worms is nonsensical. You might be passing up a fine animal that can be freed of worms in one short treatment, although a heavy infestation of worms of any kind in a young dog is dangerous and debilitating.

The extent of the infection can be readily determined by a veterinarian, and you might take his word as to whether the future health and conformation of the dog has been damaged. He can prescribe the dosage and supply the medication at the time and you will already have one of your problems solved. The kinds and varieties of worms and how to detect them is described in detail elsewhere in this book and we advise you to check the matter out further if there is any doubt in your mind as to the problems of worms in dogs.

VETERINARY INSPECTION

While your veterinarian is going over the puppy you have selected to purchase, you might just as well ask him for his opinion of it as a breed as well as the facts about its general health. While few veterinarins can claim to be breed conformation experts, they usually have a good eye for a worthy specimen and can advise you where to go for further information. Perhaps your veterinarian could also recommend other breeders if you should want another opinion. The veterinarian can point out structural faults or organic problems that affect all breeds and can usually judge whether an animal has been abused or mishandled and whether it is oversized or undersized.

I would like to emphasize here that it is only through this type of close cooperation between owners and veterinarians that we can expect to reap the harvest of modern research in the veterinary field.

One of Miss Emily Schweitzer's lovely Irish Setters photographed in 1939. Photograph by William Brown.

Westwind Scarlet Escapade on point in the field. Bred, owned and worked by Luz Holvenstot, Westwind Kennels, Long Valley, New Jersey.

Most reliable veterinarians are more than eager to learn about various breeds of purebred dogs, and we in turn must acknowledge and apply what they have proved through experience and research in their field. We can buy and breed the best dog in the world, but when disease strikes we are only as safe as our veterinarian is capable—so let's keep them informed breed by breed, and dog by dog. The veterinarian represents the difference between life and death!

THE CONDITIONS OF SALE

While it is customary to pay for the puppy before you take it away with you, you should be able to give the breeder a deposit if there is any doubt about the puppy's health. You might also (depending on local laws) postdate a check to cover the 24-hour veterinary approval. If you decide to take the puppy, the breeder is required to supply you with a pedigree, along with the puppy's registration paper. He is also obliged to supply you with complete information about the inoculations and American Kennel Club instructions on how to transfer ownership of the puppy into your name.

Champion Seaforth Dark Rex

Champion Seaforth Dark Rex, outstanding stud and show dog from the Seaforth kennels of Mr. and Mrs. George Brodie, Jr. of North Easton, Massachusetts. The Brodies consider Rex their greatest contribution to the breed in their years of showing and breeding Irish Setters. His show career was commendable, and his influence as a stud cannot be denied. His influence is still felt in the breed today, with his name behind kennels such as Thenderin, Innisfail, Tirvelda, Webline, Draherin and others.

Ch. End O'Maine Patridge, shown with handler Hollis Wilson. This Best in Show winning Irish Setter was owned by Dr. Robert F. Wilcox of La Porte, Indiana.

Some breeders will offer buyers time payment plans for convenience if the price on a show dog is very high or if deferred payments are the only way you can purchase the dog. However, any such terms must be worked out between buyer and breeder and should be put in writing to avoid later complications.

You will find most breeders cooperative if they believe you are sincere in your love for the puppy and that you will give it the proper home and the show ring career it deserves (if it is sold as a show quality specimen of the breed). Remember, when buying a show dog, it is impossible to guarantee nature. A breeder can only tell you what he *believes* will develop into a show dog. . . so be sure your breeder is an honest one.

Also, if you purchase a show prospect and promise to show the dog, you definitely should show it! It is a waste to have a beautiful dog that deserves recognition in the show ring sitting at home as a family pet, and it is unfair to the breeder. This is especially true if the breeder offered you a reduced price because of the advertising his kennel and bloodlines would receive by your showing the dog in the ring. If you want a pet, buy a pet. Be honest about it, and let the breeder decide on this basis which is the best dog for you. Your conscience will be clear and you'll both be doing a real service to the breed.

BUYING A SHOW PUPPY

If you are positive about breeding and showing your dog, make it clear that you intend to do so so that the breeder will sell you the best possible puppy. If you are dealing with an established kennel, you will have to rely partially if not entirely on their choice, since they know their bloodlines and what they can expect from the breeding. They know how their stock develops, and it would be foolish of them to sell you a puppy that could not stand up as a show specimen representing their stock in the ring.

However, you must also realize that the breeder may be keeping the best puppy in the litter to show and breed himself. If this is the case, you might be wise to select the best puppy of the opposite sex so that the dogs will not be competing against one another in the show rings for their championship title.

THE PURCHASE PRICE

Prices vary on all puppies, of course, but a good show prospect at six weeks to six months of age will sell for several hundred dollars. If the puppy is really outstanding, and the pedigree and parentage is

Irish Setters at a show in Moscow in 1972. They have no less feathering than Irish Setters in the United States, but their chin whiskers apparently go untrimmed. Photographed by Connie Vanacore.

An informal photograph of the famous Ch. St. Clouds Fermanagh III, owned by Mrs. Cheever Porter of New York City.

also outstanding, the price will be even higher. Honest breeders, however, will be around the same figure, so price should not be a deciding factor in your choice. If there is any question as to the current price range, a few telephone calls to different kennels will give you a good average. Breeders will usually stand behind their puppies; should something drastically wrong develop, such as hip dysplasia, etc., their obligation to make an adjustment is usually honored. Therefore, your cost is covered.

THE COST OF BUYING ADULT STOCK

Prices for adult dogs fluctuate greatly. Some grown dogs are offered free of charge to good homes; others are put out with owners on breeders' terms. But don't count on getting a "bargain" if it doesn't cost you anything! Good dogs are always in demand, and worthy studs or brood bitches are expensive. Prices for them can easily go up into the four-figure range. Take an expert with you if you intend to make this sort of investment. Just make sure the "expert" is free of professional jealousy and will offer an unprejudiced opinion. If you are reasonably familiar with the Standard, and get the expert's opinion, between the two you can usually come up with a proper decision.

Buying grown stock does remove some of the risk if you are planning a kennel. You will know exactly what you are getting for your foundation stock and will also save time on getting your kennel started.

16. GENETICS

No one can guarantee the workings of nature. But, with facts and theories as guides, you can plan, at least on paper, a litter of puppies that should fulfill your fondest expectations. Since the ultimate purpose of breeding is to try to improve the breed, or maintain it at the highest possible standard, such planning should be earnestly done, no matter how uncertain particular elements may be.

There are a few terms with which you should become familiar to help you understand the breeding procedure and the workings of genetics. The first thing that comes to mind is a set of formulae known as Mendelian Laws. Gregor Mendel was an Austrian cleric and botanist born July 22, 1822 in what is now named Hyncice and is in Czechoslovakia. He developed his theories on heredity by working for several years with garden peas. A paper on his work was published in a scientific journal in 1866, but for many years it went unnoticed. Today the laws derived from these experiments are basic to all studies of genetics and are employed by horticulturists and animal breeders.

To use these laws as applicable to the breeding of dogs, it is necessary to understand the physical aspects of reproduction. First, dogs possess reproductive glands called gonads. The male gonads are the testicles and there are produced the sperms (spermatozoa) that impregnate the female. Eggs (ova) are produced in the female gonads (ovaries). When whelped, the bitch possesses in rudimentary form all the eggs that will develop throughout her life, whereas spermatozoa are in continual production within the male gonads. When a bitch is mature enough to reproduce, she periodically comes in heat (estrus). Then a number of eggs descend from the ovaries via the fallopian tubes and enter the two horns of the uterus. There they are fertilized by male sperm deposited in semen while mating, or they pass out if not fertilized.

In the mating of dogs, there is what is referred to as a tie, a period during which anatomical features bind the male and female together and about 600 million spermatozoa are ejected into the female to fertilize the ripened eggs. When sperm and ripe eggs meet, zygotes are created and these one-celled future puppies descend from the fallopian tubes, attach themselves to the walls of the uterus, and begin the developmental process of cell production known as mitosis. With all inherited characteristics determined as the zygote was formed, the dam then assumes her role as an incubator for the developing organisms. She has been bred and is in whelp; in these circumstances she also serves in the exchange of gases and in furnishing nourishment for the puppies forming within.

Let us take a closer look at what is happening during the breeding process. We know that the male deposits millions of sperms within the female and that the number of ripe eggs released by the female will determine the number of puppies in the litter. Therefore, those breeders who advertise a stud as a "producer of large litters" do not know the facts or are not sticking to them. The bitch determines the size of the litter; the male sperm determines the sex of the puppies. Half of the millions of sperm involved in a mating carry the characteristic that determines development of a male and the other half carry the factor which triggers development of a female, and distribution of sex is thus decided according to random pairings of sperms and eggs.

Each dog and bitch possesses 39 pairs of chromosomes in each body cell; these pairs are split up in the formation of germ cells so that each one carries half of the hereditary complement. The chromosomes carry the genes, approximately 150,000 like peas in a pod in each chromosome, and these are the actual factors that determine inherited characteristics. As the chromosomes are split apart and rearranged as to genic pairings in the production of ova and spermatozoa, every zygote formed by the joining of an egg and a sperm receives 39 chromosomes from each to form the pattern of 78 chromosomes inherited from dam and sire which will be reproduced in every cell of the developing individual and determine what sort of animal it will be.

To understand the procedure more clearly, we must know that there are two kinds of genes—dominant and recessive. A dominant gene is one of a pair whose influence is expressed to the exclusion of the effects of the other. A recessive gene is one of a pair whose influence is subdued by the effects of the other, and characteristics determined by recessive genes become manifest only when both genes of a pairing are recessive. Most of the important qualities we wish to perpetuate in our breeding programs are carried by the dominant genes. It is the successful breeder who becomes expert at eliminating recessive or undesirable genes and building up the dominant or desirable gene patterns.

We have merely touched upon genetics here to point out the importance of planned mating. Any librarian can help you find further information, or books may be purchased offering the very latest findings on canine genetics. It is a fascinating and rewarding program toward creating better dogs.

17. BREEDING YOUR IRISH SETTER

Let us assume the time has come for your dog to be bred, and you have decided you are in a position to enjoy producing a litter of puppies that you hope will make a contribution to the breed. The bitch you purchased is sound, her temperament is excellent and she is a most worthy representative of the breed.

You have taken a calendar and counted off the ten days since the first day of red staining and have determined the tenth to fourteenth day, which will more than likely be the best days for the actual mating. You have additionally counted off 65 to 63 days before the puppies are likely to be born to make sure everything necessary for their arrival will be in good order by that time.

From the moment the idea of having a litter occurred to you, your thoughts should have been given to the correct selection of a proper stud. Here again the novice would do well to seek advice on analyzing pedigrees and tracing bloodlines for your best breedings. As soon as the bitch is in season and you see color (or staining) and a swelling of the vulva, it is time to notify the owner of the stud you selected and make appointments for the breedings. There are several pertinent questions you will want to ask the stud owners after having decided upon the pedigree. The owners, naturally, will also have a few questions they wish to ask you. These questions will concern your bitch's bloodlines, health, age, how many previous litters if any, etc.

THE HEALTH OF THE BREEDING STOCK

Some of your first questions should concern whether or not the stud has already proved himself by siring a normal healthy litter. Also inquire as to whether or not the owners have had a sperm count made to determine just exactly how fertile or potent the stud is. Also ask whether he has been X-rayed for hip dysplasia and found to be clear. Determine for yourself whether the dog has two normal testicles.

When considering your bitch for this mating, you must take into consideration a few important points that lead to a successful breeding. You and the owner of the stud will want to recall whether she has had normal heat cycles, whether there were too many runts in the lit-

A Nilsen photograph taken in 1950 of Del Rey Saga, sired by Kendare Red Duke **ex** Ch. Clodagh O'Sagstone.

ter, and whether Caesarean section was ever necessary. Has she ever had a vaginal infection? Could she take care of her puppies by herself, or was there a milk shortage? How many surviving puppies were there from the litter, and what did they grow up to be in comparison to the requirements of the breed Standard?

Don't buy a bitch that has problem heats and has never had a litter. But don't be afraid to buy a healthy maiden bitch, since chances are, if she is healthy and from good stock, she will be a healthy producer. Don't buy a monorchid male, and certainly not a cryptorchid. If there is any doubt in your mind about his potency, get a sperm count from the veterinarian. Older dogs that have been good producers and are for sale are usually not too hard to find at good established kennels. If they are not too old and have sired quality show puppies, they can give you some excellent show stock from which to establish your own breeding lines.

THE DAY OF THE MATING

Now that you have decided upon the proper male and female combination to produce what you hope will be—according to the pedigrees—a fine litter of puppies, it is time to set the date. You have selected the two days (with a one day lapse in between) that you feel are best for the breeding, and you call the owner of the stud. The bitch always goes to the stud, unless, of course, there are extenuating circumstances. You set the date and the time and arrive with the bitch *and* the money.

Standard procedure is payment of a stud fee at the time of the first breeding, if there is a tie. For the stud fee, you are entitled to two breedings with ties. Contracts may be written up with specific conditions on breeding terms, of course, but this is general procedure. Often a breeder will take the pick of a litter to protect and maintain his bloodlines. This can be especially desirable if he needs an outcross for his breeding program or if he wishes to continue his own bloodlines if he sold you the bitch to start with, and this mating will continue his line-breeding program. This should all be worked out ahead of time and written and signed before the two dogs are bred. Remember that the payment of the stud fee is for the services of the stud—not for a guarantee of a litter of puppies. This is why it is so important to

Ch. Dunguaire Bryson, whelped in July, 1950, was owned by Dr. Jack Skelskie and was 3rd ranking Sporting Dog in the nation in 1956 and 6th in the Sporting Group in 1957. Winner of 7 Bests in Show, he was the sire of 3 champions. His sire was Ch. Brymount Maydorwill Brandyson **ex** Thenderin Amaranth.

Ch. Wolfscroft My Wild Irish Rose prepares for feeding time at Dr. Wolfgang Casper's Wolfscroft Kennels in Staten Island. This delightful domestic scene was the inspiration for a painting by Gladys Emerson Cook, the famous animal artist, and featured in one of her dog books.

A litter of 12 Irish Setters sired by Lewis Starkey's Redwood Rocket out of Ward Gardner's Ch. Ruxton's Shannon of Boyne. Six of these puppies became champions. One was Ch. Sally O'Bryan of Crosshaven.

make sure you are using a proven stud. Bear in mind also that the American Kennel Club will not register a litter of puppies sired by a male that is under eight months of age. In the case of an older dog, they will not register a litter sired by a dog over 12 years of age, unless there is a witness to the breeding in the form of a veterinarian or other responsible person.

Many studs over 12 years of age are still fertile and capable of producing puppies, but if you do not witness the breeding there is always the danger of a "substitute" stud being used to produce a litter. This brings up the subject of sending your bitch away to be bred if you cannot accompany her.

The disadvantages of sending a bitch away to be bred are numerous. First of all, she will not be herself in a strange place, so she'll be difficult to handle. Transportation if she goes by air, while reasonably safe, is still a traumatic experience, and there is the danger of her being put off at the wrong airport, not being fed or watered properly, etc. Some bitches get so upset that they go out of season and the trip, which may prove expensive, especially on top of a substantial stud fee, will have been for nothing.

If at all possible, accompany your bitch so that the experience is as comfortable for her as it can be. In other words, make sure before setting this kind of schedule for a breeding that there is no stud in the area that might be as good for her as the one that is far away. Don't sacrifice the proper breeding for convenience, since bloodlines are so important, but put the safety of the bitch above all else. There is always a risk in traveling, since dogs are considered cargo on a plane.

HOW MUCH DOES THE STUD FEE COST?

The stud fee will vary considerably—the better the bloodlines, the more winning the dog does at shows, the higher the fee. Stud service from a top winning dog could run up to $500.00. Here again, there may be exceptions. Some breeders will take part cash and then, say, third pick of the litter. The fee can be arranged by a private contract rather than the traditional procedure we have described.

Here again, it is wise to get the details of the payment of the stud fee in writing to avoid trouble.

THE ACTUAL MATING

It is always advisable to muzzle the bitch. A terrified bitch may fear-bite the stud, or even one of the people involved, and the wild bitch may snap or attack the stud, to the point where he may become discouraged and lose interest in the breeding. Muzzling can be done with a lady's stocking tied around the muzzle with a half knot, crossed under the chin and knotted at the back of the neck. There is enough "give" in the stocking for her to breathe or salivate freely and yet not open her jaws far enough to bite. Place her in front of her own-

Rheola Morello and her litter of six Irish Setter puppies photographed several years ago.

er, who holds onto her collar and talks to her and calms her as much as possible.

If the male will not mount on his own initiative, it may be necessary for the owner to assist in lifting him onto the bitch, perhaps even in guiding him to the proper place. But usually, the tie is accomplished once the male gets the idea. The owner should remain close at hand, however, to make sure the tie is not broken before an adequate breeding has been completed. After a while the stud may get bored and try to break away. This could prove injurious. It may be necessary to hold him in place until the tie is broken.

Lady Nada of Ardee and a litter of her puppies.

We must stress at this point that while some bitches carry on physically, and vocally, during the tie, there is no way the bitch can be hurt. However, a stud can be seriously or even permanently damaged by a bad breeding. Therefore the owner of the bitch must be reminded that she must not be alarmed by any commotion. All concentration should be devoted to the stud and a successful and properly executed service.

Many people believe that breeding dogs is simply a matter of placing two dogs, a male and a female, in close proximity, and letting nature take its course. While often this is true, you cannot count on it. Sometimes it is hard work, and in the case of valuable stock it is essential to supervise to be sure of the safety factor, especially if one or both of the dogs are inexperienced. If the owners are also inexperienced it may not take place at all!

ARTIFICIAL INSEMINATION

Breeding by means of artificial insemination is usually unsuccessful, unless under a veterinarian's supervision, and can lead to an infection for the bitch and discomfort for the dog. The American Kennel Club requires a veterinarian's certificate to register puppies from such a breeding. Although the practice has been used for over two decades, it now offers new promise, since research has been conducted to make it a more feasible procedure for the future.

Great dogs may eventually look forward to reproducing themselves years after they have left this earth. There now exists a frozen semen concept that has been tested and found successful. The study, headed by Dr. Stephen W.J. Seager, M.V.B., an instructor at the University of Oregon Medical School, has the financial support of the American Kennel Club, indicating that organization's interest in the work. The study is being monitored by the Morris Animal Foundation of Denver, Colorado.

Dr. Seager announced in 1970 that he had been able to preserve dog semen and to produce litters with the stored semen. The possibilities of selective world-wide breedings by this method are exciting. Imagine simply mailing a vial of semen to the bitch! The perfection of line-breeding by storing semen without the threat of death interrupting the breeding program is exciting, also.

As it stands today, the technique for artificial insemination requires the depositing of semen (taken directly from the dog) into the bitch's vagina, past the cervix and into the uterus by syringe. The correct temperature of the semen is vital, and there is no guarantee of success. The storage method, if successfully adopted, will present a new era in the field of purebred dogs.

THE GESTATION PERIOD

Once the breeding has taken place successfully, the seemingly endless waiting period of about 63 days begins. For the first ten days after the breeding, you do absolutely nothing for the bitch—just spin dreams about the delights you will share with the family when the puppies arrive.

Around the tenth day it is time to begin supplementing the diet of the bitch with vitamins and calcium. We strongly recommend that you take her to your veterinarian for a list of the proper or perhaps necessary supplements and the correct amounts of each for your particular bitch. Guesses, which may lead to excesses or insufficiencies, can ruin a litter. For the price of a visit to your veterinarian, you will be confident that you are feeding properly.

The bitch should be free of worms, of course, and if there is any doubt in your mind, she should be wormed now, before the third week of pregnancy. Your veterinarian will advise you on the necessity of this and proper dosage as well.

Half a dozen of a litter of 15 Irish Setters. . . bred by Luz Holvenstot at her Westwind Kennels in Long Valley, New Jersey. Notice the uniformity in this impressive line-up.

PROBING FOR PUPPIES

Far too many breeders are overanxious about whether the breeding "took" and are inclined to feel for puppies or persuade a veterinarian to radiograph or X-ray their bitches to confirm it, Unless there is reason to doubt the normalcy of a pregnancy, this is risky. Certainly 63 days are not too long to wait, and why risk endangering the litter by probing with your inexperienced hands? Few bitches give no evidence of being in whelp, and there is no need to prove it for yourself by trying to count puppies.

ALERTING YOUR VETERINARIAN

At least a week before the puppies are due, you should telephone your veterinarian and notify him that you expect the litter and give him the date. This way he can make sure that there will be someone available to help, should there be any problems during the whelping. Most veterinarians today have answering services and alternate vets on call when they are not available themselves. Some veterinarians suggest that you call them when the bitch starts labor so that they may further plan their time, should they be needed. Discuss this matter with your veterinarian when you first take the bitch to him for her diet instructions, etc., and establish the method which will best fit in with his schedule.

DO YOU NEED A VETERINARIAN IN ATTENDANCE?

Even if this is your first litter, I would advise that you go through the experience of whelping without panicking and calling desperately for the veterinarian. Most animal births are accomplished without complications, and you should call for assistance only if you run into trouble.

When having her puppies, your bitch will appreciate as little interference and as few strangers around as possible. A quiet place, with her nest, a single familiar face and her own instincts are all that is necessary for nature to take its course. An audience of curious children squealing and questioning, other family pets nosing around, or strange adults should be avoided. Many a bitch which has been distracted in this way has been known to devour her young. This can be

Ch. Tuxedo Comanche Sunny pictured at a 1973 dog show with handler Dick Cooper. Owner is Dr. R.D. Helferty of Davison, Michigan.

Ch. Kingsize wins a Sporting Group First under the late judge Alva Rosenberg. Dick Cooper handled at this 1951 show.

the horrible result of intrusion into the bitch's privacy. There are other ways of teaching children the miracle of birth, and there will be plenty of time later for the whole family to enjoy the puppies. Let them be born under proper and considerate circumstances.

LABOR

Some litters—many first litters—do not run the full term of 63 days. So, at least a week before the puppies are actually due, and at the time you alert your veterinarian as to their arrival, start observing the bitch for signs of the commencement of labor. This will manifest itself in the form of ripples running down the sides of her body, which will come as a revelation to her as well. It is most noticeable when she is lying on her side—and she will be sleeping a great deal as the arrival date comes closer. If she is sitting or walking about, she will perhaps sit down quickly or squat peculiarly. As the ripples become more frequent, birth time is drawing near; you will be wise not to leave her. Usually within 24 hours before whelping, she will stop eating, and as much as a week before she will begin digging a nest. The bitch should be given something resembling a whelping box with layers of newspaper (black and white only) to make her nest. She will dig more and more as birth approaches, and this is the time to begin making your promise to stop interfering unless your help is specifically required. Some bitches whimper and others are silent, but whimpering does not necessarily indicate trouble.

THE ARRIVAL OF THE PUPPIES

The sudden gush of green fluid from the bitch indicates that the water or fluid surrounding the puppies has "broken" and they are about to start down the canal and come into the world. When the

A Carbery Irish Setter photographed by Thomas Fall in England several decades ago.

water breaks, birth of the first puppy is imminent. The first puppies are usually born within minutes to a half hour of each other, but a couple of hours between the later ones is not uncommon. If you notice the bitch straining constantly without producing a puppy, or if a puppy remains partially in and partially out for too long, it is cause for concern. Breech births (puppies born feet first instead of head first) can often cause delay or hold things up, and this is often a problem which requires veterinarian assistance.

FEEDING THE BITCH BETWEEN BIRTHS

Usually the bitch will not be interested in food for about 24 hours before the arrival of the puppies, and perhaps as long as two or three days after their arrival. The placenta which she cleans up after each puppy is high in food value and will be more than ample to sustain her. This is nature's way of allowing the mother to feed herself and her babies without having to leave the nest and hunt for food during the first crucial days. The mother always cleans up all traces of birth in the wilds so as not to attract other animals to her newborn babies.

However, there are those of us who believe in making food available should the mother feel the need to restore her strength during or after delivery—especially if she whelps a large litter. Raw chopmeat, beef boullion, and milk are all acceptable and may be placed near the whelping box during the first two or three days. After that, the mother will begin to put the babies on a sort of schedule. She will leave the whelping box at frequent intervals, take longer exercise periods, and begin to take interest in other things. This is where the fun begins for you. Now the babies are no longer soggy little pinkish blobs. They begin to crawl around and squeal and hum and grow before your very eyes!

It is at this time, if all has gone normally, that the family can be introduced gradually and great praise and affection given to the mother.

BREECH BIRTHS

Puppies normally are delivered head first. However, some are presented feet first, or in other abnormal positions, and this is referred to as a "breech birth." Assistance is often necessary to get the puppy out of the canal, and great care must be taken not to injure the puppy or the dam.

Aid can be given by grasping the puppy with a piece of turkish toweling and pulling gently during the dam's contractions. Be careful not to squeeze the puppy too hard; merely try to ease it out by moving it gently back and forth. Because even this much delay in delivery may mean the puppy is drowning, do not wait for the bitch to remove the sac. Do it yourself by tearing the sac open to expose the face and head. Then cut the cord anywhere from one-half to three-quarters of

Ch. Red Maureen of Janard, owned by Mr. and Mrs. L. Richard Fried of the Janard Kennels, finished her title at Brockton Fair, where she won the Sporting Group. This photograph by William Brown was taken in 1942.

an inch away from the navel. If the cord bleeds excessively, pinch the end of it with your fingers and count five. Repeat if necessary. Then pry open the mouth with your finger and hold the puppy upside-down for a moment to drain any fluids from the lungs. Next, rub the puppy briskly with turkish or paper toweling. You should get it wriggling and whimpering by this time.

If the litter is large, this assistance will help conserve the strength of the bitch and will probably be welcomed by her. However, it is best to allow her to take care of at least the first few herself to preserve the natural instinct and to provide the nutritive values obtained by her consumption of the afterbirths.

DRY BIRTHS

Occasionally the sac will break before the delivery of a puppy and will be expelled while the puppy remains inside, thereby depriving the dam of the necessary lubrication to expel the puppy normally.

Inserting vaseline or mineral oil via your finger will help the puppy pass down the birth canal. This is why it is essential that you be present during the whelping so that you can count puppies and afterbirths and determine when and if assistance is needed.

THE TWENTY-FOUR-HOUR CHECKUP

It is smart to have a veterinarian check the mother and her puppies within 24 hours after the last puppy is born. The vet can check the puppies for cleft palates or umbilical hernia and may wish to give the dam—particularly if she is a show dog—an injection of Pituitin to make sure of the expulsion of all afterbirths and to tighten up the uterus. This can prevent a sagging belly after the puppies are weaned and the bitch is being readied for the show ring.

FALSE PREGNANCY

The disappointment of a false pregnancy is almost as bad for the owner as it is for the bitch. She goes through the gestation period with all the symptoms—swollen stomach, increased appetite, swollen nipples—even makes a nest when the time comes. You may even take an oath that you noticed the ripples on her body from the labor pains. Then, just as suddenly as you made up your mind that she was definitely going to have puppies, you will know that she definitely is not! She may walk around carrying a toy as if it were a puppy for a few days, but she will soon be back to normal and acting just as if nothing happened—and nothing did!

CAESAREAN SECTION

Should the whelping reach the point where there is complication, such as the bitch's not being capable of whelping the puppies herself, the "moment of truth" is upon you and a Caesarean section may be necessary. The bitch may be too small or too immature to expel the puppies herself; or her cervix may fail to dilate enough to allow the young to come down the birth canal; or there may be torsion of the uterus, a dead or monster puppy, a sideways puppy blocking the canal, or perhaps toxemia. A Caesarean section will be the only solution. No matter what the cause, get the bitch to the veterinarian immediately to insure your chances of saving the mother and/or puppies.

The Caesarean section operation (the name derived from the idea that Julius Caesar was delivered by this method) involves the removal of the unborn young from the uterus of the dam by surgical incision into the walls through the abdomen. The operation is performed when it has been determined that for some reason the puppies cannot be delivered normally. While modern surgical methods have made the operation itself reasonably safe, with the dam being perfectly capable of nursing the puppies shortly after the completion of the surgery, the chief danger lies in the ability to spark life into the puppies immediately upon their removal from the womb. If the mother dies, the time element is even more important in saving the young, since the oxygen supply ceases upon the death of the dam, and the difference between life and death is measured in seconds.

After surgery, when the bitch is home in her whelping box with the babies, she will probably nurse the young without distress. You must be sure that the sutures are kept clean and that no redness or swelling or ooze appears in the wound. Healing will take place naturally, and no salves or ointments should be applied unless prescribed by the veterinarian, for fear the puppies will get it into their systems. If there is any doubt, check the bitch for fever, restlessness (other than the natural concern for her young) or a lack of appetite, but do not anticipate trouble.

EPISIOTOMY

Even though large dogs are generally easy whelpers, any number of reasons might occur to cause the bitch to have a difficult birth. Before automatically resorting to Caesarean section, many veterinarians are now trying the technique known as episiotomy.

Used rather frequently in human deliveries, episiotomy (pronounced A-PEASE-E-*OTT*-O-ME) is the cutting of the membrane between the rear opening of the vagina back almost to the opening of the anus. After delivery it is stitched together, and barring complications, heals easily, presenting no problem in future births.

SOCIALIZING YOUR PUPPY

The need for puppies to get out among other animals and people cannot be stressed enough. Kennel-reared dogs are subject to all sorts of idiosyncrasies and seldom make good house dogs or normal members of the world around them when they grow up.

The crucial age, which determines the personality and general behavior patterns which will predominate during the rest of the dog's life, are formed between the ages of three and ten weeks. This is particularly true during the 21st to 28th day. It is essential that the puppy be socialized during this time by bringing him into family life as much as possible. Floor surfaces, indoor and outdoor, should be experienced; handling by all members of the family and visitors is important; preliminary grooming gets him used to a lifelong necessity; light training, such as setting him up on tables and cleaning teeth and ears and cutting nails, etc., has to be started early if he is to become a show dog. The puppy should be exposed to car riding, shopping tours, a leash around its neck, children—your own and others—and in all possible ways develop relationships with humans.

It is up to the breeder, of course, to protect the puppy from harm or injury during this initiation into the outside world. The benefits

"Hang in there!" might be an appropriate title for this feeding time photograph taken by Dr. Wolfgang A. Casper at his Wolfscroft Kennels on Staten Island, New York. Note the lovely "Irish" linen cloth on which this patient mother feeds her young.

reaped from proper attention will pay off in the long run with a well-behaved, well-adjusted grown dog capable of becoming an integral part of a happy family.

REARING THE FAMILY

Needless to say, even with a small litter there will be certain considerations which must be adhered to in order to insure successful rearing of the puppies. For instance, the diet for the mother should be appropriately increased as the puppies grow and take more and more nourishment from her. During the first few days of rest while the bitch just looks over her puppies and regains her strength, she should be left pretty much alone. It is during these first days that she begins to put the puppies on a feeding schedule and feels safe enough about them to leave the whelping box long enough to take a little extended exercise.

It is cruel, however, to try and keep the mother away from the puppies any longer than she wants to be because you feel she is being too attentive or to give the neighbors a chance to peek in at the puppies. The mother should not have to worry about harm coming to her puppies for the first few weeks. The veterinary checkup will be enough of an experience for her to have to endure until she is more like herself once again.

Ch. Flornell Squire of Milson, whelped October 5, 1929, and photographed in December, 1931. Owned by Harry Hartnell, Milson Kennels, Harrison, New York.

Ja-Mar Scarlet Thunder, owned by Rudy and Marilyn De Mark of the Woodland Acre Kennels in Dover, New Jersey. Shannon was being shown to his championship during the mid-1970's and is the stud for the De Marks' kennel.

As the puppies continue to thrive and grow, you will notice that they take on individual characteristics. If you are going to keep and show one of the puppies, this is the time to start observing them for various outstanding characteristics.

EVALUATING THE LITTER

A show puppy prospect should be outgoing, (probably the first one to fall out of the whelping box!) and all efforts should be made to socialize the puppy which appears to be the most shy. Once the puppies are about three weeks old, they can and should be handled a great deal by friends and members of the family.

During the third week they begin to try to walk instead of crawl, but they are unsteady on their feet. Tails are used for balancing, and they begin to make sounds.

The crucial period in a puppy's life occurs when the puppy is from 21 to 28 days old, so all the time you can devote to them at this time will reap rewards later on in life. This is the age when several other important steps must be taken in a puppy's life. Weaning should start if it hasn't already, and it is the time to check for worms. Do not worm unnecessarily. A veterinarian should advise on worming and appropriate dosage and can also discuss with you at this time the schedule for serum or vaccination, which will depend on the size of the puppies as well as their age.

Exercise and grooming should be started at this time, with special care and consideration given to the diet. You will find that the dam will help you wean the puppies, leaving them alone more and more as she notices that they are eating well on their own. Begin by

293

leaving them with her during the night for comfort and warmth; eventually, when she shows less interest, keep them separated entirely.

By the time the fifth week of their lives arrives you will already be in love with every one of them and desperately searching for reasons to keep them all. They recognize you—which really gets to you!—and they box and chew on each other and try to eat your finger and a million other captivating antics which are special with puppies. Their stomachs seem to be bottomless pits, and their weight will rise. At eight to ten weeks, the puppies will be weaned and ready to go.

SPAYING AND CASTRATING

A wise old philosopher once said, "Timing in life is everything!" No statement could apply more readily to the age-old question which every dog owner is faced with sooner or later. . . to spay or not to spay.

For the one-bitch pet owner, spaying is the most logical answer, for it solves many problems. The pet is usually not of top breeding quality, and therefore there is no great loss to the bloodline; it takes the pressure off the family if the dog runs free with children and certainly eliminates the problem of repeated litters of unwanted puppies or a backyard full of eager males twice a year.

But for the owner or breeder, the extra time and protection which must be afforded a purebred quality bitch can be most worthwhile—even if it is only until a single litter is produced after the first heat. It is then not too late to spay, the progeny can perpetuate the bloodline, the bitch will have been fulfilled—though it is merely an old wives' tale that bitches should have at least one litter to be "normal"—and she may then be retired to her deserved role as family pet once again.

With spaying the problem of staining and unusual behavior around the house is eliminated without the necessity of having to keep her in "pants" or administering pills, sprays, or shots. . . which most veterinarians do not approve of anyway.

In the case of males, castration is seldom contemplated, which to me is highly regrettable. The owner of the male dog merely overlooks the dog's ability to populate an entire neighborhood, since they do not have the responsibility of rearing and disposing of the puppies. But when you take into consideration all the many females the male dog can impregnate it is almost more essential that the males be taken out of circulation than that the female be. The male dog will still be inclined to roam but will be less frantic about leaving the grounds, and you will find that a lot of the wanderlust has left him.

Dog breeder Jimmy Hale has his hands full at feeding time with Irish Setter puppies used in Walt Disney's movie *Big Red.*

STERILIZING FOR HEALTH

When considering the problem of spaying or castrating, the first consideration after the population explosion should actually be the health of the dog or bitch. Males are frequently subject to urinary diseases, and sometimes castration is a help. Your veterinarian can best advise you on this problem. Another aspect to consider is the kennel dog which is no longer being used at stud. It is unfair to keep him in a kennel with females in heat when there is no chance for him to be used. There are other more personal considerations for both kennel and one-dog owners, but when making the decision remember that it is final. You can always spay or castrate, but once the deed is done there is no return!

THE POWER OF PEDIGREES

Someone in the dog fancy once remarked that the definition of a show prospect puppy is one third the pedigree, one third what you see, and one third what you *hope* it will be! Well, no matter how you break down your qualifying fractions, we all quite agree that good breeding is essential if you have any plans at all for a show career for

Ch. Westwind Scarlet Temptation pictured winning at a recent show under judge Jerome Rich. Susan Holvenstot handling for owner Luz Holvenstot, Westwind Kennels, Long Valley, New Jersey. Sire was Ch. Westwind Scarlet Gay Blade.

This Irish Setter mother of 12 active pups seeks temporary refuge in her Tuttle Kennel. The kennel was developed by United Air Lines for safe sanitary aerial transport of dogs. Mother and puppies are owned by Bill Humphrey of Altadena, California. United Air Lines photo.

your dog! Many breeders will buy on pedigree alone, counting largely on what they can do with the puppy themselves by way of feeding, conditioning and training. Needless to say, that very important piece of paper commonly referred to as "the pedigree" is mighty reassuring to a breeder or buyer new at the game or to one who has a breeding program in mind and is trying to establish his own bloodline.

One of the most fascinating aspects of tracing pedigrees is the way the names of the really great dogs of the past keep appearing in the pedigrees of the great dogs of today. . . positive proof of the strong influence of heredity, and witness to a great deal of truth in the statement that great dogs frequently reproduce themselves, though not necessarily in appearance only. A pedigree represents something of value when one is dedicated to breeding better dogs.

To the novice buyer or one who is perhaps merely switching to another breed and sees only a frolicking, leggy, squirming bundle of energy in a fur coat, a pedigree can mean *everything*! To those of us who believe in heredity, a pedigree is more like an insurance policy . . . so read it carefully and take heed!

The size of this book prevents reproducing pedigrees of all the important Irish Setters which have made their mark in the breed. But we hasten to add that the Irish Setter Club of America has published an enormous hard-bound 8½ x 11 inch hardcover book called the *Irish Setter Club of America Pictorial*. This pictorial contains over five hundred pedigrees and photographs of the Irish Setter "greats" which will provide the background you need for a substantial foundation to a breeding program.

We suggest that the serious Irish Setter breeder write to the club secretary regarding the purchase of these limited editions. If they are sold out there is always the possibility of using the copy in the permanent file at the American Kennel Club library. As the breed continues to grow in popularity and registrations there will hopefully be future editions of the pedigree pictorials since they are of such great value to the breed as a study and reference source.

18. TRAINING YOUR IRISH SETTER

There are few things in the world a dog would rather do than please his master. Therefore, obedience training, or even the initial basic training, will be a pleasure for your dog, if taught correctly, and will make him a much nicer animal to live with for the rest of his life.

WHEN TO START TRAINING

The most frequently asked question by those who consider training their dog is, naturally, "What is the best age to begin training?" The answer is "not before six months." A dog simply cannot be sufficiently or permanently trained before this age and be expected to retain all he has been taught. If too much is expected of him, he can become frustrated and it may ruin him completely for any serious training later on, or even jeopardize his disposition. Most things a puppy learns and repeats before he is six months of age should be considered habit rather than training.

THE REWARD METHOD

The only proper and acceptable kind of training is the kindness and reward method which will build a strong bond between dog and owner. A dog must have confidence in and respect for his teacher. The most important thing to remember in training any dog is that the quickest way to teach, especially the young dog, is through repetition. Praise him when he does well, and scold him when he does wrong. This will suffice. There is no need or excuse for swinging at a dog with rolled up newspapers, or flailing hands which will only tend to make the dog hand shy the rest of his life. Also, make every word count. Do not give a command unless you intend to see it through. Pronounce distinctly with the fewest possible words, and use the same words for the same command every time.

Include the dog's name every time to make sure you have his undivided attention at the beginning of each command. Do not go on to another command until he has successfully completed the previous one and is praised for it. Of course, you should not mix play with the serious training time. Make sure the dog knows the difference between the two.

In the beginning, it is best to train without any distractions whatsoever. After he has learned to concentrate and is older and more proficient, he should perform the exercises with interference, so that the dog learns absolute obedience in the face of all distractions. Needless to say, whatever the distractions, you never lose control. You must be in command at all times to earn the respect and attention of your dog.

HOW LONG SHOULD THE LESSONS BE?

The lessons should be brief with a young dog, starting at five minutes, and as the dog ages and becomes adept in the first lessons, increase the time all the way up to one-half hour. Public training classes are usually set for one hour, and this is acceptable since the full hour of concentration is not placed on your dog alone. Working under these conditions with other dogs, you will find that he will not be as intent as he would be with a private lesson where the commands are directed to him alone for the entire thirty minutes.

If you should notice that your dog is not doing well, or not keeping up with the class, consider putting off training for awhile. Animals, like children, are not always ready for schooling at exactly the same age. It would be a shame to ruin a good obedience dog because you insist on starting his training at six months rather than at, say, nine months, when he would be more apt to be receptive both physically and mentally. If he has particular difficulty in learning one exercise, you might do well to skip to a different one and come back to it again at another session. There are no set rules in this basic training, except, "don't push!"

WHAT YOU NEED TO START TRAINING

From three to six months of age, use the soft nylon show leads, which are the best and safest. When you get ready for the basic training at six months of age, you will require one of the special metal-link choke chains sold for exactly this purpose. Do not let the word "choke" scare you. It is a soft, smooth chain and should be held slack whenever you are not actually using it to correct the dog. This chain should be put over the dog's head so that the lead can be attached over the dog's neck rather than underneath against his throat. It is wise when you buy your choke collar to ask the sales person to show you how it is put on. Those of you who will be taking your dog to a training class will have an instructor who can show you.

To avoid undue stress on the dog, use both hands on the lead. The dog will be taught to obey commands at your left side, and therefore, your left hand will guide the dog close to his collar on a six-foot train-

Canadian and American Ch. Webline Rio Hondo shown winning at a show under judge May Handley. Hondo is handled here by Dick Webb, who bred Hondo at his Webline Kennels in El Monte, California. Hondo was later sold to Mrs. Cheever Porter of New York City and became a top Irish Setter and #10 Sporting Dog in the nation.

ing lead. The balance of the lead will be held in your right hand. Learn at the very beginning to handle your choke collar and lead correctly. It is as important in training a dog as is the proper equipment for riding a horse.

WHAT TO TEACH FIRST

The first training actually should be to teach the dog to know his name. This, of course, he can learn at an earlier age than six months, just as he can learn to walk nicely on a leash or lead. Many puppies will at first probably want to walk around with the leash in their mouths. There is no objection to this if the dog will walk while doing it. Rather than cultivating this as a habit, you will find that if you don't make an issue of it, the dog will soon realize that carrying the lead in his mouth is not rewarding and he'll let it fall to his side where it belongs.

Ch. Caldene Judson, pictured winning at the 1944 show in Pittsburgh, Pennsylvania under judge Edwin Pickhardt. Brown photo.

Ch. Sean Warlocke of Bridgeview, owned by John and Dorothy Curry, Sr. and handled by Jack Funk. Sean is pictured winning Best of Breed at the 1970 Muncie, Indiana, dog show and finished for his championship with a 4th major win. Ritter photo.

We also let the puppy walk around by himself for a while with the lead around his neck. If he wishes to chew on it a little, that's all right too. In other words, let it be something he recognizes and associates with at first. Do not let the lead start out being a harness.

If the dog is at all bright, chances are he has learned to come on command when you call him by name. This is relatively simple with sweet talk and a reward. On lead, without a reward, and on command without a lead is something else again. If there has been, or is now, a problem, the best way to correct it is to put on the choke collar and the six-foot lead. Then walk away from the dog, and call him, "Pirate, come!" and gently start reeling him in until the dog is in front of you. Give him a pat on the head and/or reward.

Walking, or heeling, next to you is also one of the first and most important things for him to learn. With the soft lead training starting very early, he should soon take up your pace at your left side. At the command to "heel" he should start off with you and continue alongside until you stop. Give the command, "Pirate, sit!" This is taught by leaning over and pushing down on his hindquarters until he sits next to you, while pulling up gently on the collar. When you have this down pat on the straightaway, then start practicing it in circles, with turns and figure eights. When he is an advanced student, you can look forward to the heels and sits being done neatly, spontaneously, and off lead as well.

THE "DOWN" COMMAND

One of the most valuable lessons or commands you can teach your dog is to lie down on command. Some day it may save his life, and is invaluable when traveling with a dog or visiting, if behavior and manners are required even beyond obedience. While repeating the words, "Pirate, down!" lower the dog from a sitting position in front of you by gently pulling his front legs out in front of him. Place your full hand on him while repeating the command, "Pirate, down!" and hold him down to let him know you want him to *stay* down. After he gets the general idea, this can be done from a short distance away on a lead along with the command, by pulling the lead down to the floor. Or perhaps you can slip the lead under your shoe (between the heel and sole) and pull it directly to the floor. As the dog progresses in training, a hand signal with or without verbal command, or with or without lead, can be given from a considerable distance by raising your arm and extending the hand palm down.

THE "STAY" COMMAND

The stay command eventually can be taught from both a sit and a down position. Start with the sit. With the dog on your left side in the sitting position give the command, "Pirate, stay!" Reach down with the left hand open and palm side to the dog and sweep it in close to his nose. Then walk a short distance away and face him. He will at first, having learned to heel immediately as you start off, more than likely start off with you. The trick in teaching this is to make sure he hears "stay" before you start off. It will take practice. If he breaks, sit him down again, stand next to him, and give the command all over again. As he masters the command, let the distance between you and your dog increase while the dog remains seated. Once the command is learned, advance to the stay command from the down position.

THE STAND FOR EXAMINATION

If you have any intention of going on to advanced training in obedience with your dog, or if you have a show dog which you feel you will enjoy showing yourself, a most important command which should be mastered at six months of age is the stand command. This is essential for a show dog since it is the position used when the show judge goes over your dog. This is taught in the same manner as the stay command, but this time with the dog remaining up on all four feet. He should learn to stand still, without moving his feet and without flinching or breaking when approached by either you or strangers. The hand with palm open wide and facing him should be firmly placed in front of his nose with the command, "Pirate, stand!" After he learns the basic rules and knows the difference between stand and stay, ask friends, relatives, and strangers to assist you with this exercise by walking up to the dog and going over him. He should not react physically to their touch. A dog posing in this stance should show all the beauty and pride of being a sterling example of his breed.

FORMAL SCHOOL TRAINING

We mentioned previously about the various training schools and classes given for dogs. Your local kennel club, newspaper, or the yellow pages of the telephone book will put you in touch with organizations in your area where this service is performed. You and your dog will learn a great deal from these classes. Not only do they offer formal training, but the experience for you and your dog in public, with other dogs of approximately the same age and with the same purpose in mind, is excellent. If you intend to show your dog, this training is valuable ring experience for later on. If you are having difficulty with the training, remember, it is either too soon to start—or YOU are doing something wrong!

Ch. Webline Golden Jubilee, C.D., owned and bred by Mr. and Mrs. William R. Golden of Pacific Palisades, California. This glorious Irish Setter was the sire of 12 champions and was 2nd ranking Sporting Dog in the Phillips System in 1965 and #3 ranking Sporting Dog in 1966. Jubilee had 9 Bests in Show to his credit. His sire was Ch. Thenderin Chaparal Cayenne **ex** Ch. Weblyn Mi Golden Flame, C.D.

A class of young Irish Setters learn basic obedience. Whether your dog is to compete for an obedience title, or whether he is a family pet, good manners are essential. Photo by Ken Levey.

ADVANCED TRAINING AND OBEDIENCE TRIALS

The A.K.C. obedience trials are divided into three classes: Novice, Open and Utility.

In the Novice Class, the dog will be judged on the following basis:

TEST	MAXIMUM SCORE
Heel on lead	35
Stand for examination	30
Heel free—on lead	45
Recall (come on command)	30
One-minute sit (handler in ring)	30
Three-minute down (handler in ring)	30
Maximum total score	200

If the dog "qualifies" in three shows by earning at least 50% of the points for each test, with a total of at least 170 for the trial, he has earned the Companion Dog degree and the letters C.D. (Companion Dog) are entered after his name in the A.K.C. records.

After the dog has qualified as a C.D., he is eligible to enter the Open Class competition, where he will be judged on this basis:

TEST	MAXIMUM SCORE
Heel free	40
Drop on Recall	30
Retrieve (wooden dumbbell) on flat	25
Retrieve over obstacle (hurdle)	35
Broad jump	20
Three-minute sit (handler out of ring)	25
Five-minute down (handler out of ring)	25
maximum total score	200

Again he must qualify in three shows for the C.D.X. (Companion Dog Excellent) title and then is eligible for the Utility Class, where he can earn the Utility Dog (U.D.) degree in these rugged tests:

TEST	MAXIMUM SCORE
Scent discrimination (Article #1)	30
Scent discrimination (Article #2)	30
Directed retrieve	30
Signal exercise (heeling, etc., on hand signal)	35
Directed jumping (over hurdle and bar jump)	40
Group examination	35
Maximum total score	200

For more complete information about these obedience trials, write for the American Kennel Club's *Regulations and Standards for Obedience Trials*. Dogs that are disqualifed from breed shows because of alteration or physical defects are eligible to compete in these trials.

THE COMPANION DOG EXCELLENT DEGREE

There are seven exercises which must be executed to achieve the C.D.X. degree, and the percentages for achieving these are the same as for the U.D. degree. Candidates must qualify in three different obedience trials and under three different judges and must have received scores of more than 50% of the available points in each exercise, with a total of 170 points or more out of the possible 200. At that time they may add the letters C.D.X. after their name.

THE UTILITY DOG DEGREE

The Utility Dog degree is awarded to dogs which have qualified by successfully completing six exercises under three different judges

Dajo's Dannie Boy, C.D.X., had earned his C.D. title by the time he was 9 months old and his C.D.X. title by the time he was 14 months old. Owners Dale and Ruth Jones believe this makes him the youngest Irish Setter in the country to attain the C.D.X. title.

at three different obedience trials, with a score of more than 50% of available points in each exercise, and with a score of 170 or more out of a possible 200 points.

These six exercises consist of Scent Discrimination, with two different articles for which they receive thirty points each if successfully completed; Direct Retrieving, for 30 points; Signal Exercise for 35 points; Directed Jumping for 40 points and a Group Examination for 35 points.

THE TRACKING DOG DEGREE

The Tracking Dog trials are not held, as the others are, with the dog shows, and need be passed only once.

The dog must work continuously on a strange track at least 440 yards long and with two right angle turns. There is no time limit, and the dog must retrieve an article laid at the other end of the trail. There is no score given; the dog either earns the degree or fails. The dog is worked by his trainer on a long leash, usually in harness.

Charming mother and son photograph of Ch. Wolfscroft Vanguard, C.D.X., U.D. and Ch. Wolfscroft My Wild Irish Rose. Both dogs owned and photographed by Dr. Wolfgang A. Casper, Wolfscroft Kennels, Staten Island, New York.

A lovely "at home" scene at the Sid Marx house with their youngster and one of the Marx Irish Setters.

19. SHOWING YOUR IRISH SETTER

Let us assume that after a few months of tender loving care, you realize your dog is developing beyond your wildest expectations and that the dog you selected is very definitely a show dog! Of course, every owner is prejudiced. But if you are sincerely interested in going to dog shows with your dog and making a champion of him, now is the time to start casting a critical eye on him from a judge's point of view.

There is no such thing as a perfect dog. Every dog has some faults, perhaps even a few serious ones. The best way to appraise your dog's degree of perfection is to compare him with the Standard for the breed, or before a judge in a show ring.

MATCH SHOWS

For the beginner there are "mock" dog shows, called Match Shows, where you and your dog go through many of the procedures of a regular dog show, but do not gain points toward championship. These shows are usually held by kennel clubs, annually or semiannually, and much ring poise and experience can be gained there. The age limit is reduced to two months at match shows to give puppies four months of training before they compete at the regular shows when they reach six months of age. Classes range from two to four months; four to six months; six to nine months; and nine to twelve months. Puppies compete with others of their own age for comparative purposes. Many breeders evaluate their litters in this manner, choosing which is the most outgoing, which is the most poised, the best showman, etc.

For those seriously interested in showing their dogs to full championship, these match shows provide important experience for both the dog and the owner. Class categories may vary slightly, according to number of entries, but basically include all the classes that are included at a regular point show. There is a nominal entry fee and, of course, ribbons and usually trophies are given for your efforts as well. Unlike the point shows, entries can be made on the day of the show right on the show grounds. They are unbenched and provide an informal, usually congenial atmosphere for the amateur, which helps to make the ordeal of one's first adventures in the show ring a little less nerve-wracking.

THE POINT SHOWS

It is not possible to show a puppy at an American Kennel Club sanctioned point show before the age of six months. When your dog reaches this eligible age, your local kennel club can provide you with the names and addresses of the show-giving superintendents in your area who will be staging the club's dog show for them, and where you must write for an entry form.

Ch. Fleetwood Farms Grand Marshal, pictured winning Best of Winners at the 1973 First National Specialty Show held by the Irish Setter Club of America. . . and winning over the largest entry in the history of the breed. ISCA president Louis Iacobucci presents the trophy. Owners are Hugh and Virginia Rumbaugh, Fleetwood Farms, Akron, Ohio.

BEST OF WINNERS

ASHBEY PHOTO

Ch. Kinvarra Red Sean, pictured finishing under judge Clark Thompson, handled by Erwin Hutzmann. Sired by Ch. Kinvarra Kimson **ex** Tawny PiPit's Lady, Sean was bred by William McGrath and is co-owned by Mr. McGrath and William McCormack. Shafer photo.

Three generations of Best in Show Irish Setters from the famous Milson Kennels, Harrison, New York. Father, son and grandson represented by Ch. Milson Top Notcher, Ch. Milson O'Boy and Ch. Higgins Red Coat. A Walter Levick photograph.

The forms are mailed in a pamphlet called a premium list. This also includes the names of the judges for each breed, a list of the prizes and trophies, the name and address of the show-giving club and where the show will be held, as well as rules and regulations set up by the American Kennel Club which must be abided by if you are to enter.

A booklet containing the complete set of show rules and regulations may be obtained by writing to the American Kennel Club, Inc., 51 Madison Avenue, New York, N.Y., 10010.

When you write to the Dog Show Superintendent, request not only your premium list for this particular show, but ask that your name be added to their mailing list so that you will automatically receive all premium lists in the future. List your breed or breeds and they will see to it that you receive premium lists for Specialty shows as well.

Unlike the match shows where your dog will be judged on ring behavior, at the point shows he will be judged on conformation to the breed Standard. In addition to being at least six months of age (on the

Ch. St. Cloud's Fermanagh III photographed by Tauskey for owner Mrs. Cheever Porter of New York, New York.

Ch. Cherry Point Brask, sired by Ch. Thenderin Brian Tristan out of
Ch. End O'Maine Encore. Brask has won 5 Bests in Show, 1 Specialty
Best of Breed and 27 Sporting Group Firsts. Owner is Marion T. Darling; handled here by Eldon McCormack. Maurice Baker was the judge
for this show win.

day of the show) he must be a purebred for a point show. This means both of his parents and he are registered with the American Kennel Club. There must be no alterations or falsifications regarding his appearance. Females cannot have been spayed and males must have both testicles in evidence. No dyes or powders may be used to enhance the appearance, and any lameness or deformity or major deviation from the Standard for the breed constitutes a disqualification.

With all these things in mind, groom your dog to the best of your ability in the specified area for this purpose in the show hall and walk into the show ring with great pride of ownership and ready for an appraisal of your dog by the judge.

The presiding judge on that day will allow each and every dog a certain amount of time and consideration before making his decisions. It is never permissible to consult the judge regarding either

Ch. Heslop's Stylish Charm II, owned by the Osbornes.

your dog or his decision while you are in the ring. An exhibitor never speaks unless spoken to, and then only to answer such questions as the judge may ask—the age of the dog, the dog's bite, or to ask you to move your dog around the ring once again.

However, before you reach the point where you are actually in the ring awaiting the final decisions of the judge, you will have had to decide in which of the five classes in each sex your dog should compete.

Point Show Classes

The regular classes of the AKC are: Puppy, Novice, Bred-by-Exhibitor, American-Bred, Open; if your dog is undefeated in any of the regular classes (divided by sex) in which it is entered, he or she is *required* to enter the Winners Class. If your dog is placed second in the class to the dog which won Winners Dog or Winners Bitch, hold the dog or bitch in readiness as the judge must consider it for Reserve Winners.

PUPPY CLASSES shall be for dogs which are six months of age and over but under twelve months, which were whelped in the U.S.A. or Canada, and which are not champions. Classes are often divided 6 and (under) 9, and 9 and (under) 12 months. The age of a dog shall be calculated up to and inclusive of the first day of a show. For example, a dog whelped on Jan. 1st is eligible to compete in a puppy class on July 1st, and may continue to compete up to and including Dec. 31st of the same year, but is not eligible to compete Jan. 1st of the following year.

THE NOVICE CLASS shall be for dogs six months of age or over, whelped in the U.S.A. or Canada which have not, prior to the closing of entries, won three first prizes in the Novice Class, a first prize in Bred-by-Exhibitor, American-Bred or Open Class, nor one or more points toward a championship title.

THE BRED-BY-EXHIBITOR CLASS shall be for dogs whelped in the U.S.A. which are six months of age and over, which are not champions, and which are owned wholly or in part by the person or by the spouse of the person who was the breeder or one of the breeders of record. Dogs entered in the BBE Class must be handled by an owner or by a member of the immediate family of an owner, i.e., the husband, wife, father, mother, son, daughter, brother or sister.

THE AMERICAN-BRED CLASS is for all dogs (except champions) six months of age or over, whelped in the U.S.A. by reason of a mating that took place in the U.S.A.

THE OPEN CLASS is for any dog six months of age or over, except in a member specialty club show held for only American-Bred dogs, in which case the class is for American-Bred dogs only.

At the time he retired (December 15, 1968), Ch. Webline Rio Hondo had won 173 Bests of Breed, 65 Sporting Group Firsts, and 14 Bests in Show, as well as 6 Specialty Shows. Hondo was top winning Irish Setter in America for 1966. Handled by Jane Forsyth for owner Mrs. Cheever Porter of New York City.

WINNERS DOG and WINNERS BITCH: After the above male classes have been judged, the first-place winners are then *required* to compete in the ring. The dog judged "Winners Dog" is awarded the points toward his championship title.

RESERVE WINNERS are selected immediately after the Winners Dog. In case of a disqualification of a win by the AKC, the Reserve Dog moves up to "Winners" and receives the points. After all male classes are judged, the bitch classes are called.

BEST OF BREED OR BEST OF VARIETY COMPETITION is limited to Champions of Record or dogs (with newly acquired points, for a 90-day period prior to AKC confirmation) which have completed championship requirements, and Winners Dog and Winners Bitch (or the dog awarded Winners if only one Winners prize has been awarded), together with any undefeated dogs which have been shown only in non-regular classes; all compete for Best of Breed or Best of Variety (if the breed is divided by size, color, texture or length of coat hair, etc.).

BEST OF WINNERS: If the WD or WB earns BOB or BOV, it automatically becomes BOW; otherwise they will be judged together for BOW (following BOB or BOV judging).

BEST OF OPPOSITE SEX is selected from the remaining dogs of the opposite sex to Best of Breed or Best of Variety.

OTHER CLASSES may be approved by the AKC: STUD DOGS, BROOD BITCHES, BRACE CLASS, TEAM CLASS; classes consist-

Ch. Tirvelda Maidavale, one of the outstanding show dogs bred and owned by E. Irving Eldredge, Tirvelda Kennels, Middleburg, Virginia.

Ch. Candy K's Twice-A-Prince, Best in Show winning Irish Setter, bred
and owned by Dolores and Dale Hughes, Candy Kennels, El Cajon,
California.

ing of local dogs and bitches may also be included in a show if approved by the AKC (special rules are included in the AKC Rule Book).

The MISCELLANEOUS CLASS shall be for purebred dogs of such breeds as may be designated by the AKC. No dog shall be eligible for entry in this class unless the owner has been granted an Indefinite Listing Privilege (ILP) and unless the ILP number is given on the entry form. Application for an ILP shall be made on a form provided by the AKC and when submitted must be accompanied by a fee set by the Board of Directors.

All Miscellaneous Breeds shall be shown together in a single class except that the class may be divided by sex if so specified in the premium list. There shall be *no* further competition for dogs entered in this class. Ribbons for 1st, 2nd, 3rd and 4th shall be Rose, Brown, Light Green and Gray, respectively. This class is open to the following Miscellaneous dog breeds: Australian Cattle Dogs, Australian Kelpies, Border Collies, Cavalier King Charles Spaniels, Ibizan Hounds, Miniature Bull Terriers, and Spinoni Italiani.

If Your Dog Wins a Class. . .

Study the classes to make certain your dog is entered in a proper class for his or her qualifications. If your dog wins his class, the rule states: *You are required* to enter classes for Winners, Best of Breed and Best of Winners (no additional entry fees). The rule states, "No eligible dog may be withheld from competition." It is not mandatory that you stay for group judging. *If your dog wins a group, however, you must stay for Best-in-Show competition.*

THE PRIZE RIBBONS AND WHAT THEY STAND FOR

No matter how many entries there are in each class at a dog show, if you place first through fourth position you will receive a ribbon. These ribbons commemorate your win and can be impressive when collected and displayed to prospective buyers when and if you have puppies for sale, or if you intend to use your dog at public stud.

All ribbons from the American Kennel Club licensed dog shows will bear the American Kennel Club seal, the name of the show, the date and the placement. In the classes the colors are blue for first, red for second, yellow for third, and white for fourth. Winners Dog or Winners Bitch ribbons are purple, while Reserve Dog and Reserve Bitch ribbons are purple and white. Best of Winners ribbons are blue and white; Best of Breed, purple and gold; and Best of Opposite Sex ribbons are red and white.

In the six groups, first prize is a blue rosette or ribbon, second placement is red, third yellow, and fourth white. The Best In Show rosette is either red, white and blue, or incorporates the colors used in the show-giving club's emblem.

QUALIFYING FOR CHAMPIONSHIP

Championship points are given for Winners Dog and Winners Bitch in accordance with a scale of points established by the American Kennel Club based on the popularity of the breed in entries, and the number of dogs competing in the classes. This scale of points varies in different sections of the country, but the scale is published in the front of each dog show catalog. These points may differ between the dogs and the bitches at the same show. You may, however, win additional points by winning Best of Winners, if there are fewer dogs than bitches entered, or vice versa. Points never exceed five at any one show, and a total of fifteen points must be won to constitute a championship. These fifteen points must be won under at least three different judges, and you must acquire at least two major wins. Anything from a three to five point win is a major, while one and two point wins are minor wins. Two major wins must be won under two different judges to meet championship requirements.

OBEDIENCE TRIALS

Some shows also offer Obedience Trials, which are considered as separate events. They give the dogs a chance to compete and score on performing a prescribed set of exercises intended to display their training in doing useful work.

There are three obedience titles for which they may compete. First, the Companion Dog or C.D. title; second, the Companion Dog Excellent or C.D.X.; and third, the Utility Dog or U.D. Detailed information on these degrees is contained in a booklet entitled Official Obedience Regulations and may be obtained by writing to the American Kennel Club.

JUNIOR SHOWMANSHIP COMPETITION

Junior Showmanship Competition is for boys and girls in different age groups handling their own dogs or one owned by their immediate family. There are four divisions: Novice A, for the ten to 12 year olds; Novice B, for those 13 to 16 years of age, with no previous junior showmanship wins; Open C, for ten to 12 year olds; and Open D, for 13 to 16 year olds who have earned one or more JS awards.

As Junior Showmanship at the dog shows increased in popularity, certain changes and improvements had to be made. As of April 1, 1971, the American Kennel Club issued a new booklet containing the Regulations for Junior Showmanship which may be obtained by writing to the A.K.C. at 51 Madison Avenue, New York, N.Y. 10010.

Ch. Candia Dandi, sire of three champions to date, including Am. and Mex. Ch. Candy K's Katy Dunn, Am. and Mex. Ch. Candy K's M deen and Ch. Candy K's Shannon Mae. Dandi is pictured winning at a show on the way to his championship. Owners are Dolores and Dale Hughes, Candy Kennels, El Cajon, California.

DOG SHOW PHOTOGRAPHERS

Every show has at least one official photographer who will be more than happy to take a photograph of your dog with the judge, ribbons and trophies, along with your or your handler. These make marvelous remembrances of your top show wins and are frequently framed along with the ribbons for display purposes. Photographers can be paged at the show over the public address system, if you wish to obtain this service. Prices vary, but you will probably find it costs little to capture these happy moments, and the photos can always be used in the various dog magazines to advertise your dog's wins.

TWO TYPES OF DOG SHOWS

There are two types of dog shows licensed by the American Kennel Club. One is the all-breed show which includes classes for all the recognized breeds, and groups of breeds; i.e., all terriers, all toys, etc. Then there are the specialty shows for one particular breed which also offer championship points.

Ch. Dunguaire Bryson, owned by Dr. Jack H. Skelsie, was Best in Show at the 1956 Central Maine Kennel Club show. Art Baines handling for the owner under judge Earl H. Lounsbury. William Brown photograph.

Ch. Carrvale's Terry Terhune pictured winning at the 1958 International Kennel Club of Chicago show under the late judge Major Godsol. Handled by Hollis Wilson for owner William Spilios, Terry was the sire of 15 offspring and was #8 ranking Sporting Dog in the nation in 1958. This great Sporting Dog was also a Best in Show winner and was sired by Ch. Carrvale's Sergeant Terhune **ex** Tyronne Farm Sherry.

BENCHED OR UNBENCHED DOG SHOWS

The show-giving clubs determine, usually on the basis of what facilities are offered by their chosen show site, whether their show will be benched or unbenched. A benched show is one where the dog show superintendent supplies benches (cages for toy dogs). Each bench is numbered and its corresponding number appears on your entry identification slip which is sent to you prior to the show date. The number also appears in the show catalog. Upon entering the show you should take your dog to the bench where he should remain until it is time to groom him before entering the ring to be judged. After judging, he must be returned to the bench until the official time of dismissal from the show. At an unbenched show the club makes no provision whatsoever for your dog other than an enormous tent (if an outdoor show) or an area in a show hall where all crates and grooming equipment must be kept.

Benched or unbenched, the moment you enter the show grounds you are expected to look after your dog and have it under complete control at all times. This means short leads in crowded aisles or getting out of cars. In the case of a benched show, a "bench chain" is needed. It should allow the dog to move around, but not get down off the bench. It is also not considered "cute" to have small tots leading enormous dogs around a dog show where the child might be dragged into the middle of a dog fight.

Westwind Robin Hood pictured winning at the 1973 N.W. Connecticut Dog Club show. Handled by breeder-owner Luz Holvenstot, Westwind Kennels, Long Valley, New Jersey. Shafer photo.

PROFESSIONAL HANDLERS

If you are new in the fancy and do not know how to handle your dog to his best advantage, or if you are too nervous or physically unable to show your dog, you can hire a licensed professional handler who will do it for you for a specified fee. The more successful or well-known handlers charge slightly higher rates, but generally speaking there is a pretty uniform charge for this service. As the dog progresses with his wins in the show ring, the fee increases proportionately. Included in this service is professional advice on when and where to show your dog, grooming, a statement of your wins at each show, and all trophies and ribbons that the dog accumulates. Any cash award is kept by the handler as a sort of "bonus."

When engaging a handler, it is advisable to select one that does not take more dogs to a show than he can properly and comfortably handle. You want your dog to receive his individual attention and not

Ch. King Size, Best of Breed and Group Second at the June, 1952 Mississippi Valley Kennel Club show under judge Mrs. James Phillips (now Mrs. Harold Schlintz). Handler, Dick Cooper.

Ch. Delarda's Blith Spirit, C.D. owned by Madeline Blush of Baldwin, New York.

be rushed into the ring at the last moment because the handler has been busy with too many other dogs in other rings. Some handlers require that you deliver the dog to their establishment a few days ahead of the show so they have ample time to groom and train him. Others will accept well-behaved and previously trained and groomed dogs at ringside, if they are familiar with the dog and the owner. This should be determined well in advance of the show date. NEVER expect a handler to accept a dog at ringside that is not groomed to perfection!

There are several sources for locating a professional handler. Dog magazines carry their classified advertising; a note or telephone call to the American Kennel Club will put you in touch with several in your area. Usually, you will be billed after the day of the show.

DO YOU REALLY NEED A HANDLER?

The answer to the above question is sometimes yes! However, the answer most exhibitors give is, "But I can't *afford* a professional handler!" or, "I want to show my dog myself. Does that mean my dog will never do any big winning?"

Do you *really* need a handler to win? If you are mishandling a good dog that should be winning and isn't, because it is made to look simply terrible in the ring by its owner, the answer is yes. If you don't know how to handle a dog properly, why make your dog look bad when a handler could show it to its best advantage?

Some owners simply cannot handle a dog well and still wonder why their dogs aren't winning in the ring, no matter how hard they try. Others are nervous and this nervousness travels down the leash to the dog and the dog behaves accordingly. Some people are extroverts by nature, and these are the people who usually make excellent handlers. Of course, the biggest winning dogs at the shows usually have a lot of "show off" in their nature, too, and this helps a great deal.

THE COST OF CAMPAIGNING A DOG WITH A HANDLER

At present many champions are shown an average of 25 times before completing a championship. In entry fees at today's prices, that adds up to about $200. This does not include motel bills, traveling expenses, or food. There have been dog champions finished in fewer shows, say five to ten shows, but this is the exception rather than the rule. When and where to show should be thought out carefully so that you can perhaps save money on entries. Here is one of the services a professional handler provides that can mean a considerable saving. Hiring a handler can save money in the long run if you just wish to make a champion. If your dog has been winning reserves and not taking the points and a handler can finish him in five to ten shows, you would be ahead financially. If your dog is not really top quality, the length of time it takes even a handler to finish it (depending upon competition in the area) could add up to a large amount of money.

Campaigning a show specimen that not only captures the wins in his breed but wins group and Best in Show awards gets up into the big money. To cover the nation's major shows and rack up a record as one of the top dogs in the nation usually costs an owner between ten and fifteen thousand dollars a year. This includes not only the professional handler's fee for taking the dog into the ring, but the cost of conditioning and grooming, board, advertising in the dog magazines, photographs, etc.

There is great satisfaction in winning with your own dog, especially if you have trained and cared for it yourself. With today's enormous entries at the dog shows and so many worthy dogs competing for top wins, many owners who said "I'd rather do it myself!" and meant it became discouraged and eventually hired a handler anyway.

However, if you really are in it just for the sport, you can and should handle your own dog if you want to. You can learn the tricks by

Ch. Fleetwood Farms Sixty Special pictured winning in 1961 at the Central New York Kennel Club show with his handler, Charley Meyer. This dog was top-winning Irish Setter for 1961, 1962 and 1963. Owned by Hugh and Virginia Rumbaugh, Fleetwood Farms, Akron, Ohio. Evelyn Shafer photograph.

American, Bermudian, and Canadian Ch. Tirvelda Middle Brother pictured winning the Sporting Group at the 1971 South Shore Kennel Club show under judge Nelson Groh. Brother is owner-handled by Helen Olivio of New York. Ashbey photo.

attending training classes, and you can learn a lot by carefully observing the more successful professional handlers as they perform in the ring. Model yourself after the ones that command respect as being the leaders in their profession. But, if you find you'd really rather be at ringside looking on, then do get a handler so that your worthy dog gets his deserved recognition in the ring. To own a good dog and win with it is a thrill, so good luck, no matter how you do it.

20. FEEDING AND NUTRITION

FEEDING PUPPIES

There are many diets today for young puppies, including all sorts of products on the market for feeding the newborn, for supplementing the feeding of the young and for adding this or that to diets, depending on what is lacking in the way of a complete diet.

When weaning puppies, it is necessary to put them on four meals a day, even while you are tapering off with the mother's milk. Feeding at six in the morning, noontime, six in the evening and midnight is about the best schedule, since it fits in with most human eating plans. Meals for the puppies can be prepared immediately before or after your own meals, without too much of a change in your own schedule.

6 A.M.

Two meat and two milk meals serve best and should be served alternately, of course. Assuming the 6 A.M. feeding is a milk meal, the contents should be as follows: Goat's milk is the very best milk to feed puppies but is expensive and usually available only a drug stores, unless you live in farm country where it could be readily available fresh and still less expensive. If goat's milk is not available, use evaporated milk (which can be changed to powdered milk later on) diluted two parts evaporated milk and one part water, along with raw egg yoke, honey or Karo syrup, sprinkled with high-protein baby cereal and some wheat germ. As the puppies mature, cottage cheese may be added or, at one of the two milk meals, it can be substituted for the cereal.

NOONTIME

A puppy chow which has been soaked in warm water or beef broth according to the time specified on the wrapper should be mixed with raw or simmered chopped meat in equal proportions with vitamin powder added.

6 P.M.

Repeat the milk meal—perhaps varying the type of cereal from wheat to oats, or corn or rice.

MIDNIGHT

Repeat the meat meal. If raw meat was fed at noon, the evening meal might be simmered.

Please note that specific proportions on this suggested diet are not given. However, it's safe to say that the most important ingredients are the milk and cereal, and the meat and puppy chow which forms the basis of the diet. Your veterinarian can advise on the portion sizes if there is any doubt in your mind as to how much to use.

If you notice that the puppies are cleaning their plates you are perhaps not feeding enough to keep up with their rate of growth. Increase the amount at the next feeding. Observe them closely; puppies should each "have their fill," because growth is very rapid at this age. If they have not satisfied themselves, increase the amount so that they do not have to fight for the last morsel. They will not overeat if they know there is enough food available. Instinct will usually let them eat to suit their normal capacity.

Rudy and Marilyn De Mark's Mos'n Acre Wedgewood takes time out at their Woodland Acre Kennel in Dover, New Jersey. Taura was being shown to a championship during the mid-1970's.

If there is any doubt in your mind as to any ingredient you are feeding, ask yourself, "Would I give it to my own baby?" If the answer is no, then don't give it to your puppies. At this age, the comparison between puppies and human babies can be a good guide.

If there is any doubt in your mind, I repeat: ask your veterinarian to be sure.

Many puppies will regurgitate their food, perhaps a couple of times, before they manage to retain it. If they do bring up their food, allow them to eat it again, rather than clean it away. Sometimes additional saliva is necessary for them to digest it, and you do not want them to skip a meal just because it is an unpleasant sight for you to observe.

This same regurgitation process holds true sometimes with the bitch, who will bring up her own food for her puppies every now and then. This is a natural instinct on her part which stems from the days when dogs were giving birth in the wilds. The only food the mother could provide at weaning time was too rough and indigestible for her puppies. Therefore, she took it upon herself to pre-digest the food until it could be taken and retained by her young. Bitches today will sometimes resort to this, especially bitches which love having litters and have a strong maternal instinct. Some dams will help you wean their litters and even give up feeding entirely once they see you are taking over.

WEANING THE PUPPIES

When weaning the puppies the mother is kept away from the little ones for longer and longer periods of time. This is done over a period of several days. At first she is separated from the puppies for several hours, then all day, leaving her with them only at night for comfort and warmth. This gradual separation aids in helping the mother's milk to dry up gradually, and she suffers less distress after feeding a litter.

If the mother continues to carry a great deal of milk with no signs of its tapering off, consult your veterinarian before she gets too uncomfortable. She may cut the puppies off from her supply of milk too abruptly if she is uncomfortable, before they should be completely on their own.

There are many opinions on the proper age to start weaning puppies. If you plan to start selling them between six and eight weeks, weaning should begin between two and three weeks of age. Here again, each bitch will pose a different situation. The size and weight of the litter should help determine the time, and your veterinarian will have an opinion, as he determines the burden the bitch is carrying by the size of the litter and her general condition. If she is being pulled down by feeding a large litter, he may suggest that you start at two weeks. If she is glorying in her motherhood without any apparent

Ch. Kinvarra Macaroon, bred by George E. Brodie, Seaforth Kennels, and owned by Mr. and Mrs. Walter Ochsner of Oak Ridge, Tennessee.

taxing of her strength, he may suggest three to four weeks. You and he will be the best judges. But remember, there is no substitute that is as perfect as mother's milk—and the longer the puppies benefit from it, the better. Other food yes, but mother's milk first and foremost for the healthiest puppies!

FEEDING THE ADULT DOG

The puppies' schedule of four meals a day should drop to three by six months and then to two by nine months; by the time the dog reaches one year of age, it is eating one meal a day.

The time when you feed the dog each day can be a matter of the dog's preference or your convenience, so long as once in every 24 hours the dog receives a meal that provides him with a complete, balanced diet. In addition, of course, fresh clean water should be available at all times.

There are many brands of dry food, kibbles and biscuits on the market which are all of good quality. There are also many varieties of canned dog food which are of good quality and provide a balanced diet for your dog. But, for those breeders and exhibitors who show their dogs, additional care is given to providing a few "extras" which enhance the good health and good appearance of show dogs.

A good meal or kibble mixed with water or beef broth and raw meat is perhaps the best ration to provide. In cold weather many

336

breeders add suet or corn oil (or even olive or cooking oil) to the mixture and others make use of the bacon fat after breakfast by pouring it over the dog's food.

Salting a dog's food in the summer helps replace the salt he "pants away" in the heat. Many breeders sprinkle the food with garlic powder to sweeten the dog's breath and prevent gas, especially in breeds that gulp or wolf their food and swallow a lot of air. I prefer garlic powder; the salt is too weak and the clove is too strong.

There are those, of course, who cook very elaborately for their dogs, which is not necessary if a good meal and meat mixture is provided. Many prefer to add vegetables, rice, tomatoes, etc., in with everything else they feed. As long as the extras do not throw the nutritional balance off, there is little harm, but no one thing should be fed to excess. Occasionally liver is given as a treat at home. Fish, which

Ch. Seaforth's Faig-A-Baille, Best in Show-winning Irish Setter, pictured here going Best of Winners at a New England Irish Setter Club Specialty show on the way to his championship. Judge was Dr. Jay Calhoon. Owners, Mr. and Mrs. George E. Brodie, Jr. of the Seaforth Kennels, North Easton, Massachusetts.

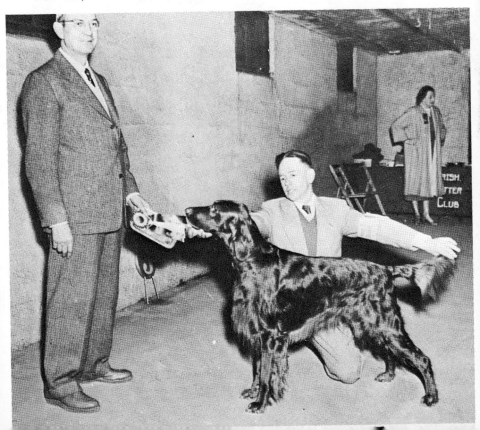

Ch. Knightscroft Symphony, owned by Helen Naylor of Blue Ball, Pennsylvania, with handler Harold Correll. Photo by William Brown.

most veterinarians no longer recommend even for cats, is fed to puppies, but should not be given in excess of once a week. Always remember that no one thing should be given as a total diet. Balance is most important; a 100 per cent meat diet can kill a dog.

THE ALL MEAT DIET CONTROVERSY

In March of 1971, the National Research Council investigated a great stir in the dog fancy about the all-meat dog-feeding controversy. It was established that meat and meat by-products constitute a complete balanced diet for dogs only when it is further fortified with vitamins and minerals.

Therefore, a good dog chow or meal mixed with meat provides the perfect combination for a dog's diet. While the dry food is a complete diet in itself, the fresh meat additionally satisfies the dog's anatomically and physiologically meat-oriented appetite. While dogs are actually carnivores, it must be remembered that when they were feeding themselves in the wild they ate almost the entire animal they captured, including its stomach contents. This provided some of the vitamins and minerals we must now add to the diet.

In the United States, the standard for diets which claim to be "complete and balanced" is set by the Subcommittee on Canine Nutrition of the National Research Council (NRC) of the National Academy of Sciences. This is the official agency for establishing the nutritional requirements of dog foods. Most foods sold for dogs and cats meet these requirements, and manufactuers are proud to say so on their labels, so look for this when you buy. Pet food labels must be approved by the Association of American Feed Control Officials, Pet Foods Committee. Both the Food and Drug Administration and the Federal Trade Commission of the AAFCO define the word "balanced" when referring to dog food as:

"Balanced is a term which may be applied to pet food having all known required nutrients in a proper amount and proportion based upon the recommendations of a recognized authority (The National Research Council is one) in the field of animal nutrition, for a given set of physiological animal requirements."

With this much care given to your dog's diet, there can be little reason for not having happy well-fed dogs in proper weight and proportions for the show ring.

OBESITY

As we mentioned before, there are many "perfect" diets for your dogs on the market today. When fed in proper proportions, they should keep your dogs in "full bloom." However, there are those owners who, more often than not, indulge their own appetites and are inclined to overfeed their dogs as well. A study in Great Britain in the early 1970's found that a major percentage of obese people also had obese dogs. The entire family was overfed and all suffered from the same condition.

Obesity in dogs is a direct result of the animal's being fed more food that he can properly "burn up" over a period of time, so it is stored as fat or fatty tissue in the body. Pet dogs are more inclined to become obese than show dogs or working dogs, but obesity also is a factor to be considered with the older dog, since his exercise is curtailed.

A lack of "tuck up" on a dog, or not being able to feel the ribs, or great folds of fat which hang from the underside of the dog can all be considered as obesity. Genetic factors may enter into the picture, but usually the owner is at fault.

The life span of the obese dog is decreased on several counts. Excess weight puts undue stress on the heart as well as the joints. The dog becomes a poor anesthetic risk and has less resistance to viral or bacterial infections. Treatment is seldom easy or completely effective, so emphasis should be placed on not letting your dog get FAT in the first place!

ORPHANED PUPPIES

The ideal solution to feeding orphaned puppies is to be able to put them with another nursing dam who will take them on as her own. If this is not possible within your own kennel, or a kennel that you know of, it is up to you to care for and feed the puppies. Survival is possible but requires a great deal of time and effort on your part.

Your substitute formula must be precisely prepared, always served heated to body temperature and refrigerated when not being fed. Esbilac, a vacuum-packed powder, with complete feeding instructions on the can, is excellent and about as close to mother's milk as you can get. If you can't get Esbilac, or until you do get Esbilac, there are two alternative formulas that you might use.

Mix one part boiled water with five parts of evaporated milk and add one teaspoonful of di-calcium phosphate per quart of formula. Di-calcium phosphate can be secured at any drug store. If they have it in tablet form only, you can powder the tablets with the back part of a tablespoon. The other formula for newborn puppies is a combination of eight ounces of homogenized milk mixed well with two egg yolks.

You will need baby bottles with three-hole nipples. Sometimes doll bottles can be used for the newborn puppies, which should be fed at six-hour intervals. If they are consuming sufficient amounts, their stomachs should look full, or slightly enlarged, though never distended. The amount of formula to be fed is proportionate to the size, age, growth and weight of the puppy, and is indicated on the can of Esbilac or on the advice of your veterinarian. Many breeders like to keep a baby scale nearby to check the weight of the puppies to be sure they are thriving on the formula.

At two to three weeks you can start adding Pablum or some other high protein baby cereal to the formula. Also, baby beef can be licked from your finger at this age, or added to the formula. At four weeks the surviving puppies should be taken off the diet of Esbilac and put on a more substantial diet, such as wet puppy meal or chopped beef. However, Esbilac powder can still be mixed in with the food for additional nutrition. The jarred baby foods of pureed meats make for a smooth changeover also, and can be blended into the diet.

HOW TO FEED THE NEWBORN PUPPIES

When the puppy is a newborn, remember that it is vitally important to keep the feeding procedure as close to the natural mother's routine as possible. The newborn puppy should be held in your lap in

American and Canadian Ch. Verbu Killee Oogh, C.D.X., another of Emily Schweitzer's obedience-trained Irish Setters.

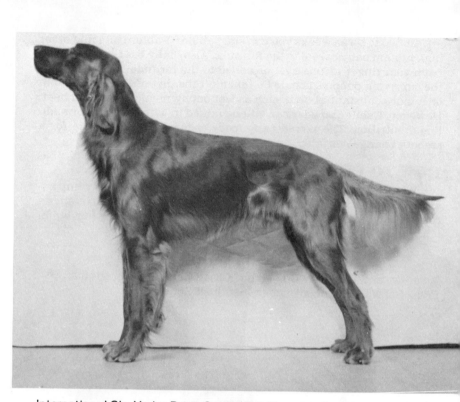

International Ch. Verbu Peter Oogh, C.D.X., owned, trained and bred by Emily Schweitzer, Verbu Kennels, Dundee, Illinois.

your hand in an almost upright position with the bottle at an angle to allow the entire nipple area to be full of the formula. Do not hold the bottle upright so the puppy's head has to reach straight up toward the ceiling. Do not let the puppy nurse too quickly or take in too much air and possibly get the colic. Once in a while, take the bottle away and let him rest a while and swallow several times. Before feeding, test the nipple to see that the fluid does not come out too quickly, or by the same token, too slowly so that the puppy gets tired of feeding before he has had enough to eat.

When the puppy is a little older, you can place him on his stomach on a towel to eat, and even allow him to hold on to the bottle or to "come and get it" on his own. Most puppies enjoy eating and this will be a good indication of how strong an appetite he has and his ability to consume the contents of the bottle.

It will be necessary to "burp" the puppy. Place a towel on your shoulder and hold the puppy on your shoulder as if it were a human

A lovely head study of the famous Ch. Thenderin Nomand, owned by Mr. and Mrs. George Brodie, Jr., Seaforth Kennels, North Easton, Massachusetts.

baby, patting and rubbing it gently. This will also encourage the puppy to defecate. At this time, you should observe for diarrhea or other intestinal disorders. The puppy should eliminate after each feeding with occasional eliminations between times as well. If the puppies do not eliminate on their own after each meal, massage their stomachs and under their tails gently until they do.

You must keep the puppies clean. If there is diarrhea or if they bring up a little formula, they should be washed and dried off. Under no circumstances should fecal matter be allowed to collect on their skin or fur.

All this—plus your determination and perseverance—might save an entire litter of puppies that would otherwise have died without their real mother.

GASTRIC TORSION

Gastric torsion, or bloat, sometimes referred to simply as "twisted stomach," has become more and more prevalent. Many dogs that in the past had been thought to die of blockage of the stomach or intestines because they had swallowed toys or other foreign objects are now suspected of having been the victims of gastric torsion and the bloat that followed.

Though life can be saved by immediate surgery to untwist the organ, the rate of fatality is high. Symptoms of gastric torsion are unusual restlessness, excessive salivation, attempts to vomit, rapid respiration, pain and the eventual bloating of the abdominal region.

The cause of gastric torsion can be attributed to overeating, excess gas formation in the stomach, poor function of the stomach or intestine, or general lack of exercise. As the food ferments in the stomach, gases form which may twist the stomach in a clockwise direction so that the gas is unable to escape. Surgery, where the stomach is untwisted counter-clockwise, is the safest and most successful way to correct the situation.

To avoid the threat of gastric torsion, it is wise to keep your dog well exercised to be sure the body is functioning normally. Make sure that food and water are available for the dog at all times, thereby reducing the tendency to overeat. With self-service dry feeding, where the dog is able to eat intermittently during the day, there is not the urge to "stuff" at one time.

If you notice any of the symptoms of gastric torsion, call your veterinarian immediately! Death can result within a matter of hours!

21. GENERAL CARE AND MANAGEMENT

TATTOOING

Ninety per cent success has been reported on the return of stolen or lost dogs that have been tattooed. More and more this simple, painless, inexpensive method of positive identification for dogs is being reported all over the United States. Long popular in Canada, along with nose prints, the idea gained interest in this country when dognapping started to soar as unscrupulous people began stealing dogs for resale to research laboratories. Pet dogs that wander off and lost hunting dogs have always been a problem. The success of tattooing has been significant.

Tattooing can be done by the veterinarian for a minor fee. There are several dog "registries" that will record your dog's number and help you locate it should it be lost or stolen. The number of the dog's American Kennel Club registration is most often used on thoroughbred dogs, or the owner's Social Security number in the case of mixed breeds. The best place for the tattoo is the groin. Some prefer the inside of an ear, and the American Kennel Club has rules that the judges officiating at the AKC dog shows not penalize the dog for the tattoo mark.

The tattoo mark serves not only to identify your dog should it be lost or stolen, but offers positive identification in large kennels where several litters of the same approximate age are on the premises. It is a safety measure against unscrupulous breeders "switching" puppies. Any age is a proper age to tattoo, but for safety's sake, the sooner the better.

The buzz of the needle might cause your dog to be apprehensive, but the pricking of the needle is virtually painless. The risk of infection is negligible when done properly, and the return of your beloved pet may be the reward for taking the time to insure positive identification for your dog. Your local kennel club will know of a dog registry in your area.

Champion trio bred by the Candy Kennels of Dolores and Dale Hughes in El Cajon, California. From left to right: Ch. Candy K's King of the road, American and Mexican Ch. Candy K's Silky Sullivan and Ch. Candy K's Donavan.

OUTDOOR HOUSEBREAKING

If you are particular about your dog's behavior in the house, where you expect him to be clean and respectful of the carpets and furniture, you should also want him to have proper manners outdoors. Just because the property belongs to you doesn't necessarily mean he should be allowed to empty himself any place he chooses. Before long the entire yard will be fouled and odorous and the dog will be completely irresponsible on other people's property as well. Dogs seldom recognize property lines.

If your dog does not have his own yard fenced in, he should be walked on leash before being allowed to run free and before being penned up in his own yard. He will appreciate his own run being kept clean. You will find that if he has learned his manners outside, his manners inside will be better. Good manners in "toilet training" are especially important with big dogs!

OTHER IMPORTANT OUTDOOR MANNERS

Excessive barking is perhaps the most objectionable habit a dog indulges in out of doors. It annoys neighbors and makes for a noisy dog in the house as well. A sharp jerk on the leash will stop a dog from excessive barking while walking; trees and shrubs around a dog run will cut down on barking if a dog is in his own run. However, it is unfair to block off his view entirely. Give him some view—preferably of his own home—to keep his interest. Needless to say, do not leave a dog that barks excessively out all night.

You will want your dog to bark at strangers, so allow him this privilege. Then after a few "alerting" barks tell the dog to be quiet (with the same word command each time). If he doesn't get the idea, put him on leash and let him greet callers with you at the door until he does get the idea.

Do not let your dog jump on visitors either. Leash training may be necessary to break this habit as well. As the dog jumps in the air, pull back on the lead so that the dog is returned to the floor abruptly. If he attempts to jump up on your, carefully raise your knee and push him away by leaning against his chest.

The four-month-old Dajo's Red Jacket, bred and owned by Dale and Ruth Jones of Dajos Kennels, Puyallup, Washington.

Do not let your dog roam free in the neighborhood no matter how well he knows his way home. Especially do not let your dog roam free to empty himself on the neighbors' property or gardens!

A positive invitation to danger is to allow your dog to chase cars or bicycles. Throwing tin cans or chains out of car windows at them has been suggested as a cure, but can also be dangerous if they hit the dog instead of the street. Streams of water from a garden hose or water pistol are the least dangerous, but leash control is still the most scientific and most effective.

If neighbors report that your dog barks or howls or runs from window to window while you are away, crate training or room training for short periods of time may be indicated. If you expect to be away for longer periods of time, put the dog in the basement or a single room where he can do the least damage. The best solution of all is to buy him another dog or cat for companionship. Let them enjoy each other while you are away and have them both welcome you home!

GERIATRICS

If you originally purchased good healthy stock and cared for your dog throughout his life, there is no reason why you cannot expect your dog to live to a ripe old age. With research and the remarkable foods produced for dogs, especially this past decade or so, his chances of longevity have increased considerably. If you have cared for him well, your dog will be a sheer delight in his old age, just as he was while in his prime.

We can assume you have fed him properly if he is not too fat. Have you ever noticed how fat people usually have fat dogs because

Shawn Duke of Avondale, C.D. pictured with owner Donna A. McKendree, McKendree Kennels, Jacksonville, Florida.

they indulge their dogs' appetite as they do their own? If there has been no great illness, then you will find that very little additional care and attention are needed to keep him well. Exercise is still essential, as is proper food, booster shots, and tender loving care.

Even if a heart condition develops, there is still no reason to believe your dog cannot live to an old age. A diet may be necessary, along with medication and limited exercise, to keep the condition under control. In the case of deafness, or partial blindness, additional care must be taken to protect the dog, but neither infirmity will in any way shorten his life. Prolonged exposure to temperature variances, overeating, excessive exercise, lack of sleep, or being housed with younger, more active dogs may take an unnecessary toll on the dog's energies and introduce serious trouble. Good judgment, periodic veterinary checkups and individual attention will keep your dog with you for many added years.

When discussing geriatrics, the question of when a dog becomes old or aged usually is asked. We have all heard the old saying that one year of a dog's life is equal to seven years in a human. This theory is strictly a matter of opinion, and must remain so, since so many outside factors enter into how quickly each individual dog "ages." Recently, a new chart was devised which is more realistically equivalent:

DOG	MAN
6 months	10 years
1 year	15 years
2 years	24 years
3 years	28 years
4 years	32 years
5 years	36 years
6 years	40 years
7 years	44 years
8 years	48 years
9 years	52 years
10 years	56 years
15 years	76 years
21 years	100 years

It must be remembered that such things as serious illnesses, poor food and housing, general neglect and poor beginnings as puppies will take their toll on a dog's general health and age him more quickly than a dog that has led a normal, healthy life. Let your veterinarian help you determine an age bracket for your dog in his later years.

While good care should prolong your dog's life, there are several "old age" disorders to be on the lookout for no matter how well he may be doing. The tendency toward obesity is the most common, but constipation is another. Aging teeth and a slowing down of the digestive processes may hinder digestion and cause constipation, just as any major change in diet can bring on diarrhea. There is also the possibility of loss or impairment of hearing or eyesight which will also tend to make the dog wary and distrustful. Other behavioral changes may result as well, such as crankiness, loss of patience and lack of interest; these are the most obvious changes. Other ailments may manifest themselves in the form of rheumatism, arthritis, tumors and warts, heart disease, kidney infections, male prostatism and female disorders. Of course, all of these require a veterinarian's checking the degree of seriousness and proper treatment.

Take care to avoid infectious diseases. When these hit the older dog, they can debilitate him to an alarming degree, leaving him open to more serious complications and a shorter life.

DOG INSURANCE

Much has been said for and against canine insurance, and much more will be said before this kind of protection for a dog becomes universal and/or practical. There has been talk of establishing a Blue Cross-type plan similar to that now existing for humans. However, the best insurance for your dog is *you*! Nothing compensates for tender, loving care. Like the insurance policies for humans, there will be a lot of fine print in the contracts revealing that the dog is not covered after all. These limited conditions usually make the acquisition of dog insurance expensive and virtually worthless.

Grandsire and grandson take a morning siesta at Westwind Kennels, Long Valley, New Jersey. Westwind Scarlet Blaze and Westwind Scarlet Jetfire were bred and are owned by Luz Holvenstot.

Verbu Christopher Oogh, U.D., owned by Virginia Hardin of North-brook, Illinois.

Blanket coverage policies for kennels or establishments which board or groom dogs can be an advantage, especially in transporting dogs to and from their premises. For the one-dog owner, however, whose dog is a constant companion, the cost for limited coverage is not necessary.

THE HIGH COST OF BURIAL

Pet cemeteries are mushrooming across the nation. Here, as with humans, the sky can be the limit for those who wish to bury their pets ceremoniously. The costs of satin-lined caskets, grave stones, flowers, etc. run the gamut of prices to match the emotions and means of the owner. This is strictly a matter of what the bereaved owner wishes to do.

IN THE EVENT OF YOUR DEATH. . .

This is a morbid thought perhaps, but ask yourself the question, "If death were to strike at this moment, what would become of my beloved dogs?"

Perhaps you are fortunate enough to have a relative, friend or spouse who could take over immediately, if only on a temporary basis. Perhaps you have already left instructions in your last will and testament for your pet's dispensation, as well as a stipend for their perpetual care.

Provide definite instructions before a disaster occurs and your dogs are carted off to the pound, or stolen by commercially minded neighbors with "resale" in mind. It is a simple thing to instruct your lawyer about your wishes in the event of sickness or death. Leave instructions as to feeding, etc., posted on your kennel room or kitchen bulletin board, or wherever your kennel records are kept. Also, tell several people what you are doing and why. If you prefer to keep such instructions private, merely place them in sealed envelopes in a known place with directions that they are to be opened only in the event of your demise. Eliminate the danger of your animals suffering in the event of an emergency that prevents your personal care of them.

KEEPING RECORDS

Whether or not you have one dog, or a kennel full of them, it is wise to keep written records. It takes only a few moments to record dates of inoculations, trips to the vet, tests for worms, etc. It can avoid confusion or mistakes, or having your dog not covered with immunization if too much time elapses between shots because you have to guess at the last shot.

Make the effort to keep all dates in writing rather than trying to commit them to memory. A rabies injection date can be a problem if you have to recall that "Fido had the shot the day Aunt Mary got back from her trip abroad, and, let's see, I guess that was around the end of June."

In an emergency, these records may prove their value if your veterinarian cannot be reached and you have to use another, or if you move and have no case history on your dog for the new veterinarian. In emergencies, you do not always think clearly or accurately, and if dates, and types of serums used, etc., are a matter of record, the veterinarian can act more quickly and with more confidence.

22. YOUR DOG, YOUR VETERINARIAN, AND YOU

The purpose of this chapter is to explain why you should never attempt to be your own veterinarian. Quite the contrary, we urge emphatically that you establish good liaison with a reputable veterinarian who will help you maintain happy, healthy dogs. Our purpose is to bring you up to date on the discoveries made in modern canine medicine and to help you work with your veterinarian by applying these new developments to your own animals.

Ch. Wamlay's Colonel, winner of Best of Breed at the first Combined Setter Specialty Show in New York City on February 7, 1960. Colonel's sire was Ch. Seaforth's Rex McDonald **ex** Wamlay's Sheherazade.

Candy K's Modeen pictured winning a 5-point major as Winners Bitch at the Orange Empire Kennel Club show under judge Roy Ayers. Handled and co-owned by Dale and Dolores Hughes, Candy Kennels, El Cajon, California.

We have provided here "thumbnail" histories of many of the most common types of diseases your dog is apt to come in contact with during his lifetime. We feel that if you know a little something about the diseases and how to recognize their symptoms, your chances of catching them in the preliminary stages will help you and your veterinarian effect a cure before a serious condition develops.

Today's dog owner is a realistic, intelligent person who learns more and more about his dog—inside and out—so that he can care for and enjoy the animal to the fullest. He uses technical terms for parts of the anatomy, has a fleeting knowledge of the miracles of surgery and is fully prepared to administer clinical care for his animals at home. This chapter is designed for study and/or reference and we hope you will use it to full advantage.

We repeat, we do *not* advocate your playing "doctor." This includes administering medication without veterinary supervision, or even doing your own inoculations. General knowledge of diseases, their symptoms and side effects will assist you in diagnosing diseases for your veterinarian. He does not expect you to be an expert, but will appreciate your efforts in getting a sick dog to him before it is too late and he cannot save its life.

ASPIRIN: A DANGER

There is a common joke about doctors telling their patients, when they telephone with a complaint, to take an aspirin, go to bed and let him know how things are in the morning! Unfortunately, that is exactly the way it turns out with a lot of dog owners who think aspirins are cureails and give them to their dogs indiscriminately. Then they call the veterinarian when the dog has an unfavorable reaction.

Aspirins are not panaceas for everything—certainly not for every dog. In an experiment, fatalities in cats treated with aspirin in one laboratory alone numbered ten out of 13 within a two-week period. Dogs' tolerance was somewhat better, as far as actual fatalities, but there was considerable evidence of ulceration in varying degrees on the stomach linings when necropsy was performed.

Aspirin has been held in the past to be almost as effective for dogs as for people when given for many of the everyday aches and pains. The fact remains, however, that medication of any kind should be administered only after veterinary consultation and a specific dosage suitable to the condition is recommended.

While aspirin is chiefly effective in reducing fever, relieving minor pains and cutting down on inflammation, the acid has been proven harmful to the stomach when given in strong doses. Only your veterinarian is qualified to determine what the dosage is, or whether it should be administered to your particular dog at all.

WHAT THE THERMOMETER CAN TELL YOU

You will notice in reading this chapter dealing with the diseases of dogs that practically everything a dog might contract in the way of sickness has basically the same set of symptoms. Loss of appetite, diarrhea, dull eyes, dull coat, warm and/or runny nose, and FEVER!

Therefore, it is most advisable to have a thermometer on hand for checking temperature. There are several inexpensive metal rectal-type thermometers that are accurate and safer than the glass variety which can be broken. This may happen either by dropping, or perhaps even breaking off in the dog because of improper insertion or an aggravated condition with the dog that makes him violently resist the injection of the thermometer. Either kind should be lubricated with Vaseline to make the insertion as easy as possible, after it has been sterilized with alcohol.

Ch. Cardinn Gorgeous George was Best Sporting dog at the 1956 Golden Gate Kennel Club show, handled by his breeder-owner, Johnny McMillan, to this win under judge Phyllis Ryan. Bernice Behrendts presents the trophy. The dog's record to this date was one Best in Show, five Sporting Groups, three Specialties and 30 Bests of Breed.

The normal temperature for a dog is 101.5° Fahrenheit, as compared to the human 98.6°. Excitement as well as illness can cause this to vary a degree or two, but any sudden or extensive rise in body temperature must be considered as cause for alarm. Your first indication will be that your dog feels unduly "warm" and this is the time to take the temperature, not when the dog becomes very ill or manifests additional serious symptoms. With a thermometer on hand, you can check temperatures quickly and perhaps prevent some illness from becoming serious.

COPROPHAGY

Perhaps the most unpleasant of all phases of dog breeding is to come up with a dog that takes to eating stool. This practice, which is referred to politely as coprophagy, is one of the unsolved mysteries in the dog world. There simply is no explanation to why some dogs do it.

However, there are several logical theories, all or any of which may be the cause. Some say nutritional deficiencies; another says that dogs inclined to gulp their food (which passes through them not entirely digested) find it still partially palatable. There is another

Ch. Crosshaven O'Hollywood Hills, Best in Show winner at the 1946 Ventura County Kennel Club show. Bred, owned and handled by Mrs. E. Cuthbertson. Trophy presented by the President of the Ventura Chamber of Commerce. The judge at this event was Charles Gilbert. Joan Ludwig photo.

theory that the preservatives used in some meat are responsible for an appealing odor that remains through the digestive process. Then again poor quality meat can be so tough and unchewable that dogs swallow it whole and it passes through them in large undigested chunks.

There are others who believe the habit is strictly psychological, the result of a nervous condition or insecurity. Others believe the dog cleans up after itself because it is afraid of being punished as it was when it made a mistake on the carpet as a puppy. Others claim boredom is the reason, or even spite. Others will tell you a dog does not want its personal odor on the premises for fear of attracting other hostile animals to itself or its home.

The most logical of all explanations and the one most veterinarians are inclined to accept is that it is a deficiency of dietary enzymes. Too much dry food can be bad and many veterinarians suggest trying meat tenderizers, monosodium glutamate, or garlic powder which gives the stool a bad odor and discourages the dog. Yeast or certain vitamins or a complete change of diet are even more often suggested. By the time you try each of the above you will probably discover that the dog has outgrown the habit anyway. However, the condition cannot be ignored if you are to enjoy your dog to the fullest.

There is no set length of time that the problem persists, and the only real cure is to walk the dog on leash, morning and night and after every meal. In other words, set up a definite eating and exercising schedule before coprophagy is an established pattern.

MASTURBATION

A source of embarrassment to many dog owners, masturbation can be eliminated with a minimum of training.

The dog which is constantly breeding anything and everything, including the leg of the piano or perhaps the leg of your favorite guest, can be broken of the habit by stopping its cause.

The over-sexed dog—if truly that is what he is—which will never be used for breeding can be castrated. The kennel stud dog can be broken of the habit by removing any furniture from his quarters or keeping him on leash and on verbal command when he is around people, or in the house where he might be tempted to breed pillows, people, etc.

Hormone imbalance may be another cause and your veterinarian may advise injections. Exercise can be of tremendous help. Keeping the dog's mind occupied by physical play when he is around people will also help relieve the situation.

Females might indulge in sexual abnormalities like masturbation during their heat cycle, or again, because of a hormone imbalance. But if they behave this way because of a more serious problem, a hysterectomy may be indicated.

Ch. Verbu Maureen, C.D., the only Irish Setter bitch to win Best of Breed at both the Combined Setter Specialty and Westminster. She was also the winner of several field trial awards. Bred and owned by Emily Schweitzer, Verbu Kennels, Dundee, Illinois.

Ch. Del Rey Saga, Best in Show at an Irish Setter Club of Southern California Specialty show under judge Lewis Starkey over an entry of 80. Left to right: owner Virginia A. Backstrom, Van Ayl Kennels, owner of Saga; judge Starkey, and Walter Tetley, the Leroy of the Gildersleeve radio program, presenting the trophy.

Best Sporting Dog and Best American Bred in Show at a Harbor Cities Kennel Club show under judge Alva Rosenberg was Margevan's Athos, owned by Mary G. Fesler of California. Photographed by Joan Ludwig.

A sharp "no!" command when you can anticipate the act, or a sharp "no!" when caught in the act will deter most dogs if you are consistent in your correction. Hitting or other physical abuse will only confuse a dog.

RABIES

The greatest fear in the dog fancy today is still the great fear it has always been—rabies!

What has always held true about this dreadful disease still holds true today. The only way rabies can be contracted is through the saliva of a rabid dog entering the bloodstream of another animal or person. There is, of course, the Pasteur treatment for rabies which is very effective. There was of late the incident of a little boy bitten by a rabid bat having survived the disease. However, the Pasteur treatment is administered immediately if there is any question of exposure. Even more than dogs being found to be rabid, we now know that the biggest carriers are bats, skunks, foxes, rabbits and other warm-blooded animals, which pass it from one to another, since they do not have the benefit of inoculation. Dogs that run free should be inoculated for protection against these animals. For city or house dogs that never leave their owner's side, it may not be as necessary.

Best in Show at the Farmington Valley Kennel Club show under judge Miss Adele S. Colgate several years ago was Ch. Kinvarra Ensign. Owned by the Kinvarra Kennels, Art Baines handling.

For many years, Great Britain, because it is an island and because of the country's strictly enforced six-month quarantine, was entirely free of rabies. But in 1969, a British officer brought back his dog from foreign duty and the dog was found to have the disease soon after being released from quarantine. There was a great uproar about it, with Britain killing off wild and domestic animals in a great scare campaign, but the quarantine is once again down to six months and things seem to have returned to a normal, sensible attitude.

Health departments in rural towns usually provide rabies inoculations free of charge. If your dog is outdoors a great deal, or exposed to other animals that are, you might wish to call the town hall and get information on the program in your area. One cannot be too cautious about this dread disease. While the number of cases diminishes each year, there are still thousands being reported and there is still the constant threat of an outbreak where animals roam free. And never forget, there is no cure.

Ch. Sir Kevin of End O'Lane, Best in Show at the 1960 Greater Lafayette Kennel Club show under judge Mrs. Anna Young. H. Martin handled for owner John Alan Goudge of Hammond, Indiana. Mr. Carl Thompson, Club president, presented the trophy.

Rabies is caused by a neurotropic virus which can be found in the saliva, brain and sometimes the blood of the warm-blooded animal afflicted. The incubation period is usually two weeks or as long as six months, which means you can be exposed to it without any visible symptoms. As we have said, while there is still no known cure, it can be controlled. It is up to every individual to help effect this control by reporting animal bites, educating the public to the dangers and symptoms and prevention of it, so that we may reduce the fatalities.

There are two kinds of rabies; one form is called "furious," and the other is referred to as "dumb." The mad dog goes through several stages of the disease. His disposition and behavior change radically and suddenly; he becomes irritable and vicious; the eating habits alter, and he rejects food for things like stones and sticks; he be-

A Tauskey portrait of Knockross O'Boy, owned by W.L. Newhall

comes exhausted and drools saliva out of his mouth almost constantly. He may hide in corners, look glassy eyed and suspicious, bite at the air as he races around snarling and attacking with his tongue hanging out. At this point paralysis sets in, starting at the throat so that he can no longer drink water though he desires it desperately; hence, the term hydrophobia is given. He begins to stagger and eventually convulse and death is imminent.

In "dumb" rabies paralysis is swift; the dog seeks dark, sheltered places and is abnormally quiet. Paralysis starts with the jaws, spreads down the body and death is quick. Contact by humans or other animals with the drool from either of these types of rabies on open skin can produce the fatal disease, so extreme haste and proper diagnosis is essential. In other words, you do not have to be bitten by a rabid dog to have the virus enter your system. An open wound or cut that comes in touch with the saliva is all that is needed.

The incubation and degree of infection can vary. You usually contract the disease faster if the wound is near the head, since the virus travels to the brain through the spinal cord. The deeper the wound, the more saliva is injected into the body, the more serious the infection. So, if bitten by a dog under any circumstances—or any warm-blooded animal for that matter—immediately wash out the wound with soap and water, bleed it profusely, and see your doctor as soon as possible.

Also, be sure to keep track of the animal that bit, if at all possible. When rabies is suspected the public health officer will need to send the animal's head away to be analyzed. If it is found to be rabies free, you will not need to undergo treatment. Otherwise, your doctor may advise that you have the Pasteur treatment, which is extremely painful. It is rather simple, however, to have the veterinarian examine a dog for rabies without having the dog sent away for positive diagnosis of the disease. A ten-day quarantine is usually all that is necessary for everyone's peace of mind.

Rabies is no respecter of age, sex or geographical location. It is found all over the world from North Pole to South Pole, and has nothing to do with the old wives' tale of dogs going mad in the hot summer months. True, there is an increase in reported cases during summer, but only because that is the time of the year for animals to roam free in good weather and during the mating season when the battle of the sexes is taking place. Inoculation and a keen eye for symptoms and bites on our dogs and other pets will help control the disease until the cure is found.

VACCINATIONS

If you are to raise a puppy, or a litter of puppies, successfully, you must adhere to a realistic and strict schedule of vaccination. Many puppyhood diseases can be fatal—all of them are debilitating.

365

The magnificent Ch. Laurel Ridge Star Rocket with handler Art Baines, photographed by Evelyn M. Shafer.

Ch. Red Dawn of Sunny Acre, Best Sporting Dog at the 1950 Muncie, Indiana Kennel Club show under judge Earl Z. Adair. Handled by Dick Cooper for owner Hayden Martin of Crown Point, Indiana.

According to the latest statistics, 98 per cent of all puppies are being inoculated after 12 weeks of age against the dread distemper, hepatitis and leptospirosis and manage to escape these horrible infections. Orphaned puppies should be vaccinated every two weeks until the age of 12 weeks. Distemper and hepatitis live-virus vaccine should be used, since they are not protected with the colostrum normally supplied to them through the mother's milk. Puppies weaned at six to seven weeks should also be inoculated repeatedly because they will no longer be receiving mother's milk. While not all will receive protection from the serum at this early age, it should be given and they should be vaccinated once again at both nine and 12 weeks of age.

Leptospirosis vaccination should be given at four months of age with thought given to booster shots if the disease is known in the area, or in the case of show dogs which are exposed on a regular basis to many dogs from far and wide. While annual boosters are in order for distemper and hepatitis, every two or three years is sufficient for leptospirosis, unless there is an outbreak in your immediate area. The cne exception should be the pregnant bitch since there is reason to believe that inoculation might cause damage to the fetus.

Strict observance of such a vaccination schedule will not only keep your dog free of these debilitating diseases, but will prevent an epidemic in your kennel, or in your locality, or to the dogs which are competing at the shows.

SNAKEBITE

As field trials and hunts and the like become more and more popular with dog enthusiasts, the incident of snakebite becomes more of a likelihood. Dogs that are kept outdoors in runs or dogs that work the fields and roam on large estates are also likely victims.

Most veterinarians carry snakebite serum, and snakebite kits are sold to dog owners for just such purpose. To catch a snakebite in time might mean the difference between life and death, and whether your area is populated with snakes or not, it behooves you to know what to do in case it happens to you or your dog.

Your primary concern should be to get to a doctor or veterinarian immediately. The victim should be kept as quiet as possible (excitement or activity spreads the venom through the body more quickly) and if possible the wound should be bled enough to clean it out before applying a tourniquet, if the bite is severe.

First of all, it must be determined if the bite is from a poisonous or non-poisonous snake. If the bite carries two horseshoe shaped pinpoints of a double row of teeth, the bite can be assumed to be non-poisonous. If the bite leaves two punctures or holes—the result of the two fangs carrying venom—the bite is very definitely poisonous and time is of the essence.

Recently, physicians have come up with an added help in the case of snakebite. A first aid treatment referred to as hypothermia, which is the application of ice to the wound to lower body temperature to a point where the venom spreads less quickly, minimizes swelling, helps prevent infection and has some influence on numbing the pain. If ice is not readily available, the bite may be soaked in ice-cold water. But even more urgent is the need to get the victim to a hospital or a veterinarian for additional treatment.

EMERGENCIES

No matter how well you run your kennel or keep an eye on an individual dog, there will almost invariably be some emergency at some time that will require quick treatment until you get the animal to the veterinarian. The first and most important thing to remember is to keep calm! You will think more clearly and your animal will need to know he can depend on you to take care of him. However, he will be frightened and you must beware of fear biting. Therefore, do not shower him with kisses and endearments at this time, no matter how

Ch. Kalarama Pagan ictured winning Best of Breed at the Goshen, New York show in 1961. Pagan as also Winners Dog at an Irish Setter of New England Specialty Show. The sire was Ch. Thenderin Nomad **ex** Seaforth's Kalarama Jody, C.D.

sympathetic you feel. Comfort him reassuringly, but keep your wits about you. Before getting him to the veterinarian try to alleviate the pain and shock.

If you can take even a minor step in this direction it will be a help toward the final cure. Listed here are a few of the emergencies which might occur and what you can do AFTER you have called the vet and told him your are coming.

BURNS

If you have been so foolish as not to turn your pot handles toward the back of the stove—for your children's sake as well as your dog's—and the dog is burned, apply ice or ice cold water and treat for shock. Electrical or chemical burns are treated the same; but with an acid or alkali burn, use, respectively, a bicarbonate of soda or vinegar solution. Check the advisability of covering the burn when you call the veterinarian.

DROWNING

Most animals love the water, but sometimes get in "over their heads." Should your dog take in too much water, hold him upside down and open his mouth so that water can empty from the lungs, then apply artificial respiration, or mouth-to-mouth resuscitation. Then treat for shock by covering him with a blanket, administering a stimulant such as coffee with sugar, and soothing him with voice and hand.

FITS AND CONVULSIONS

Prevent the dog from thrashing about and injuring himself, cover with a blanket and hold down until you can get him to the veterinarian.

FROSTBITE

There is no excuse for an animal getting frostbite if you are on your toes and care for the animal. However, should frostbite set in, thaw out the affected area slowly with a circulatory motion and stimulation. Use vaseline to help keep the skin from peeling off and/or drying out.

HEART ATTACK

Be sure the animal keeps breathing by applying artificial respiration. A mild stimulant may be used and give him plenty of air. Treat for shock as well, and get to the veterinarian quickly.

Westwind Scarlet Winterfire, sired by Ch. Titian Intrepid **ex** Ch. Knockross Sally. Bred and owned by Luz Holvenstot, Westwind Kennels, Long Valley, New Jersey.

SUFFOCATION

Artificial respiration and treat for shock with plenty of air.

SUN STROKE

Cooling the dog off immediately is essential. Ice packs, submersion in ice water, and plenty of cool air are needed.

WOUNDS

Open wounds or cuts which produce bleeding must be treated with hydrogen peroxide and tourniquets should be used if bleeding is excessive. Also, shock treatment must be given, and the animal must be kept warm.

Ch. Headliner The Flaming Beauty, owned by the Hon. Katharine St. George and Mrs. Priscilla Ryan, wins Best in Show at the 1962 Champaign, Illinois Kennel Club show under the late judge Alva Rosenberg; Jack Funk handling. Mr. George Curzon, president of the Club, completes the picture.

THE FIRST AID KIT

It would be sheer folly to try to operate a kennel or to keep a dog without providing for certain emergencies that are bound to crop up when there are active dogs around. Just as you would provide a first aid kit for people you should also provide a first aid kit for the animals on the premises.

The first aid kit should contains the following items:

> BFI or other medicated powder
> jar of Vaseline
> Q-tips
> bandage—1 inch gauze
> adhesive tape
> Band-Aids
> cotton
> boric acid powder

First in the Sporting Group at the 1953 Westchester Kennel Club show was Ch. Kinvarra Deacon Malone, owned and handled by James Taylor. This win was made under judge Virgil D. Johnson.

A trip to your veterinarian is always safest, but there are certain preliminaries for cuts and bruises of a minor nature that you can care for yourself.

Cuts, for instance, should be washed out and medicated powder or Vaseline applied with a bandage. The lighter the bandage the better so that the most air possible can reach the wound. Q-tips can be used for removing debris from the eyes after which a mild solution of boric acid wash can be applied. As for sores, use dry powder on wet sores, and Vaseline on dry sores. Use cotton for washing out wounds and drying them.

A particular caution must be given here on bandaging. Make sure that the bandage is not too tight to hamper the dog's circulation. Also, make sure the bandage is made correctly so that the dog does not bite at it trying to get it off. A great deal of damage can be done to a wound by a dog tearing at a bandage to get it off. If you notice the dog is starting to bite at it, do it over or put something on the bandage that smells and tastes bad to him. Make sure, however, that the solution does not soak through the bandage and enter the wound. Sometimes, if it is a leg wound, a sock or stocking slipped on the dog's leg will cover the bandage edges and will also keep it clean.

HOW NOT TO POISON YOUR DOG

Ever since the appearance of Rachel Carson's book *Silent Spring,* people have been asking, "Just how dangerous are chemicals?" In the animal world where disinfectants, room deodorants, parasitic sprays, solutions and aerosols are so widely used, the question has taken on even more meaning. Veterinarians are beginning to ask, "What kind of disinfectant do you use?" or "Have you any fruit trees that have been sprayed recently?" When animals are brought in to their offices in a toxic condition, or for unexplained death, or when entire litters of puppies die mysteriously, there is good reason to ask such questions.

The popular practice of protecting animals against parasites has given way to their being exposed to an alarming number of commercial products, some of which are dangerous to their very lives. Even flea collars can be dangerous, especially if they get wet or somehow touch the genital regions or eyes. While some products are a great deal more poisonous than others, great care must be taken that they be applied in proportion to the size of the dog and the area to be covered. Many a dog has been taken to the vet with an unusual skin problem that was a direct result of having been bathed with a detergent rather than a proper shampoo. Certain products that are safe for dogs can be fatal for cats. Extreme care must be taken to read all ingredients and instructions carefully before use on any animal.

The same caution must be given to outdoor chemicals. Dog owners must question the use of fertilizers on their lawns. Lime, for in-

Ch. Margevans Real McCoy, owned by William J. Robb of San Francisco, winning Best in Show at the 1952 San Joaquin Kennel Club show in Stockton, California. Judge was Hessie Ballantine; the handler is Jim McManus.

stance, can be harmful to a dog's feet. The unleashed dog that covers the neighborhood on his daily rounds is open to all sorts of tree and lawn sprays and insecticides that may prove harmful to him, if not as a poison, as a producer of an allergy. Many puppy fatalities are reported when they consume mothballs.

There are various products found around the house which can be lethal, such as rat poison, boric acid, hand soap, detergents, and insecticides. The garage too may provide dangers: antifreeze for the car, lawn, garden and tree sprays, paints, etc., are all available for tipping over and consuming. All poisons should be placed on high shelves for the sake of your children as well as your animals.

Perhaps the most readily available of all household poisons are plants. Household plants are almost all poisonous, even if taken in small quantities. Some of the most dangerous are the elephant ear, the narcissus bulb, any kind of ivy leaves, burning bush leaves, the jimson weed, the dumb cane weed, mock orange fruit, castor beans, Scotch broom seeds, the root or seed of the plant called four o'clock, cyclamen, pimpernel, lily of the valley, the stem of the sweet pea, rhododendrons of any kind, spider lily bulbs, bayonet root, foxglove leaves, tulip bulbs, monkshood roots, azalea, wisteria, poinsettia leaves, mistletoe, hemlock, locoweed and arrowglove. In all, there are over 500 poisonous plants in the United States. Peach, elderberry and cherry trees can cause cyanide poisoning if the bark is consumed. Rhubarb leaves either raw or cooked can cause death or violent convulsions. Check out your closets, fields and grounds around your home to see what might be of danger to your pets.

Ch. Muffin of Sunnymeath pictured here winning at the May, 1969 Windham County Kennel Club show under the late Hollis Wilson. Handled by owner Mrs. Marion B. Neville, Red Barn Kennels, Blauvelt, New York. Shafer photo.

KEOMAH
KENNEL CLU[...]
OCTOBER 10
BEST IN
SHOW

Ch. Hollywood Hills Honor, Best in Show at a 1960 Canadian dog show. The judge was Mr. G. Davis; Laurence Garvic presents the trophy. Owner-handled by Thomas G. Threlkeld of Halifax, Nova Scotia.

#4 Sporting Dog in the nation in 1964 was Ch. Cherry Point Brask, Best in Show winner and sire of 12 champion offspring. His sire was Ch. Thenderin Brian Tristan **ex** Ch. End O'Maine Encore. Owned by Mrs. Cheever Porter of New York City, Brask was whelped November 2, 1958.

Best in Show at the 1965 Keomah Kennel Club show was Virginia Hardin's Ch. Runwild Finnagain, handled by Dick Cooper. Photo by Ritter.

Sporting Group winner at a Westchester Kennel Club show was Ch. Shawnlea's Fanfare, owned by May H. Hanley and shown by Robert Forsyth to this important win under judge Joseph Quirk. Fanfare was later owned by Mrs. Cheever Porter of New York City.

SYMPTOMS OF POISONING

Be on the lookout for vomiting, hard or labored breathing, whimpering, stomach cramps, and trembling as a prelude to the convulsions. Any delay in a visit to your veterinarian can mean death. Take along the bottle or package or a sample of the plant you suspect to be the cause to help the veterinarian determine the correct antidote.

The most common type of poisoning, which accounts for nearly one-fourth of all animal victims, is staphylococcic-infected food. Salmonella ranks third. These can be avoided by serving fresh food and not letting it lie around in hot weather.

There are also many insect poisonings caused by animals eating cockroaches, spiders, flies, butterflies, etc. Toads and some frogs give off a fluid which can make a dog foam at the mouth—and even kill him—if he bites just a little too hard!

Some misguided dog owners think it is "cute" to let their dogs enjoy a cocktail with them before dinner. There can be serious effects resulting from encouraging a dog to drink—sneezing fits, injuries as a result of intoxication, and heart stoppage are just a few. Whiskey for medicinal purposes, or beer for brood bitches should be administered only on the advice of your veterinarian.

There have been cases of severe damage and death when dogs emptied ash trays and consumed cigarettes, resulting in nicotine poisoning. Leaving a dog alone all day in a house where there are cigarettes available on a coffee table is asking for trouble. Needless to say, the same applies to marijuana. The narcotic addict who takes his dog along with him on "a trip" does not deserve to have a dog. All the ghastly side effects are as possible for the dog as for the addict, and for a person to submit an animal to this indignity is indeed despicable. Don't think it doesn't happen. Ask the veterinarians that practice near some of your major hippie havens! Unfortunately, in all our major cities the practice is becoming more and more a problem for the veterinarian.

Be on the alert and remember that in the case of any type of poisoning, the best treatment is prevention.

Best in Show at the 1959 all-breed Duluth Kennel Club show was Ch. Wautoma, owned by Mrs. Cheever Porter of New York City. Colonel Edward D. McQuown was the judge at this event. Handler was famous Irish Setter man Hollis Wilson. Mrs. J.E. Brown, club president, completes the picture. Yoho photograph.

THE CURSE OF ALLERGY

The heartbreak of a child being forced to give up a beloved pet because he is suddenly found to be allergic to it is a sad but true story. Many families claim to be unable to have dogs at all; others seem to be able only to enjoy them on a restricted basis. Many children know animals only through occasional visits to a friend's house or the zoo.

While modern veterinary science has produced some brilliant allergists, such as Dr. Edward Baker of New Jersey, the field is still working on a solution for those who suffer from exposure to their pets. There is no permanent cure as yet.

Over the last quarter of a century there have been many attempts at a permanent cure, but none has proven successful, because the treatment was needed too frequently, or was too expensive to maintain over extended periods of time.

Luz Holvenstot and her Westwind Scarlet Royal Blaze make a beautiful picture as they pose near their Westwind Kennel in Long Valley, New Jersey.

However, we find that most people who are allergic to their animals are also allergic to a variety of other things as well. By eliminating the other irritants, and by taking medication given for the control of allergies in general, many are able to keep pets on a restricted basis. This may necessitate the dog's living outside the house, being groomed at a professional grooming parlor instead of by the owner, or merely being kept out of the bedroom at night. A discussion of this "balance" factor with your medical and veterinary doctors may give new hope to those willing to try.

A paper presented by Mathilde M. Gould, M.D., a New York allergist, before the American Academy of Allergists in the 1960's, and reported in the September-October 1964 issue of the *National Humane Review* magazine, offered new hope to those who are allergic by a method referred to as hyposensitization. You may wish to write to the magazine and request the article for discussion with your medical and veterinary doctors on your individual problem.

Ch. Fleetwood Farms Sixty Special, pictured winning at the January 1962 Jacksonville Dog Fanciers Association show, with handler Charley Meyer. The judge was Haskell Schuffman. Owners are Hugh and Virginia Rumbaugh, Fleetwood Farms, Akron, Ohio.

English Best in Show winning puppy at 7 months of age was Dallinghoo Ebenezer, whelped in 1972 and owned by Mrs. C.M. Girling of Beds., England. Sired by Margretwoods Caretaker **ex** Dallinghoo Candida.

Canadian Ch. Red Echo of Ardee pointing pheasants. This dog is the sire of a number of field trial winners.

English show dog Dallinghoo Jethro, born in 1974, is pictured here at three months of age. The sire was Margretwoods Caretaker **ex** Dallinghoo Candida. Owned and bred by Mrs. C.M. Girling, Dallinghoo Kennels, Beds., England.

Best Sporting Dog at the 1956 Westchester Kennel Club show was Ch. Dunguaire Bryson. Owned by Dr. Jack H. Skelsie of East Longmeadow, Massachusetts, he is handled by Mrs. Audrey Baines to this win under judge Paul Palmer.

DO ALL DOGS CHEW?

All young dogs chew! Chewing is the best possible method of cutting teeth and exercising gums. Every puppy goes through this teething process. True, it can be destructive if not watched carefully, and it is really the responsibility of every owner to prevent the damage before it occurs.

When you see a puppy pick up an object to chew, immediately remove it from his mouth with a sharp "No!" and replace the object with a Nylon or rawhide bone which should be provided for him to do his serious chewing. Puppies take anything and everything into their mouths so they should be provided with proper toys which they cannot chew up and swallow.

BONES

There are many opinions on the kind of bones a dog should have. Anyone who has lost a puppy or dog because of a bone chip puncturing the stomach or intestinal wall will say "no bones" except for the

Nylon or rawhide kind you buy in pet shops. There are those who say shank or knuckle bones are permissible. Use your own judgment, but when there are adequate processed bones which you know to be safe, why risk a valuable animal? Cooked bones, soft enough to be pulverized and put in the food can be fed if they are reduced almost to a powder. If you have the patience for this sort of thing, okay. Otherwise, stick to the commercial products.

As for dogs and puppies chewing furniture, shoes, etc., replace the object with something allowable and safe and put yourself on record as remembering to close closet doors. Keep the puppy in the same room with you so you can stand guard over the furniture.

Electrical cords and sockets, or wires of any kind, present a dangerous threat to chewers. Glass dishes which can be broken are hazardous if not picked up right after feeding.

Chewing can also be a form of frustration or nervousness. Dogs sometimes chew for spite, if owners leave them alone too long or too often. Bitches will sometimes chew if their puppies are taken away from them too soon; insecure puppies often chew thinking they're nursing. Puppies which chew wool or blankets or carpet corners or certain types of materials may have a nutritional deficiency or something lacking in their diet, such as craving the starch that might be left in material after washing. Perhaps the articles have been near something that tastes good and they retain the odor.

The act of chewing has no connection with particular breeds or ages, any more than there is a logical reason for dogs to dig holes outdoors or dig on wooden floors indoors.

So we repeat, it is up to you to be on guard at all times until the need—or habit—passes.

HIP DYSPLASIA

Hip dysplasia, or HD, is one of the most widely discussed of all animal afflictions, since it has appeared in varying degrees in just about every breed of dog. True, the larger breeds seem most susceptible, but it has hit the small breeds and is beginning to be recognized in cats as well.

While HD in man has been recorded as far back as 370 B.C., HD in dogs was more than likely referred to as rheumatism until veterinary research came into the picture. In 1935, Dr. Otto Schales, at Angell Memorial Hospital in Boston, wrote a paper on hip dysplasia and classified the four degrees of dysplasia of the hip joint as follows:

Grade 1—slight (poor fit between ball and socket)

Grade 2—moderate (moderate but obvious shallowness of the socket)

Grade 3—severe (socket quite flat)

Grade 4—very severe (complete displacement of head of femur at early age)

HD is an incurable, hereditary, though not congenital disease of the hip sockets. It is transmitted as a dominant trait with irregular manifestations. Puppies appear normal at birth but the constant wearing away of the socket means the animal moves more and more on muscle, thereby presenting a lameness, a difficulty in getting up and severe pain in advanced cases.

The degree of severity can be determined around six months of age, but its presence can be noticed from two months of age. The problem is determined by X-ray, and if pain is present it can be relieved temporarily by medication. Exercise should be avoided since motion encourages the wearing away of the bone surfaces.

Dogs with HD should not be shown or bred, if quality in the breed is to be maintained. It is essential to check a pedigree for dogs known to be dysplastic before breeding, since this disease can be dormant for many generations.

ELBOW DYSPLASIA

The same condition can also affect the elbow joints and is known as elbow dysplasia. This also causes lameness, and dogs so affected should not be used for breeding.

PATELLAR DYSPLASIA

Some of the smaller breeds of dogs also suffer from patella dysplasia, or dislocation of the knee. This can be treated surgically, but the surgery by no means abolishes the hereditary factor. Therefore, these dogs should not be used for breeding.

All dogs—in any breed—should be X-rayed before being used for breeding. The X-ray should be read by a competent veterinarian, and the dog declared free and clear.

HD PROGRAM IN GREAT BRITAIN

The British Veterinary Association (BVA) has made an attempt to control the spread of HD by appointing a panel of members of their profession who have made a special study of the disease to read X-rays. Dogs over one year of age may be X-rayed and certified as free. Forms are completed in triplicate to verify the tests. One copy remains with the panel, one copy is for the owner's veterinarian, and one for the owner. A record is also sent to the British Kennel Club for those wishing to check on a particular dog for breeding purposes.

THE UNITED STATES REGISTRY

In the United States we have a central Hip Dysplasia Foundation, known as the OFA (Orthopedic Foundation for Animals). This HD control registry was formed in 1966. X-rays are sent for expert evaluation by qualified radiologists.

Ch. Webline Free N Easy pictured winning a 1973 Specialty Show under judge Kurt Mueller. Easy was bred and owned by Mr. and Mrs. C.R. Webb, Webline Kennels, El Monte, California, and handled by Dick Webb.

All you need do for complete information on getting an X-ray for your dog is to write to the Orthopedic Foundation for Animals at 817 Virginia Ave., Columbia, Mo., 65201, and request their dysplasia packet. There is no charge for this kit. It contains an envelope large enough to hold your X-ray film (which you will have taken by your own veterinarian), and a drawing showing how to position the dog properly for X-ray. There is also an application card for proper identification of the dog. Then, hopefully, your dog will be certified "normal." You will be given a registry number which you can put on his pedigree, use in your advertising, and rest assured your breeding program is in good order.

All X-rays should be sent to the address above. Any other information you might wish to have may be requested from Mrs. Robert Bower, OFA, Route 1, Constantine, Mo., 49042.

We cannot urge strongly enough the importance of doing this. While it involves time and effort, the reward in the long run will more than pay for your trouble. To see the heartbreak of parents and children when their beloved dog has to be put to sleep because of severe hip dysplasia as the result of bad breeding is a sad experience. Don't let this happen to your or to those who will purchase your puppies!

Additionally, we should mention that there is a method of palpation to determine the extent of affliction. This can be painful if the animal is not properly prepared for the examination. There have also been attempts to replace the animal's femur and socket. This is not only expensive, but the percentage of success is small.

For those who refuse to put their dog down, there is a new surgical technique which can relieve pain, but in no way constitutes a cure. This technique involves the severing of the pectinius muscle which for some unknown reason brings relief from pain over a period of many months—even up to two years. Two veterinary colleges in the United States are performing this operation at the present time. However, the owner must also give permission to "de-sex" the dogs at the time of the muscle severance. This is a safety measure to help stamp out hip dysplasia, since obviously the condition itself remains and can be passed on.

23. THE BLIGHT OF PARASITES

Anyone who has ever spent countless hours peering down intently at his dog's warm, pink stomach waiting for a flea to appear will readily understand why we call this chapter the "blight of parasites." For it is that dreaded onslaught of the pesky flea that heralds the subsequent arrival of worms.

If you have seen even one flea scoot across that vulnerable expanse of skin you can be sure there are more fleas lurking on other favorite areas of your dog. They seldom travel alone. So it is now an established fact that *la puce*, as the French would say when referring to the flea, has set up housekeeping on your dog and it is going to demand a great deal of your time before you manage to evict them completely, and probably just temporarily, no matter which species your dog is harboring.

Fleas are not always choosy about their host, but chances are your dog has what is commonly known as *Ctenocephalides canis*, the dog flea. If you are a lover of cats also, your dog might even be playing host to a few *Ctenocephalides felis*, the cat flea, or vice versa! The only thing you can be really sure of is that your dog is supporting an entire community of them, all hungry and all sexually oriented, and you are going to have to be persistent in your campaign to get rid of them.

One of the chief reasons they are so difficult to catch is that what they lack in beauty and eyesight (they are blind at birth, throughout infancy and see very poorly or are blind during adulthood,) they make up for in their fantastic ability to jump and scurry about.

While this remarkable ability to jump—some say 150 times the length of their bodies—stands them in good stead with circus entrepeneurs and has given them claim to fame as chariot pullers and acrobats in side show attractions, the dog owner can be reduced to tears at the very thought of the onset of fleas.

Modern research has provided a remedy in the form of flea sprays, dips, collars and tags which can be successful in varying degrees. But there are those who swear by the good old-fashioned methods of removing them by hand, which can be a challenge to your sanity as well as your dexterity.

Ch. McKendrees Bold Venture, pictured winning Best in Show at a Central Florida Kennel Club show under judge James Culp. Venture is a product of four generations of home-bred winners for the McKendree Kennels of Harold and Norma McKendree of Jacksonville, Florida. Stanley, as he is called, finished his championship in April, 1974 by going Best of Breed and 3rd in the Group from the classes with an entry of 117 Irish Setters. In addition to his other wins, he was Best of Breed at the 1975 Westminster Kennel Club show, handled by the McKendree's 19-year-old daughter Jan, pictured with him above.

Since the fleas' conformation (they are built like envelopes, long and flat) with their spiny skeletal system on the outside of their bodies is specifically provided for slithering through hair forests, they are given a distinct advantage to start with. Two antennae on the head select the best spot for digging and then two mandibles penetrate the skin and hit a blood vessel. It is also at this moment that the flea brings into play his spiny contours to prop himself against a few surrounding hairs which prevent him from being scratched off as he puts the bite on your dog. A small tubular tongue is then lowered into the hole to draw out blood and another tube is injected into the hole to pump the saliva of the flea into the wound which prevents the blood from clotting. This allows the flea to drink freely. Simultaneously your dog jumps into the air and gets one of those back legs into action scratching endlessly and in vain.

Now while you may catch an itinerant flea as he mistakenly shortcuts across your dog's stomach, the best hunting grounds are usually in the deep fur down along the dog's back from neck to the base of the tail. However, the flea like every other creature on earth must have water, so several times during its residency it will make its way to the moister areas of your dog, such as the corners of the mouth, the eyes or the genital areas. This is when the flea collars and tags are useful. The fumes from them prevent the fleas from passing the neck to get to the head of your dog.

Your dog can usually support several generations of fleas if he doesn't scratch himself to death or go out of his mind with the itching in the interim. The population of the flea is insured by the strong mating instinct and the wise personal decision of the female flea as to the best time to deposit her eggs. She has the useful capacity to store semen until the time is right to lay the eggs after some previous brief encounter with a passing member of the opposite sex.

When that time comes for her to lay the eggs, she does so without so much as a backward glance and moves on. The dog, during a normal day's wandering, shakes the eggs off along his way, and there the eggs remain until hatched and the baby fleas are ready to jump back on a dog. If any of the eggs remain on the dog, chances are your dog will help them emerge from their shells with his scratching when some adult flea passes in the vicinity.

Larval fleas look like very small and slender maggots; they begin their lives feasting off their own egg shells until your dog comes along and offers the return to the world of adult fleas, whose excrement provides the predigested blood pellets they must have to thrive. They cannot survive on fresh blood, nor are they capable at this tender age of digging for it themselves. We are certain that the expression "two can eat as cheaply as one" originated after some curious scientist made a detailed study of the life cycle of the flea.

After a couple of weeks of this free loading, the baby flea makes his own cocoon and becomes a pupa. This stage lasts long enough for the larval flea to grow legs, mandibles, and sharp spines and to flatten out and in general get to be identifiable as the commonly known and obnoxious *Ctenocephalides canis*. The process can take several weeks or several months, depending on weather conditions, heat, moisture, etc., but generally three weeks is all that is required to enable it to start chomping on your dog in its own right.

And so the life of the flea is renewed and begun again, and if you don't have plans to stem the tide, you will certainly see a population explosion that will make the human one resemble an endangered species. Getting rid of fleas can be accomplished by the aforementioned spraying of the dog, or the flea collars and tags, but air, sunshine and a good shaking out of beds, bedding, carpets, cushions, etc., certainly must be undertaken to get rid of the eggs or larvae lying around the premises.

However, if you love the thrill of the chase, and have the stomach for it, you can still try to catch them on safari across your dog's stomach. Your dog will love the attention, that is, if you don't keep pinching a bit of skin instead of that little blackish critter. Chances are

Ch. Suffield's Hiawatha, the Irish Setter bitch which can boast the amazing bench show record of 37 championship points at 22 American Kennel Club shows in 5 different states under 11 different judges. She was 11 times Best of Winners and 3 times Best of Breed as well as Best of Winners and Best of Opposite Sex at the largest Irish Setter benching in the United States. Owned by J. Allen Clark of Glen Falls, New York.

Ch. Carrvales Terry Terhune, owned by the Tarawil Kennels in Palatine, Illinois, wins Best of Breed at the Western Irish Setter Club show
in Chicago during the 1950's under judge Major Bryant Godsol. Hollis
Wilson handles for owners.

great you will come up with skin rather than the flea and your dog
will lose interest and patience.

Should you be lucky enough to get hold of one, you must either
squeeze it to death (which isn't likely) or break it in two with a sharp,
strong fingernail (which also isn't likely) or you must release it
underwater in the toilet bowl and flush immediately. This prospect is
only slightly more likely. We strongly suggest that you shape up,
clean up, shake out and spray—on a regular basis.

There are those people, however, who are much more philosophi-
cal about the flea, since, like the cockroach, it has been around since
the beginning of the world. For instance, that old-time philosopher,
David Harum, who has been much quoted with his remark, "A reasonable amount of fleas is good for a dog. They keep him from broodin'
on bein' a dog." We would rather agree with John Donne who in his
Devotions reveals that, "The flea, though he kill none, he does all the
harm he can." This is especially true if your dog is a show dog! If the
scratching doesn't ruin the coat, the inevitable infestations of the parasites the fleas will leave with your dog will!

So we readily see that dogs can be afflicted by both internal and
external parasites. The external parasites are known as the aforementioned fleas, plus ticks and lice; while all of these are bothersome, they can be treated. However, the internal parasites, or worms
of various kinds, are usually well-infested before discovery and require more substantial means of ridding the dog of them completely.

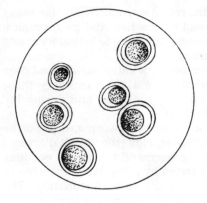

**Round Worm
(Ascarid)**

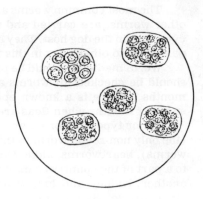

Tapeworm

Hookworm

Whipworm

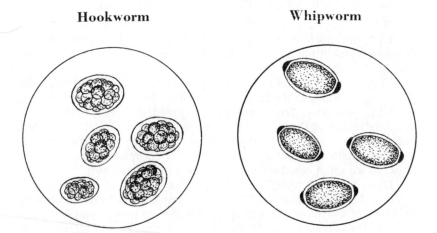

Eggs of certain parasites commonly seen in dogs.

INTERNAL PARASITES

The most common worms are the round worms. These, like many other worms, are carried and spread by the flea and go through a cycle within the dog host. They are excreted in egg or larval form and passed on to other dogs in this manner.

Worm medicine should be prescribed by a veterinarian, and dogs should be checked for worms at least twice a year, or every three months if there is a known epidemic in your area, and during the summer months when fleas are plentiful.

Major types of worms are hookworms, whipworms, tapeworms (the only non-round worm in this list), ascarids (the "typical" round worms), heartworms, kidney and lung worms. Each can be peculiar to a part of the country or may be carried by a dog from one area to another. Kidney and lung worms are quite rare, fortunately. The others are not. Symptoms for worms might be vomiting intermittently, eating grass, lack of pep, bloated stomach, rubbing their tail along the ground, loss of weight, dull coat, anemia and pale gums, eye discharge, or unexplained nervousness and irritability. A dog with worms will usually eat twice as much as he normally would also.

Never worm a sick dog, or a pregnant bitch after the first two weeks she has been bred, and never worm a constipated dog. . . it will retain the strong medicine within the body for too long a time. The best, safest way to determine the presence of worms is to test for them before they do excessive damage.

HOW TO TEST FOR WORMS

Worms can kill your dog if the infestation is severe enough. Even light infestations of worms can debilitate a dog to the point where he is more susceptible to other serious diseases that can kill, if the worms do not.

Today's medication for worming is relatively safe and mild, and worming is no longer the traumatic experience for either dog or owner that it used to be. Great care must be given, however, to the proper administration of the drugs. Correct dosage is a "must" and clean quarters are essential to rid your kennel of these parasites. It is almost impossible to find an animal that is completely free of parasites, so we must consider worming as a necessary evil.

However mild today's medicines may be, it is inadvisable to worm a dog unnecessarily. There are simple tests to determine the presence of worms and this chapter is designed to help you learn how to make these tests yourself. Veterinarians charge a nominal fee for this service, if it is not part of their regular office visit examination. It is a simple matter to prepare fecal slides that you can read yourself on a periodic basis. Over the years it will save you much time and money, especially if you have more than one dog or a large kennel.

All that is needed by way of equipment is a microscope with 100x power. These can be purchased in the toy department in a department or regular toy store for a few dollars, depending on what else you want to get with it, but the basic, least expensive sets come with the necessary glass slides and attachments.

After the dog has defecated, take an applicator stick, or a toothpick with a flat end, or even an old-fashioned wooden matchstick, and gouge off a piece of the stool about the size of a small pea. Have one of the glass slides ready with a large drop of water on it. Mix the two together until you have a cloudy film over a large area of the slide. This smear should be covered with another slide, or a cover slip—though it is possible to obtain readings with just the one open slide. Place your slide under the microscope and prepare to focus in on it. To read the slide you will find that your eye should follow a certain pattern. Start at the top and read from left to right, then right back to the left side and then left over to the right side once again until you have looked at every portion of the slide from the top left to the bottom right side, as illustrated here:

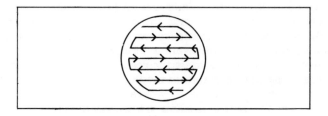

Make sure that your smear is not too thick or watery or the reading will be too dark and confused to make proper identification. Included in this chapter are drawings which will show you what to look for when reading the slides to identify the four most common varieties of worms. If you decide you would rather not make your own fecal examinations, but would prefer to have the veterinarian do it, the proper way to present a segment of the stool for him to examine is as follows:

After the dog has defecated, a portion of the stool, say a square inch from different sections of it, should be placed in a glass jar or plastic container, and labeled with the dog's name and address of the owner. If the sample cannot be examined within three to four hours after passage, it should be refrigerated. Your opinion as to what variety of worms you suspect is sometimes helpful to the veterinarian and may be noted on the label of the jar you submit to him for the examination.

Checking for worms on a regular basis is advisable not only for the welfare of the dog but for the protection of your family, since most worms are transmissible, under certain circumstances, to humans.

24. DICTIONARY OF DOG DISEASES

AN AID TO DIAGNOSIS

—A—

ABORTION—The premature expulsion of embryos from the uterus. If part of a fetus is left in the uterus, serious infection may occur. The first indication of this will be high fever, dry nose and lethargy. The immediate services of a veterinarian are necessary.

ABSCESS—A skin eruption characterized by a localized collection of pus formed as a result of disintegrating tissues of the body. Abscesses may be acute or chronic. An acute abscess forms rapidly and will more than likely burst within a week. It is accompanied by pain, redness, heat and swelling, and may cause a rise in temperature. An abscess is usually the result of infection of a bacterial nature. Treatment consists of medication in the form of antibiotics and salves, ointments, powders or a poultice designed to bring it to a head. A chronic abscess is a slow-developing headless lump surrounded by gathering tissue. This infection is usually of internal origin, and painless unless found in a sensitive area of the body. The same antibiotics and medications are used. Because abscesses of this nature are slow in developing, they are generally slow in dissolving.

ACARUS—One of the parasitic mites which cause mange.

ACHONDROPLASIA—A disease which results in the stunting of growth, or dwarfing of the limbs before birth.

ADENOMA—A non-inflammatory growth or benign tumor found in a prominent gland; most commonly found in the mammary gland of the bitch.

AGALACTIA—A contagious, viral disease resulting in lowered or no production of milk by a nursing bitch. It usually appears in warm weather, and is accompanied by fever and loss of appetite. Abscesses may also form. In chronic cases the mammary gland itself may atrophy.

ALARIASIS—An infection caused by flukes (*Alaria arisaemoides*), which are ingested by the dog. They pass on to the bronchial tract and into the small intestine where they grow to maturity and feed on intestinal contents.

Hugh and Virginia Rumbaugh's glorious Ch. Starheir's Aaron Ardee, who defeated over 68,000 competitors of all breeds to amass his show record. Handled by Dick Cooper, Aaron has been a top contender in the Irish Setter breed for several years. He is pictured here winning a Group First in 1973 under judge Henry Stoecker.

Ch. Glendee's Bourbon on the Rocks, Irish Setter owned by Mr. and Mrs. Thorne D. Harris, pictured winning Best in Show at the 1970 Huntsville, Alabama, Kennel Club show. Handled by Mrs. Harris, the judge was Herman Cox. Presenting the trophy is club president Harvey J. Eastman, Jr. Earl Graham photo.

ALLERGY—Dogs can be allergic as well as people to outdoor or indoor surroundings, such as carpet fuzz, pillow stuffings, food, pollen, etc. Recent experiments in hyposensitization have proved effective in many cases when injections are given with follow-up "boosters." Sneezing, coughing, nasal discharges, runny, watery eyes, etc., are all symptomatic.

ALOPECIA—A bare spot, or lack of full growth of hair on a portion of the body; another name for baldness and can be the end result of a skin condition.

AMAUROSIS—Sometimes called "glass eye." A condition that may occur during a case of distemper if the nervous system has been affected, or head injuries sustained. It is characterized by the animal bumping into things or by a lack of coordination. The condition is incurable and sooner or later the optic nerve becomes completely paralyzed.

ANALGESIA—Loss of ability to feel pain with the loss of consciousness or the power to move a part of the body. The condition may be induced by drugs which act on the brain or central nervous system.

ANAL SAC OBSTRUCTION—The sacs on either side of the rectum, just inside the anus, at times may become clogged. If the condition persists, it is necessary for the animal to be assisted in their opening, so that they do not become infected and/or abscess. Pressure is applied by the veterinarian and the glands release a thick, horrible-smelling excretion. Antibiotics or a "flushing" of the glands if infected is the usual treatment, but at the first sign of discomfort in the dog's eliminating, or a "sliding along" the floor, it is wise to check for clogged anal glands.

ANASARCA—Dropsy of the connective tissues of the skin. It is occasionally encountered in fetuses and makes whelping difficult.

ANEMIA—A decrease of red blood cells which are the cells that carry oxygen to the body tissues. Causes are usually severe infestation of parasites, bad diet, or blood disease. Transfusions and medications can be given to replace red blood cells, but the disease is sometimes fatal.

ANEURYSM—A rupture or dilation of a major blood vessel, causing a bulge or swelling of the affected part. Blood gathers in the tissues forming a swelling. It may be caused by strain, injury, or when arteries are weakened by debilitating disease or old age. Surgery is needed to remove the clot.

ANESTROUS—When a female does not come into heat.

ANTIPERISTALSIS—A term given to the reverse action of the normal procedures of the stomach or intestine, which brings their contents closer to the mouth.

ANTIPYRETICS—Drugs or methods used to reduce temperature during fevers. These may take the form of cold baths, purgatives, etc.

ANTISPASMODICS—Medications which reduce spasms of the muscular tissues and soothe the nerves and muscles involved.

ANTISIALICS—Term applied to substances used to reduce excessive salivation.

ARSENIC POISONING—Dogs are particularly susceptible to this type of poisoning. There is nausea, vomiting, stomach pains and convulsions, even death in severe cases. An emetic may save the animal in some cases. Salt or dry mustard (1 tablespoon mixed with 1 teaspoonful of water) can be effective in causing vomiting until the veterinarian is reached.

Ch. Tirvelda's Hunter's Moon and owner Celeste Gavin in a setting appropriate to the breed.

Ch. Riley of Woolridge, owned by Paul A. Saucier, wins Best in Show at the 1960 Mid-Kentucky Kennel Club show under judge Dr. Frederick D. Rutherford. The handler is Paul A Saucier; club president Jack Jahr presents the trophy.

American and Canadian Ch. Mid'Oak's Kelly, pictured winning at a recent show with handler Pat Tripp. Kelly is owned by Dale and Ruth Jones who own the Dajos Kennels in Puyallup, Washington.

ARTHRITIS—A painful condition of the joints which results in irritation and inflammation. A disease that pretty much confines itself to older dogs, especially in the larger breeds. Limping, irritability and pain are symptomatic. Anti-inflammatory drugs are effective after X-ray determines the severity. Heat and rest are helpful.

ASCITES—A collection of serous fluid in the abdominal cavity, causing swelling. It may be a result of heavy parasitic infestation or a symptom of liver, kidney, tuberculosis or heart diseases.

ASPERGILLOSIS—A disease contracted from poultry and often mistaken for tuberculosis since symptoms are quite similar. It attacks the nervous system and sometimes has disastrous effects on the respiratory system. This fungus growth in the body tissue spreads quickly and is accompanied by convulsions. The dog rubs his nose and there is a bloody discharge.

ASTHMA—Acute distress in breathing. Attacks may occur suddenly at irregular intervals and last as long as half an hour. The condition may be hereditary or due to allergy or heart condition. Antihistamines are effective in minor attacks.

ATAXIA—Muscular incoordination or lack of movement causing an inhibited gait, although the necessary organs and muscle power are coherent. The dog may have a tendency to stagger.

ATOPY—Manifestations of atopy in the dog are a persistent scratching of the eyes and nose. Onsets are usually seasonal—the dog allergic to, say, ragweed will develop the condition when ragweed is in season, or say, house dust all year round. Most dogs afflicted with atopy are multi-sensitive and are affected by something several months out of the year. Treatment is by antihistamines or systemic corticosteroids, or both.

Best in Show at the 1970 Keomah Kennel Club event was Ch. Jubilee Farms Gouelu, owned by Mr. A.J. Peterka, Jr. Handled for owner by Pete Kordus for this win under judge Forest N. Hall. Patricia Van Arkel presents the trophy. Lloyd Olson photograph.

—B—

BABESIA GIBSONI (or Babesiosis)—A parasitic disease of the tropics, reasonably rare in the U.S.A. to date. Blood tests can reveal its presence and like other parasitic infections the symptoms are loss of appetite, no pep, anemia and elevations in temperature as the disease advances, and enlarged spleen and liver are sometimes evident.

BALANITIS—The medical term for a constant discharge of pus from the penis which causes spotting of clothing or quarters or causes the dog to clean himself constantly. When bacteria gather at the end of the sheath, it causes irritations in the tissue and pus. If the condition becomes serious, the dog may be cauterized or ointment applied.

BLASTOMYCOSIS—A rare infectious disease involving the kidneys and liver. The animal loses its appetite and vomits. Laboratory examination is necessary to determine presence.

BRADYCARDIA—Abnormal slowness of the heartbeat and pulse.

BRONCHITIS—Inflammation of the mucus lining in the respiratory tract, the windpipe or trachea, and lungs. Dampness and cold are usually responsible and the symptoms usually follow a chill, or may be present with cases of pneumonia or distemper. Symptoms are a nagging dry cough, fever, quickened pulse rate, runny nose, perhaps vomiting, and congested nasal passages which must be kept open. Old dogs are particularly affected. It is a highly transmissible disease and isolation from other animals is important. Antibiotics are given.

BRUCELLA CANIS—An infectious disease associated with abortion in bitches in the last quarter of gestation, sterility or stillbirths. A comparable is testicle trouble in male dogs. It is highly contagious and can be diagnosed through blood tests and animals having the infection should be isolated.

—C—

CANCER (tumors, neoplasia, etc.)—A growth of cells which serve no purpose is referred to as a cancer. The growth may be malignant or benign. Malignancy is the spreading type growth and may invade the entire body. Treatment, if the condition is diagnosed and caught in time, may be successful by surgical methods, drugs, or radioactive therapy. Haste in consulting your veterinarian cannot be urged too strongly.

CANKER (Otitis)—A bacterial infection of the ear where the ear may drain, have a dreadful odor, and ooze a dark brown substance all the way out to the ear flap. Cause of canker can be from mites, dirt, excessive hair growth in the ear canal, wax, etc. A daily cleaning and administering of antifungal ointment or powder are in order until the condition is cured. Symptoms are the dog shaking his head, scratching his ear and holding the head to the side.

CARIES—A pathologic change causing destruction of the enamel on teeth and subsequent invasion of the dentine; in other words, a cavity in a tooth. This may result in bad breath, toothache, digestive disorders, etc., depending upon the severity. Cavities in dogs are rare, though we hear more and more of false teeth being made for dogs and occasionally even root canal work for show dogs.

CASTRATION—Surgical removal of the male gonads or sex organs. An anesthesia is necessary and the animal must be watched for at least a week to see that hemorrhage does not occur. It is best performed at an early age—anywhere from three to nine months. Older dogs suffering from a hormonal imbalance or cancer of the gonads are castrated.

CATARACT—An opaque growth covering the lens of the eye. Surgical removal is the only treatment. Cataract may be a result of an injury to the eye or in some cases may be an inherited trait.

CELLULITIS—Inflammation of the loose subcutaneous tissue of the body. A condition which can be symptomatic of several other diseases.

CHEILITIS—Inflammation of the lips.

CHOLECYSTITIS—A condition affecting the gall bladder. The onset is usually during the time an animal is suffering from infectious canine hepatitis. Removal of the gall bladder, which thickens and becomes highly vascular, can effect a complete cure.

CHOREA—Brain damage as a result of distemper which has been severe is characterized by convulsive movements of the legs. It is progressive and if it affects the facial muscles, salivating or difficulty in eating or moving the jaws may be evident. Sedatives may bring relief, but the disease is incurable.

CHOROIDITIS—Inflammation of the choroid coat of the eye which is to be regarded as serious. Immediate veterinary inspection is required.

COCCIDIOSIS—An intestinal disease of parasitic nature and origin. Microscopic organisms reproduce on the walls of the intestinal tract and destroy tissue. Bloody diarrhea, loss of weight and appetite and general lethargy result. Presence of parasites is determined by fecal examination. Sulfur drugs are administered and a complete clean up of the premises is in order since the parasite is passed from one to to another through floor surfaces or eating utensils.

COLOSTRUM—A secretion of the mammary glands for the first day or so after the bitch gives birth. It acts as a purgative for the young, and contains antibodies against distemper, hepatitis and other bacteria.

CONJUNCTIVITIS—Inflammation of the conjunctiva of the eye.

CONVULSIONS—A fit, or violent involuntary contractions of groups of muscles, accompanied by unconsciousness. They are in themselves a symptom of another disease, especially traceable to one affecting the brain; i.e., rabies, or an attack of encephalitis or distemper. It may also be the result of a heavy infestation of parasites or toxic poisonings. Care must be taken that the animal does not injure itself and a veterinarian must be consulted to determine and eliminate the cause.

American, Bermudian and Canadian Ch. Mahogany's Socair Buacaill, C.D., pictured winning Best of Breed at the 1969 Bronx County Kennel Club show. Cochise is owner-handled by Helen Olivio of New York.

CRYPTORCHID—A male animal in which neither testicle is present or descended. This condition automatically bars a dog from the show ring.

CYANOSIS—A definite blueness seen in and around the mucous membranes of the face; i.e. tongue, lips and eyes. It is usually synonymous with a circulatory obstruction or heart condition.

CYSTITIS—A disease of the urinary tract which is characterized by inflammation and/or infection in the bladder. Symptoms are straining, frequent urination with little results or with traces of blood, and perhaps a fever. Antibiotics, usually in the sulfur category, as well as antiseptics are administered. This is a condition which is of great discomfort to the animal and is of lengthy duration. Relief must be given by a veterinarian, who will empty bladder by means of catheter or medication to relax the bladder so that the urine may be passed.

407

DEMODECTIC MANGE—A skin condition caused by a parasitic mite, *Demodex*, living in hair follicles. This is a difficult condition to get rid of and is treated internally as well as externally. It requires diligent care to free the animal of it entirely.

DERMATITIS—There are many forms of skin irritations and eruptions but perhaps the most common is "contact dermatitis." Redness and itching are present. The irritation is due to something the animal has been exposed to and to which it is allergic. The irritant must be identified and removed. Antihistamines and anti-inflammatory drugs are administered, and in severe cases sedatives or tranquilizers are prescribed to lessen the dog's scratching.

DIABETES (Insipidus)—A deficiency of antidiuretic hormone produced by the posterior pituitary gland. It occurs in older animals and is characterized by the animal's drinking excessive amounts of water and voiding frequently. Treatment is by periodic injection of an antidiuretic drug for the rest of the animal's life.

DIABETES (Mellitus)—Sometimes referred to as sugar diabetes, this is a disorder of the metabolism of carbohydrates caused by lack of insulin production by the cells of the pancreas. Symptoms are the same as in the insipidus type, and in severe cases loss of weight, vomiting or coma may occur. Blood and urine analysis confirm its presence. It is treated by low carbohydrate diet, oral medication and/or insulin injections.

Ch. Blarneywood Country Squire, whelped in August, 1960 and owned by Mrs. Marion Darling, was the sire of 20 champion offspring. The sire was Ch. Draherin Irish Chieftan **ex** Kinvarra Shiela. Squire was 3rd ranking Sporting Dog in the nation in 1965 and #4 in 1966 according to the Phillips System.

DIGITOXIN—A medication given to a dog with congestive heart failure. Dosage is, of course, adjusted to severeness of condition and size of the individual animal.

DISC ABNORMALITIES (Intervertebral)—Between each bone in the spine is a connecting structure called an intervertebral disc. When the disc between two vertebrae becomes irritated and protrudes into the spinal canal it forms lesions and is painful. (This is a disease which particularly affects the Dachshund because of its long back in comparison to length of legs.) Paralysis of the legs, reluctance to move, and loss of control of body functions may be symptoms. X-ray and physical examination will determine extent of the condition. Massage helps circulation and pain relievers may be prescribed. Surgery is sometimes successful and portable two-wheel carts which support the hindquarters help.

DISTEMPER—Highly transmissible disease of viral origin which spreads through secretions of nose, eyes or direct oral contact. May be fatal in puppies under 12 weeks. Symptoms of this disease are alternately high and low fevers, runny eyes and nose, loss of appetite and general lassitude, diarrhea and loss of weight. This disease sometimes goes into pneumonia or convulsions if the virus reaches the brain. Chorea may remain if infection has been severe or neglected. Antibiotics are administered and fluids and sedation may be advised by your veterinarian. If the dog has been inoculated, the disease may remain a light case, BUT it is not to be treated lightly. Warmth and rest are also indicated.

DROPSY—Abnormal accumulation of fluid in the tissues or body cavities. Also referred to as edema when accumulations manifest themselves below the skin. In the stomach region it is called ascites. Lack of exercise or poor circulation, particularly in older dogs, may be the cause. While the swellings are painless, excess accumulations in the stomach can cause digestive distress or heart disturbances, and may be associated with diabetes. Occasional diarrhea, lack of appetite, loss of weight, exhaustion, emaciation and death may occur if the condition is not treated.

DYSGERMINOMA—A malignant ovarian tumor. Symptoms are fever, vaginal discharge, vomiting and diarrhea. Tumors vary in size, though more commonly are of the large size and from reports to date, the right ovary is more commonly affected. Radiotherapy may be successful; if not, surgery is required.

—E—

EAR MANGE—Otodectic mange, or parasitic otitis externa. Ear mites suck lymph fluids through the walls of the ear canal. Infections are high when mites are present and a brownish, horrible smelling ooze is present deep down in the canal all the way out to the flap where the secretion has a granular texture. The dog shakes his head, rubs and scrapes. In extreme cases convulsions

The 1949 Irish Setter Club of the Pacific Specialty Show saw Best of Breed won by Ch. McGowan's Dugan, owned by Mr. and Mrs. Davis and handled by Jim McManus, on the right, and Ch. Lady Kathleen O'Hagginwood Best of Opposite Sex, handled by Harry Sangster for owners Mr. and Mrs. James Phillips. The judge is Mrs. Hayes Blake Hoyt. Athos Nilsen photo.

or brain damage may result. The ear must be cleaned daily and drugs of an antibiotic and anti-inflammatory nature must be given.

ECLAMPSIA—A toxemia of pregnancy. Shortly before the time a bitch whelps her puppies, her milk may go bad. She will pant as a result of high fever, and go into convulsions. The puppies must be taken away from the mother immediately. This is usually the result of an extreme lack of calcium during pregnancy. Also known as milk fever.

ECTROPION—All breeders of dogs with drooping eyelids or exaggerated haws will be familiar with this condition, where the lower eyelid turns out. It can be a result of an injury, as well as hereditary in some breeds, but can be corrected surgically.

ECZEMA—Eczema is another form of skin irritation which may confine itself to redness and itching, or go all the way to a scaly skin surface or open wet sores. This is sometimes referred to as "hot spots." A hormone imbalance or actual diet deficiency may prevail. Find the cause and remove it. Medicinal baths and ointments usually provide a cure, but cure is a lengthy process and the condition frequently recurs.

EDEMA—Abnormal collections of fluids in the tissues of the body.

ELBOW DYSPLASIA—Term applies to a developmental abnormality of the elbow joints. It is hereditary.

EMPHYSEMA—Labored breathing caused by distended or ruptured lungs. May be acute or chronic and is not uncommon.

EMPYEMA—Accumulation of pus or purulent fluid, in a body cavity resembling an abscess. Another term for pleurisy.

ENCEPHALITIS—Brain fever associated with meningitis. An inflammation of the brain caused by a virus, rabies or perhaps tuberculosis. It may also be caused by poisonous plants, bad food or lead poisoning. Dogs go "wild," running in circles, falling over, etc. Paralysis and death frequently result. Cure depends on extent of infection and speed with which it is diagnosed and treated.

ENDOCARDITIS—Inflammation and bacterial infection of the smooth membrane that lines the inside of the heart.

ENTERITIS—Intestinal inflammation of serious import. It can be massive or confine itself to one spot. Symptoms are diarrhea, bloody at times, vomiting, and general discomfort. Antibiotics are prescribed and fluids, if the diarrhea and vomiting have been excessive. Causes are varied; may follow distemper or other infections or bacterial infection through intestinal worms.

Ch. Mahogany Boy's Monty, Best Dog in Show at the Greater Miami dog show in Miami several years ago. Left to right are Mabel Hammond, president of the club, Jim Mulvey, show announcer, L.B. Schelver, handler, owner Samuel Kolow of Needham, Massachusetts and the late Alva Rosenberg, judge.

ENTROPION—A turning in of the margin of the eyelids. As a result, the eyelashes rub on the eyeball and cause irritation resulting in a discharge from the eye. Here again it is a condition peculiar to certain breeds—particularly Chow Chows—or may be the result of an injury which failed to heal properly. Infection may result as the dog will rub his eyes and cause a swelling. It is painful, but can be cured surgically.

ENTEROTOXEMIA—A result of toxins and gases in the intestine. As bacteria increase in the intestine, intermittent diarrhea and/or constipation results from maldigestion. If the infection reaches the kidney through the circulatory system, nephritis results. The digestive system must be cleaned out by use of castor oil or colonic irrigation, and outwardly by antibiotics.

Ch. Tonleighs Lord Shawn, a Best of Breed winner at Westminster several years ago. This lovely Group winner was sired by Ch. Seaforth's Poetry of Motion **ex** Tonleighs Sunbeam.

Smokey's Cinder of Glenarm, Best of Breed at the 1960 Combined Setter Specialty show. Owned by Mr. and Mrs. R.I. Pusey, Jr. of Hanover, Virginia.

EOSINOPHILIC MYOSITIS—Inflammation of the muscles dogs use for chewing. Persistent attacks usually lasting one or more weeks. They come and go over long periods of time, coming closer and closer together. Difficulty in swallowing, swelling of the face, or even the dog holding his mouth open will indicate the onset of an attack. Anti-inflammatory drugs are the only known treatment. Cause unknown, outlook grave.

EPILEPSY—The brain is the area affected and fits and/or convulsions may occur early or late in life. It cannot be cured; however, it can be controlled with medication. Said to be hereditary. Convulsions may be of short duration or the dog may just appear to be dazed. It is rarely fatal. Care must be taken to see that the dog does not injure itself during an attack.

EPIPHORA—A constant tearing which stains the face and fur of dogs. It is a bothersome condition which is not easily remedied either with outside medication or by surgical tear duct removal. There has been some success in certain cases reported from a liquid medication given with the food and prescribed by veterinarians. This condition may be caused by any one or more of a number of corneal irritations, such as nasal malfunction or the presence of foreign matter in the superficial gland of the third eyelid. After complete examination as to the specific cause, a veterinarian can decide whether surgery is indicated.

ESOPHAGEAL DIVERTICULUM—Inflammation or sac-like protrusions on the walls of the esophagus resembling small hernias. It is uncommon in dogs, but operable, and characterized by gagging, listlessness, temperature and vomiting in some cases.

—F—

FALSE PREGNANCY (or pseudopregnancy)—All the signs of the real thing are present in this heart-breaking and frustrating condition. The bitch may even go into false labor near the end of the 63-day cycle and build a nest for her hoped-for puppies. It may be confirmed by X-ray or a gentle feeling for them through the stomach area. Hormones can be injected to relieve the symptoms.

FROSTBITE—Dead tissue as a result of extreme cold. The tissues become red, swollen and painful, and may peel away later, causing open lesions. Ointments and protective coverings should be administered until irritation is alleviated.

FUSOSPIROCHETAL DISEASE—Bad breath is the first and most formidable symptom of this disease of the mouth affecting the gums. Bloody saliva and gingivitis or ulcers in the mouth may also be present, and the dog may be listless due to lack of desire to eat. Cleaning the teeth and gums daily with hydrogen peroxide in prescribed dosage by the veterinarian is required. Further diagnosis of the disease can be confirmed by microscopic examination of smears, though these fusiform bacteria might be present in the mouth of a dog which never becomes infected. Attempts to culture these anaerobes have been unsuccessful.

—G—

GASTRIC DILATION—This is an abnormal swelling of the abdomen due to gas or overeating. Consumption of large amounts of food especially if dry foods are eaten, and then large quantities of water make the dog "swell." The stomach twists so that both ends are locked off. Vomiting is impossible, breathing is hampered and the dog suffers pain until the food is expelled. Dogs that gulp their food and swallow air with it are most susceptible. Immediate surgery may be required to prevent the stomach from bursting. Commonly known as bloat.

GASTRITIS—Inflammation of the stomach caused by many things— spoiled food which tends to turn to gas, overeating, eating foreign bodies, chemicals or even worms. Vomiting is usually the first symptom though the animal will usually drink great quantities of water which more often than not it throws back up. A 24-hour fast which eliminates the cause is the first step toward cure. If vomiting persists chunks of ice cubes put down the throat may help. Hopefully the dog will lick them himself. Keep the dog on a liquid diet for another 24 hours before resuming his regular meals.

GASTRO-ENTERITIS—Inflammation of the stomach and intestines. There is bleeding and ulceration in the stomach and this serious condition calls for immediate veterinary help.

GASTRODUODENITIS—Inflammation of the stomach and duodenum.

GINGIVITIS or gum infection—Badly tartared teeth are usually the cause of this gum infection characterized by swelling, redness at the gum line, bleeding and bloody saliva. Bad breath also. Improper diet may be a cause of it. Feeding of only soft foods as a steady diet allows the tartar to form and to irritate the gums. To effect a cure, clean the teeth and perhaps the veterinarian will also recommend antibiotics.

Ch. Rusthill's Irish Taoiseach, a Best of Breed winner over specials. Owned by Robert E. Brennan, Brenmor Kennels, Willoughby Hills, Ohio.

GLAUCOMA—Pressure inside the eyeball builds up, the eyeball becomes hard and bulgy and a cloudiness of the entire corneal area occurs. The pupil is dilated and the eye is extremely sensitive. Blindness is inevitable unless treatment is prompt at the onset of the disease. Cold applications as well as medical prescriptions are required with also the possibility of surgery, though with no guarantee of success.

GLOSSITIS—Inflammation of the tongue.

GOITER—Enlargement of the thyroid gland, sometimes requiring surgery. In minor cases, medication—usually containing iodine—is administered.

—H—

HARELIP—A malformation of the upper lip characterized by a cleft palate. Difficulty in nursing in exaggerated cases can result in starvation or puny development. Operations can be performed late in life.

HEART DISEASE—Heart failure is rare in young dogs, but older dogs which show an unusual heavy breathing after exercise or are easily tired may be victims of heart trouble, and an examination is in order. As it grows worse, wheezing, coughing or gasping may be noticed. Other symptoms indicating faulty circulation may manifest themselves as the animal retains more body fluids as the circulation slows down. Rest, less exercise, and non-fattening diets are advised and medication to remove excess fluids from the body are prescribed. In many cases, doses of digitalis may be recommended.

HEARTWORM (*Dirofilaria immitis*)—This condition does not necessarily debilitate a working dog or a dog that is extremely active. It is diagnosed by a blood test and a microscopic examination to determine the extent of the microfilariae. If positive, further differentials are made for comparison with other microfilariae. Treatment consists of considerable attention to the state of nutrition, and liver and kidney functions are watched closely in older dogs. Medication is usually treatment other than surgery and consists of dithiazine iodine therapy over a period of two weeks. Anorexia and/or fever may occur and supplemental vitamins and minerals may be indicated. Dogs with heavy infestations are observed for possible foreign protein reaction from dying and decomposing worms, and are watched for at least three months.

HEATSTROKE—Rapid breathing, dazed condition, vomiting, temperature, and collapse in hot weather indicate heatstroke. It seems to strike older dogs especially if they are overweight or have indulged in excessive activity. Reduce body temperature immediately by submerging dog in cold water, apply ice packs, cold enemas, etc. Keep dog cool and quiet for at least 24 hours.

HEMATOMA—A pocket of blood that may collect in the ear as a result of an injury or the dog's scratching. Surgery is required to remove the fluid and return skin to cartilage by stitching.

HEMOPHILIA—Excessive bleeding on the slightest provocation. Only male subjects are susceptible and it is a hereditary disease passed on by females. Blood coagulants are now successfully used in certain cases.

HEPATITIS, Infectious canine—This disease of viral nature enters the body through the mouth and attacks primarily the liver. Puppies are the most susceptible to this disease and run a fever and drink excessive amounts of water. Runny eyes, nose, vomiting, and general discomfort are symptoms. In some cases blood build-

Ch. Shawnlea's Fanfare, owned by Mrs. Cheever Porter of New York City and handled by Jane Forsyth. Fanfare was whelped on May 13, 1955 and died May 12, 1969 after having won 75 Bests of Breed and 28 Best Sporting Dog awards, as well as four Bests in Show. Fanfare was bred by May H. Hanley and is pictured here winning Best in Show at the Long Island Kennel Club show in May, 1960.

Ch. Kalibanks King of Eatontown, owned by Arlene Miller, now Mrs. Clark Thompson, wins Best in Show at the 1961 Ladies Dog Club show held at Wellesley, Massachusetts, under the late judge Albert Van Court. Brother O'Brien presents the trophy and Lorna Demidoff, club president, completes the picture. Shafer photograph.

ers or even blood transfusions are administered since the virus has a tendency to thin the blood. This depletion of the blood often leaves the dog open to other types of infection and complete recovery is a lengthy process. Antibiotics are usually given and supplemental diet and blood builders are a help. Vaccination for young puppies is essential.

HERNIA (diaphragmatic)—An injury is usually responsible for this separation or break in the wall of the diaphragm. Symptoms depend on severity; breathing may become difficult, there is some general discomfort or vomiting. X-rays can determine the extent of damage and the only cure is surgery.

HERNIA (umbilical)—Caused by a portion of the abdominal viscera protruding through a weak spot near the navel. Tendency toward hernia is said to be largely hereditary.

Ch. End O'Maine Reddy Go, whelped May 19, 1959. Owned by Mr. and Mrs. William Randall, Reddy was a multiple Best in Show winner and the sire of 5 champion get. In 1963 he was 6th ranking Sporting Dog in the nation. His sire was Ch. Yorkhill Achilles ex End O'Maine Morning Bird.

HIP DYSPLASIA—or HD is a wearing away of the ball and socket of the hip joint. It is a hereditary disease. The symptoms of this bone abnormality are a limp and an awkwardness in raising or lowering the body. X-ray will establish severity and it is wise in buying or selling a dog of any breed to insist on a radiograph to prove the animal is HD clear. The condition can be detected as early as three months and if proven the dog should have as little exercise as possible. There is no cure for this condition. Only pain relievers can be given for the more severe cases. No animal with HD should be used for breeding.

HOOKWORM—Hookworms lodge in the small intestines and suck blood from the intestinal wall. Anemia results from loss of blood. Loss of weight, pale gums, and general weakness are symptoms. Microscopic examination of the feces will determine presence.

Emphasis on diet improvement and supplements to build up the blood is necessary and, of course, medication for the eradication of the hookworms. This can be either oral or by veterinary injection.

HYDROCEPHALUS—A condition also known as "water head" since a large amount of fluid collects in the brain cavity, usually before birth. This may result in a difficult birth and the young are usually born dead or die shortly thereafter. Euthanasia is recommended on those that do survive since intelligence is absent and violence to themselves or to others is liable to occur.

HYDRONEPHROSIS—Due to a cystic obstruction the kidney collects urine which cannot be passed through the ureter into the bladder, causing the kidney to swell (sometimes to five times its normal size) and giving pain in the lumbar region. The kidney may atrophy, if the condition goes untreated.

—I—

ICHTHYOSIS—A skin condition over elbows and hocks. Scaliness and cracked skin cover the area particularly that which comes in contact with hard surfaces. Lubricating oils well rubbed into the skin and keeping the animal on soft surfaces are solutions.

IMPETIGO—Skin disease seen in puppies infested by worms, distemper, or teething problems. Little soft pimples cover the surface of the skin. Sulfur ointments and ridding the puppy of the worms are usually sufficient cure as well.

INTERDIGITAL CYSTS—Growths usually found in the legs. They are painful and cause the dog to favor the paw or not walk on it at all. Surgery is the only cure and antibiotic ointments to keep dirt and infection out are necessary.

INTESTINAL OBSTRUCTIONS—When a foreign object becomes lodged in the intestines and prevents passage of stool constipation results from the blockage. Hernia is another cause of obstruction or stoppage. Pain, vomiting, loss of appetite are symptoms. Fluids, laxatives or enemas should be given to remove blockage. Surgery may be necessary after X-ray determines cause. Action must be taken since death may result from long delay or stoppage.

IRITIS—Inflammation of the iris or colored part of the eye. May be caused by the invasion of foreign bodies or other irritants.

—J—

JAUNDICE—A yellow discoloration of the skin. Liver malfunction causes damage by bile seeping into the circulatory system and being dispensed into the body tissue, causing discoloration of the skin. It may be caused by round worms, liver flukes or gall stones. It may be either acute or chronic and the animal loses ambition, convulses or vomits, sometimes to excess. It may be cured once the cause has been eliminated. Neglect can lead to death.

Dajos The Cajun Queen, pictured above winning Best in Sweepstakes at the 1974 Irish Setter Club of America Specialty Show under judge Marsha Hall Brown. Owners are Dale and Ruth Jones, Puyallup, Washington.

—K—

KERATITIS—Infection of the cornea of the eye. Distemper or hepatitis may be a cause. Sensitivity to light, watery discharge and pain are symptomatic. Treatment depends on whether the lesion is surface irritation or a puncture of the cornea. Warm compresses may help until the veterinarian prescribes the final treatment. Sedatives or tranquilizers may be prescribed to aid in preventing the dog from rubbing the eye.

KIDNEY WORM—The giant worm that attacks the kidney and kidney tissue. It can reach a yard in length. The eggs of this rare species of worm are passed in the dog's urine rather than the feces. These worms are found in raw fish. It is almost impossible to detect them until at least one of the kidneys is completely destroyed or an autopsy reveals its presence. There is no known cure at this point and, therefore, the only alternative is not to feed raw fish.

—L—

LEAD POISONING—Ingestion of lead-based paints or products such as linoleum containing lead is serious. Symptoms are vomiting, behavior changes and/or hysteria or even convulsions in severe cases. It can be cured by medication if caught early enough. Serious damage can be done to the central nervous system. Blood samples are usually taken to determine amount in the blood. Emetics may be required if heavy intake is determined.

LEPTOSPIROSIS—This viral infection is dangerous and bothersome because it affects many organs of the body before lodging itself in the kidneys. Incubation is about two weeks after exposure to the urine of another affected dog. Temperature, or subtemperature, pain and stiffness in the hindquarters are not uncommon, nor is vomiting. Booster shots after proper vaccination at a young age are usually preventative, but once afflicted, antibiotics are essential to cure.

LOCKJAW (tetanus)—Death rate is very high in this bacterial disease. Puncture wounds may frequently develop into lockjaw. Symptoms are severe. As the disease progresses high fever and stiffness in the limbs becomes serious though the dog does not lose consciousness. Sedatives must be given to help relax the muscles and dispel the spasms. When the stiffness affects the muscles of the face, intravenous feeding must be provided. If a cure is effected, it is a long drawn out affair. Lockjaw bacteria are found in soil and in the feces of animals and humans.

LYMPHOMA (Hodgkins disease)—Malignant lymphoma most frequently is found in dogs under four years of age, affects the lymph glands, liver and spleen. Anorexia and noticeable loss of weight are apparent as well as diarrhea. Depending on area and organ, discharge may be present. The actual neoplasm or tumorous growth may be surrounded by nodules or neoplastic tissue which should be surgically removed under anesthesia.

—M—

MAMMARY NEOPLASMS—25 per cent of all canine tumors are of mammary origin. About half of all reported cases are benign. They are highly recurrent and, when cancerous, fatalities are high. Age or number of litters has nothing to do with the condition itself or the seriousness.

MANGE—The loss of a patch of hair usually signals the onset of mange, which is caused by any number of types of microscopic mites. The veterinarian will usually take scrapings to determine which of the types it is. Medicated baths and dips plus internal and external medication is essential as it spreads rapidly and with care can be confined to one part of the body. Antibiotics are prescribed.

Ch. Gala Glens September Dawn pictured winning Best of Opposite Sex at a Westminster Kennel Club show under judge Virginia Miller. Dawn was handled by Wendy Wolforth for owner Patricia P. Gallagher, Gala Glen Kennels, Melbourne, Florida.

MASTITIS (mammary gland infection)—After the birth of her young, a bitch may be beset by an infection causing inflammation of the mammary glands which produce milk for the puppies. Soreness and swelling make it painful for her when the puppies nurse. Abscess may form and she will usually run a fever. Hot compresses and antibiotics are necessary and in some instances hormone therapy.

MENINGITIS—Inflammation affecting the membranes covering the brain and/or spinal cord. It is a serious complication which may result from a serious case of distemper, tuberculosis, hardpad, head injury, etc. Symptoms are delirium, restlessness, high temperature, and dilated pupils in the eyes. Paralysis and death are almost certain.

METRITIS—This infection, or inflammation of the uterus, causes the dog to exude a bloody discharge. Vomiting and a general lassitude are symptoms. Metritis can occur during the time the bitch is in season or right after giving birth. Antibiotics are used, or in severe cases hysterectomy.

MONORCHIDISM—Having only one testicle.

MOTION SICKNESS—On land, on sea, or in the air, your dog may be susceptible to motion sickness. Yawning, or excessive salivation, may signal the onset, and there is eventual vomiting. One or all of the symptoms may be present and recovery is miraculously fast once the motion ceases. Antinauseant drugs are available for animals which do not outgrow this condition.

MYELOMA—Tumor of the bone marrow. Lameness and evidence of pain are symptoms as well as weight loss, depression and palpable tumor masses. Anemia or unnatural tendency to bleed in severe cases may be observed. The tumors may be detected radiographically, but no treatment has yet been reported for the condition.

—N—

NEONATAL K-9 HERPESVIRUS INFECTION—Though K-9 herpesvirus infection, or CHV, has been thought to be a disease of the respiratory system in adult dogs, the acute necrotizing and hemorrhagic disease occurs only in infant puppies. The virus multiplies in the respiratory system and female genital tracts of older dogs. Puppies may be affected in the vaginal canal. Unfortunately the symptoms resemble other neonatal infections, even hepatitis, and only after autopsy can it be detected.

NEPHROTIC SYNDROME—Symptoms may be moist or suppurative dermatitis, edema or hypercholesteremia. It is a disease of the liver and may be the result of another disease. Laboratory data and biopsies may be necessary to determine the actual cause if it is other than renal disease. This is a relatively uncommon thing in dogs, and liver and urinal function tests are made to determine its presence.

A Bit of Barney Duke of Harvard, pictured winning under judge R. Cowan at the 1974 Brevard Kennel Club show on the way to his championship. Handled by Katie Gallagher for owner Barbara Parks, Lindale Kennels, Dillard, Georgia.

Full speed ahead for this working Irish Setter in the mountains of Spain: Westwind Scarlet Robin Hood, bred by Luz Holvenstot of the Westwind Kennels in Long Valley, New Jersey, who sold and exported the dog to a client in Spain.

NEURITIS—Painful inflammation of a nerve.

NOSEBLEED (epistaxis)—A blow or other injury which causes injury to the nasal tissues is usually the cause. Tumors, parasites, foreign bodies, such as thorns or burs or quills, may also be responsible. Ice packs will help stem the tide of blood, though coagulants may also be necessary. Transfusions in severe cases may be indicated.

—O—

ORCHITIS—Inflammation of the testes.

OSTEOGENESIS IMPERFECTA—Or "brittle bones" is a condition that can be said to be both hereditary and dietary. It may be due to lack of calcium or phosphorus or both. Radiographs show "thin" bones with deformities throughout the skeleton. Treatment depends on cause.

OSTEOMYELITIS (enostosis)—Bone infection may develop after a bacterial contamination of the bone, such as from a compound fracture. Pain and swelling denote the infection and wet sores may accompany it. Lack of appetite, fever and general inactivity can be expected. Antibiotics are advised after X-ray determines severity. Surgery eliminates dead tissue or bone splinters to hasten healing.

OTITIS—Inflammation of the ear.

—P—

PANCREATITIS—It is difficult to palpate for the pancreas unless it is enlarged, which it usually is if this disease is present. Symptoms

Canadian Ch. Colnbrook's Annabelle, owned by David E. Powell of Vancouver, Canada, is pictured winning at a Bermuda Kennel Club show. Sired by Canadian and American Ch. Jo-Ett's Marvelda Blazer **ex** Canadian and American Ch. Cherry Point Holly, Annabelle was whelped in April, 1970. Her Canadian, Bermudian and U.S. show record includes 4 Bests of Breed and 24 Bests of Opposite Sex.

to note are as in other gastronomic complaints such as vomiting, loss of appetite, anorexia, stomach pains and general listlessness. This is a disease of older dogs though it has been diagnosed in young dogs as well. Blood, urine and stool examination and observation of the endocrine functions of the dog are in order. Clinical diseases that may result from a serious case of pancreatitis are acute pancreatitis which involves a complete degeneration of the pancreas, atrophy, fibrous and/or neoplasia, cholecystitis. Diabetes mellitus is also a possibility.

PATELLAR LUXATION—"Trick knees" are frequent in breeds that have been "bred down" from Standard to Toy size, and is a condition where the knee bone slips out of position. It is an off again, on again condition that can happen as a result of a jump or excessive exercise. It if is persistent, anti-inflammatory drugs may be given or in some cases surgery can correct it.

PERITONITIS—Severe pain accompanies this infection or inflammation of the lining of the abdominal cavity. Extreme sensitivity to touch, loss of appetite and vomiting occur. Dehydration and weight loss is rapid and anemia is a possibility. Antibiotics should

Ch. Westwind Scarlet Arabesque, photographed in July, 1970 with owner Luz Holvenstot of Long Valley, New Jersey.

kill the infection and a liquid diet for several days is advised. Pain-killers may be necessary or drainage tubes in severe cases.

PHLEBITIS—Inflammation of a vein.

PLACENTA—The afterbirth which accompanies and has been used to nourish the fetus. It is composed of three parts; the chorion, amnion, and allantois.

POLYCYTHEMIA VERA—A disease of the blood causing an elevation of hemoglobin concentration. Blood-letting has been effective. The convulsions that typify the presence can be likened to epileptic fits and last for several minutes. The limbs are stiff and the body feels hot. Mucous membranes are congested, the dog may shiver, and the skin has a ruddy discoloration. Blood samples must be taken and analyzed periodically. If medication to reduce the production of red blood cells is given, it usually means the dog will survive.

PROCTITIS—Inflammation of the rectum.

PROSTATITIS—Inflammation of the prostate gland.

PSITTACOSIS—This disease which affects birds and people has been diagnosed in rare instances in dogs. A soft, persistent cough indicates the dog has been exposed, and a radiograph will show a cloudy portion on the affected areas of the lung. Antibiotics such as aureomycin have been successful in the known cases and cure has been effected in two to three weeks' time. This is a highly contagious disease, to the point where it can be contracted during a post mortem.

PYOMETRA—This uterine infection presents a discharge of pus from the uterus. High fever may turn to below normal as the infection persists. Lack of appetite with a desire for fluids and frequent urination are evidenced. Antibiotics and hormones are known cures. In severe cases, hysterectomy is performed.

—R—

RABIES (hydrophobia)—The most deadly of all dog diseases. The Pasteur treatment is the only known cure for humans. One of the viral diseases that affects the nervous system and damages the brain. It is contracted by the intake, through a bite or cut, of saliva from an infected animal. It takes days or even months for the symptoms to appear, so it is sometimes difficult to locate, or isolate, the source. There are two reactions in a dog to this disease. In the paralytic type of rabies the dog can't swallow and salivates from a drooping jaw, and progressive paralysis eventually overcomes the entire body. The animal goes into coma and eventually dies. In the furious type of rabies the dog turns vicious, eats strange objects, in spite of a difficulty in swallowing, foams at the mouth, and searches out animals or people to attack—hence the expression "mad dog." Vaccination is available for dogs that run loose.

Examination of the brain is necessary to determine actual diagnosis.

RECTAL PROLAPSE—Diarrhea, straining from constipation or heavy infestations of parasites are the most common cause of prolapse which is the expulsion of a part of the rectum through the anal opening. It is cylindrical in shape, and must be replaced within the body as soon as possible to prevent damage. Change in diet, medication to eliminate the cause, etc. will effect a cure.

RETINAL ATROPHY—A disease of the eye that is highly hereditary and may be revealed under ophthalmoscopic examination. Eventual blindness inevitably results. Dogs with retinal atrophy should not be used for breeding. Particularly prominent in certain breeds where current breeding trends have tended to change the shape of the head.

RHINITIS—Acute or chronic inflammation of the mucous membranes of the nasal passages. It is quite common in both dogs and cats. It is seldom fatal, but requires endless "nursing" on the part of the owner for survival, since the nose passages must be kept open so the animal will eat. Dry leather on the nose though there is excessive discharge, high fever, sneezing, etc., are symptoms. Nose discharge may be bloody and the animal will refuse to eat, making it listless. The attacks may be recurrent and medication must be administered.

RICKETS—The technical name for rickets is osteomalacia and is due to not enough calcium in the body. The bones soften and the legs become bowed or deformed. Rickets can be cured if caught in early stages by improvement in diet.

RINGWORM—The dread of the dog and cat world! This is a fungus disease where the hair falls out in circular patches. It spreads rapidly and is most difficult to get rid of entirely. Drugs must be administered "inside and out!" The cure takes many weeks and much patience. Ultraviolet lights will show hairs green in color so it is wise to have your animal, or new puppy, checked out by the veterinarian for this disease before introducing him to the household. It is contracted by humans.

ROOT CANAL THERAPY—Injury to a tooth may be treated by prompt dental root canal therapy which involves removal of damaged or necrotic pulp and placing of opaque filling material in the root canal and pulp chamber.

—S—

SALIVARY CYST—Surgery is necessary when the salivary gland becomes clogged or non-functional, causing constant salivation. A swelling becomes evident under the ear or tongue. Surgery will release the accumulation of saliva in the duct of the salivary gland, though it is at times necessary to remove the salivary gland in its

Ch. Verbu Erin pictured winning at the 1966 Eastern Irish Setter Association show under judge William C. Thompson, author of *The Irish Setter in Word and Picture*. Handled by Robert Walgate for owner-breeder Emily Schweitzer, Verbu Kennels, Dundee, Illinois.

Two Irish Setters celebrate St. Patrick's Day at a 1966 party held at the City Squire Motor Inn in New York City. The event was the second annual St. Patrick's Day party for dogs of Irish descent. On the left is Baby Brown's Princess Bianca; at right Champion Phantom Brook's Brian Boru pauses a moment to pose for the photographer before beginning his meal.

entirety. Zygomatic salivary cysts are usually a result of obstructions in the four main pairs of salivary glands in the mouth. Infection is more prevalent in the parotid of the zygomatic glands located at the rear of the mouth, lateral to the last upper molars. Visual symptoms may be protruding eyeballs, pain when moving the jaw, or a swelling in the roof of the mouth. If surgery is necessary, it is done under general anesthesia and the obstruction removed by dissection. Occasionally, the zygomatic salivary gland is removed as well. Stitches or drainage tubes may be necessary or dilation of the affected salivary gland. Oral or internal antibiotics may be administered.

SCABIES—Infection from a skin disease caused by a sarcoptic mange mite.

SCURF (dandruff)—A scaly condition of the body in areas covered with hair. Dead cells combined with dried sweat and sebaceous oil gland materials.

SEBORRHEA—A skin condition also referred to as "stud tail," though studding has nothing to do with the condition. The sebaceous or oil-forming glands are responsible. Accumulation of dry skin, or scurf, is formed by excessive oily deposits while the hair becomes dry or falls out altogether.

SEPTICEMIA—When septic organisms invade the bloodstream, it is called septicemia. Severe cases are fatal as the organisms in the

Ch. Delarda's Heritage pictured winning Best of Breed at the 1974 Long Island Kennel Club show, owner-handled by Madeline Blush of Baldwin, New York. Shafer photo.

Ch. Cu Machree Tim, owned by Mr. and Mrs. R.S. Meriam, was Best in Show under judge William Ross Proctor. Photograph includes the kennel club president, Charles H. Werber, Jr., Charlie Meyer, Tim's handler, judge Proctor, and William E. Buckely, club officer and then president of the American Kennel Club.

Ch. Argo Lane Lad of Ulster, owned by the Argo Lane Kennels in War-
ren, Michigan, wins Best in Show at the 1962 Mahoning-Shenango
Kennel Club show in Youngstown, Ohio, under judge Henry Stoecker.
Owned and handled by Joseph Frydrych.

blood infiltrate the tissues of the body and all the body organs are affected. Septicemia is the result of serious wounds, especially joints and bones. Abscess may form. High temperature and/or shivering may herald the onset, and death occurs shortly thereafter since the organisms reproduce and spread rapidly. Close watch on all wounds, antibiotics and sulfur drugs are usually prescribed.

SHOCK (circulatory collapse)—The symptoms and severity of shock vary with the cause and nervous system of the individual dog. Severe accident, loss of blood, and heart failure are the most common cause. Keep the dog warm, quiet and get him to a veterinarian right away. Symptoms are vomiting, rapid pulse, thirst, diarrhea, "cold, clammy feeling" and then eventually physical collapse. The veterinarian might prescribe plasma transfusion, fluids, perhaps oxygen, if pulse continues to be too rapid. Tranquilizers and sedatives are sometimes used as well as antibiotics and steroids. Relapse is not uncommon, so the animal must be observed carefully for several days after initial shock.

SINUSITIS—Inflammation of a sinus gland that inhibits breathing.

SNAKEBITE—The fact must be established as to whether the bite was poisonous or non-poisonous. A horse-shoe shaped double row of toothmarks is a non-poisonous bite. A double, or two-hole puncture, is a poisonous snake bite. Many veterinarians now carry anti-venom serum and this must be injected intramuscularly almost immediately. The veterinarian will probably inject a tranquilizer and other antibiotics as well. It is usually a four-day wait before the dog is normal once again, and the swelling completely gone. During this time the dog should be kept on medication.

SPIROCHETOSIS—Diarrhea which cannot be checked through normal anti-diarrhea medication within a few days may indicate spirochetosis; while spirochetes are believed by some authorities to be present and normal to gastrointestinal tracts, unexplainable diarrhea may indicate its presence in great numbers. Large quantities could precipitate diarrhea by upsetting the normal balance of the organ, though it is possible for some dogs which are infected to have no diarrhea at all.

SPONDYLITIS—Inflammation and loosening of the vertebrae.

STOMATITIS—Mouth infection. Bleeding or swollen gums or excessive salivation may indicate this infection. Dirty teeth are usually the cause. Antibiotics and vitamin therapy are indicated; and, of course, scraping the teeth to eliminate the original cause. See also GINGIVITIS.

STRONGYLIDOSIS—Disease caused by strongyle worms that enter the body through the skin and lodge in the wall of the small intestine. Bloody diarrhea, stunted growth, and thinness are general symptoms, as well as shallow breathing. Heavy infestation or neglect leads to death. Isolation of an affected animal and medication

Ch. Cu Machru Tim, whelped in June 1952, was sired by Ch. Thenderin's Brian Tristan **ex** Ch. Tattersall Tenaj. In 1956 he was #6 Sporting Dog in the nation and had won 2 Bests in Show. Sire of 3 champions, he was owned by Mr. and Mrs. Richard Meriam. Shafer photo.

Opposite:
Waiting to go into the show ring. . . Ch. Seaforth's Dark Rex, bred and owned by Barbara and George Brodie, Jr. of North Easton, Massachusetts.

will help eliminate the problem, but the premises must also be cleaned thoroughly since the eggs are passed through the feces.

SUPPOSITORY—A capsule comprised of fat or glycerine introduced into the rectum to encourage defecation. A paper match with the ignitible sulfur end torn off may also be used. Medicated suppositories are also used to treat inflammation of the intestine.

—T—

TACHYCARDIA—An abnormal acceleration of the heartbeat. A rapid pulse signaling a disruption in the heart action. Contact a veterinarian at once.

TAPEWORM—There are many types of tapeworms, the most common being the variety passed along by the flea. It is a white, segmented worm which lives off the wall of the dog's intestine and keeps growing by segments. Some of these are passed and can be

Ch. Tirvelda Distant Drummer started his show career at the age of 3 years in February, 1975 by winning the Combined Setter Specialty show in New York City. Soon after he won his third Specialty Show and won the Sporting Group at the Detroit Kennel Club show. Bred and owned by E. Irving Eldredge, Tirvelda, Middleburg, Virginia.

seen in the stool or adhering to the hairs on the rear areas of the dog or even in his bedding. It is a difficult worm to get rid of since, even if medication eliminates segments, the head may remain in the intestinal wall to grow again. Symptoms are virtually the same as for other worms: debilitation, loss of weight, occasional diarrhea, and general listlessness. Medication and treatment should be under the supervision of a veterinarian.

TETANUS (lockjaw)—A telarius bacillus enters the body through an open wound and spreads where the air does not touch the wound. A toxin is produced and affects the nervous system, particularly the brain or spine. The animal exhibits a stiffness, slows down considerably and the legs may be extended out beyond the body even when the animal is in a standing position. The lips have a twisted appearance. Recovery is rare. Tetanus is not common in dogs, but it can result from a bad job of tail docking or ear cropping, as well as from wounds received by stepping on rusty nails.

THALLOTOXICOSIS or thallium poisoning—Thallium sulfate is a cellular-toxic metal used as a pesticide or rodenticide and a ready cause of poisoning in dogs. Thallium can be detected in the urine by a thallium spot test or by spectrographic analysis by the veterinarian. Gastrointestinal disturbances signal the onset with vomiting, diarrhea, anorexia and stomach cramps. Sometimes a cough or difficulty in breathing occurs. Other intestinal disorders may also manifest themselves as well as convulsions. In mild cases the disease may be simply a skin eruption, depending upon the damage to the kidneys. Enlarged spleens, edema or nephrosis can develop. Antibiotics and a medication called dimercaprol are helpful, but the mortality rate is over 50 per cent.

THROMBUS—A clot in the blood vessel or the heart.

TICK PARALYSIS— Seasonal tick attacks or heavy infestations of ticks can result in a dangerous paralysis. Death is a distinct reality at this point and immediate steps must be taken to prevent total paralysis. The onset is observed usually in the hindquarters. Lack of coordination, a reluctance to walk, and difficulty in getting up can be observed. Complete paralysis kills when infection reaches the respiratory system. The paralysis is the result of the saliva of the tick excreted as it feeds.

TOAD POISONING—Some species of toads secrete a potent toxin. If while chasing a toad your dog takes it in his mouth, more than likely the toad will release the toxin from its parotid glands which will coat the mucous membranes of the dog's throat. The dog will salivate excessively, suffer prostration, cardiac arrhythmia. Some tropical and highly toxic species cause convulsions that result in death. Caught in time, there are certain drugs that can be used to counteract the dire effects. Try washing the dog's mouth with large amounts of water and get him to a veterinarian quickly.

Ch. Dix Mac Downy of Tercor and Ch. Dix Mac Berry of Tercor win Best Brace in Show at the 1960 Westminster Kennel Club show with their handler Harold Correll. Owned by the McCunes.

TONSILLECTOMY—Removal of the tonsils. A solution called epinephrine, injected at the time of surgery, makes excessive bleeding almost a thing of the past in this otherwise routine operation.

TOXEMIA—The presence of toxins in the bloodstream, which normally should be eliminated by the excretory organs.

TRICHIASIS—A disease condition of the eyelids, the result of neglect of earlier infection or inflammation.

—U—

UREMIA—When poisonous materials remain in the body, because they are not eliminated through the kidneys, and are recirculated in the bloodstream. A nearly always fatal disease—sometimes within hours—preceded by convulsions and unconsciousness. Veterinary care and treatment are urgent and imperative.

Charles Meyer and the Best in Show Irish Setter Lloyds Saint Patrick, winner at the 1948 Fredericksburg Kennel Club show. He was owned by Mrs. Jessie Lloyd of Lake Success, New York.

URINARY BLADDER RUPTURE—Injury or pelvic fractures are the most common causes of a rupture in this area. Anuria usually occurs in a few days when urine backs up into the stomach area. Stomach pains are characteristic and a radiograph will determine the seriousness. Bladder is flushed with saline solution and surgery is usually required. Quiet and little exercise is recommended during recovery.

—V—

VENTRICULOCORDECTOMY—Devocalization of dogs, also known as aphonia. In diseases of the larynx this operation may be used. Portions of the vocal cords are removed by manual means or by electrocautery. Food is withheld for a day prior to surgery and premedication is administered. Food is again provided 24 hours after the operation. At the end of three or four months, scar tissue develops and the dog is able to bark in a subdued manner. Complications from surgery are few, but the psychological effects on the animal are to be reckoned with. Suppression of the barking varies from complete to merely muted, depending on the veterinarian's ability and each individual dog's anatomy.

—W—

WHIPWORMS—Parasites that inhabit the large intestine and the cecum. Two to three inches in length, they appear "whip-like" and symptoms are diarrhea, loss of weight, anemia, restlessness or even pain, if the infestation is heavy enough. Medication is best prescribed by a veterinarian. Cleaning of the kennel is essential, since infestation takes place through the mouth. Whipworms reach maturity within thirty days after intake.

25. PURSUING A CAREER IN DOGS

One of the biggest joys for those of us who love dogs is to see someone we know or someone in our family grow up in the fancy and go on to enjoy the sport of dogs in later life. Many dog lovers, in addition to leaving codicils in their wills, are providing in other ways for veterinary scholarships for deserving youngsters who wish to make their association with dogs their profession.

Unfortunately, many children who have this earnest desire are not always able to afford the expense of an education that will take them through veterinary school, and they are not eligible for scholarships. In recent years, however, we have had a great innovation in this field—a college course for those interested in earning an Animal Science degree, which costs less than half of what it costs to complete veterinary courses. These students have been a boon to the veterinarians, and a number of colleges are now offering the program.

With each passing year, the waiting rooms of veterinarians have become more crowded, and the demands on the doctors' time for research, consultation, surgery and treatment have consumed more and more of the working hours over and above his regular office hours. The tremendous increase in the number of dogs and cats and other domestic animals, both in cities and in the suburbs, has resulted in an almost overwhelming consumption of veterinarians' time.

Until recently most veterinary help consisted of kennel men or women who were restricted to services more properly classified as office maintenance rather than actual veterinary assistance. Needless to say, their part in the operation of a veterinary office is both essential and appreciated, as are the endless details and volumes of paperwork capably handled by office secretaries and receptionists. However, still more of a veterinarian's duties could be handled by properly trained semiprofessionals.

With exactly this additional service in mind, many colleges are now conducting two-year courses in animal science for the training of such semiprofessionals, thereby opening a new field for animal technologists. The time saved by the assistance of these trained semiprofessionals will relieve veterinarians of the more mechanical chores and will allow them more time for diagnosing and general servicing of their clients.

"Delhi Tech," the State University Agricultural and Technical College at Delhi, New York, has recently graduated several classes of these technologists, and many other institutions of learning are offering comparable two-year courses at the college level. Entry requirements are usually that each applicant must be a graduate of an approved high school or have taken the State University admissions examination. In addition, each applicant for the Animal Science Technology program must have some previous credits in mathematics and science, with chemistry an important part of the science background.

The program at Delhi was a new educational venture dedicated to the training of competent technicians for employment in the biochemical field and has been generously supported by a five-year grant, designated as a "Pilot Development Program in Animal Science." This grant provided both personal and scientific equipment with such obvious good results when it was done originally pursuant to a contract with the United States Department of Health, Education, and Welfare. Delhi is a unit of the State University of New York and is accredited by the Middle States Association of Colleges and Secondary Schools. The campus provides offices, laboratories and animal quarters and is equipped with modern instruments to train technicians in laboratory animal care, physiology, pathology, microbiology, anesthesia, X-ray and germ-free techniques. Sizable animal colonies are maintained in air-conditioned quarters: animals housed include mice, rats, hamsters, guinea-pigs, gerbils and rabbits, as well as dogs and cats.

First-year students are given such courses as livestock production, dairy food science, general, organic and biological chemistry, mammalian anatomy, histology and physiology, pathogenic microbiology and quantitative and instrumental analysis, to name a few. Second year students matriculate in general pathology, animal parasitology, animal care and anesthesia, introductory psychology, animal breeding, animal nutrition, hematology and urinalysis, radiology, genetics, food sanitation and meat inspection, histological techniques, animal laboratory practices and axenic techniques. These, of course, may be supplemented by electives that prepare the student for contact with the public in the administration of these duties. Such recommended electives include public speaking, botany, animal reproduction and other related subjects.

In addition to Delhi and the colleges which got in early on the presentation of these courses, more and more universities are offering training for animal technologists. Students at the State University of Maine, for instance, receive part of their practical training at the Animal Medical Center in New York City, and after this actual experience can perform professionally immediately upon entering a veterinarian's employ.

Ch. Verbu Red Mollie, pictured at 14 years of age. Owned by Miss Emily Schweitzer, Dundee, Illinois.

Under direct veterinary supervision they are able to perform all of the following procedures as a semi-professional:

*Recording of vital information relative to a case. This would include such information as the client's name, address, telephone number and other facts pertinent to the visit. The case history would include the breed, age of the animal, its sex, temperature, etc.

*Preparation of the animal for surgery

*Preparation of equipment and medicaments to be used in surgery.

*Preparation of medicaments for dispensing to clients on prescription of the attending veterinarian.

*Administration and application of certain medicines.

*Administration of colonic irrigations.

*Application or changing of wound dressings.

*Cleaning of kennels, exercise runs and kitchen utensils.

*Preparation of food and the feeding of patients.

*Explanation to clients on the handling and restraint of their pets, including needs for exercise, house training and elementary obedience training.

*First-aid treatment for hemorrhage, including the proper use of tourniquets

*Preservation of blood, urine and pathologic material for the purpose of laboratory examination

*General care and supervision of the hospital or clinic patients to insure their comfort.

*Nail trimming and grooming of patients.

High school graduates with a sincere affection and regard for animals and a desire to work with veterinarians and perform such clinical duties as mentioned above will find they fit in especially well. Women particularly will be useful since, over and beyond the strong maternal instinct that goes so far in the care and the recovery phase when dealing with animals, women will find the majority of the positions will be in the small animal field, their dexterity will also fit in well. Students having financial restrictions that preclude their education and licensing as full-fledged veterinarians can in this way pursue careers in an area close to their actual desire. Their assistance in the pharmaceutical field, where drug concerns deal with laboratory animals, covers another wide area for trained assistance. The career opportunities are varied and reach into job opportunities in medical centers, research institutions and government health agencies; at present, the demand for graduates far exceeds the current supply of trained personnel.

As far as the financial remunerations, yearly salaries are estimated at an average of $5,000.00 for a starting point. As for the estimate of basic college education expenses, they range from $1800.00 to $2200.00 per year for out-of-state residents, and include tuition, room and board, college fees, essential textbooks and limited personal expenses. These personal expenses, of course, will vary with individual students, as well as the other expenses, but we present an average. It is obvious that the costs are about half of the costs involved in becoming a full-fledged veterinarian, however.

A Russian-bred Irish Setter bitch named Lara, photographed at five months of age; this puppy was presented as a gift to American Connie Vanacore while she visited Russia with her father in 1972.

Ch. Red Barn Princess Caitlin pictured winning the Breed at the 1969 Hunterdon Hills Kennel Club show with breeder-owner-handler Mrs. Marion Neville, Red Barn Kennels, Blauvelt, New York.

PART TIME KENNEL WORK

Youngsters who do not wish to go on to become veterinarians or animal technicians can get valuable experience and extra money by working part-time after school and weekends, or full-time during summer vacations, in a veterinarian's office. The exposure to animals and office procedure will be time well spent.

Another great help to veterinarians has been the housewife who loves animals and wishes to put in some time at a job away from the house, especially if her children are grown or away at college. If she can clean up in her own kennel she can certainly clean up in a veterinarian's office, and she will learn much about handling and caring for her own animals while she is making money.

Kennel help is also an area that is wide open for retired men. They are able to help out in many areas where they can learn and stay active, and most of the work allows them to set their own pace.

The gentility that age and experience brings is also beneficial to the animals they will deal with; for their part, the men find great reward in their contribution to animals and will be keeping their hand in the business world as well.

PROFESSIONAL HANDLERS

For those who wish to participate in the sport of dogs and whose interests or abilities do not center around the clinical aspects of the fancy, there is yet another avenue of involvement.

For those who excel in the show ring, who enjoy being in the limelight and putting their dogs through their paces, a career in professional handling may be the answer. Handling may include a weekend of showing a few dogs for special clients, or it may be a full-time career which can also include boarding, training, conditioning, breeding and showing of dogs for several clients.

Depending on how deeply your interest runs, the issue can be solved by a lot of preliminary consideration before it becomes necessary to make a decision. The first move would to to have a long, serious talk with a successful professional handler to learn the pros and cons of such a profession. Watching handlers in action from ringside as they perform their duties can be revealing. A visit to their kennels for

Laura F. Delano's Ch. Patricia Girl of Knocknagree, a famous Irish Setter of yesteryear.

Ch. Cherry Point Brask, owned by Mrs. Cheever Porter of New York City, had amassed a show record of 143 Bests of Breed, 51 Best Sporting Group, and 8 Bests in Show before his retirement in October, 1965.

an on-the-spot revelation of the behind-the-scenes responsibilities is essential! And working for them full or part time would be the best way of all to resolve any doubt you might have!

Professional handling is not all glamour in the show ring. There is plenty of "dirty work" behind the scenes 24 hours of every day. You must have the necessary ability and patience for this work, as well as the ability and patience to deal with CLIENTS—the dog owners who value their animals above almost anything else and would expect a great deal from you in the way of care and handling. The big question you must ask yourself first of all is: do you *really* love dogs enough to handle it. . .

DOG TRAINING

Like the professional handler, the professional dog trainer has a most responsible job! You not only need to be thoroughly familiar with the correct and successful methods of training a dog but also

Ch. Kalibanks King of Eatontown pictured winning Best in Show in August, 1960. Handled by Charley Meyer for owner Arlene D. Miller, now Mrs. Arlene Thompson. Shafer photo.

The Best in Show winning Irish Setter Ch. Rosecroft Premier, handled by Harry Hartnett and owned by Mrs. Cheever Porter of New York City.

must have the ability to communicate with dogs. True, it is very rewarding work, but training for the show ring, obedience, or guard dog work must be done exactly right for successful results to maintain a business reputation.

Training schools are quite the vogue nowadays, with all of them claiming success. But careful investigation should be made before enrolling a dog. . . and even more careful investigation should be made of their methods and of their actual successes before becoming associated with them.

GROOMING PARLORS

If you do not wish the 24-hour a day job which is required by a professional handler or professional trainer, but still love working with and caring for dogs, there is always the very profitable grooming business. Poodles started the ball rolling for the swanky, plush grooming establishments which sprang up like mushrooms all over the major cities, many of which seem to be doing very well. Here again, handling dogs and the public is necessary for a successful operation, as well as skill in the actual grooming of the dogs, and of all breeds.

While shops flourish in the cities, some of the suburban areas are now featuring mobile units which by appointment will visit your home with a completely equipped shop on wheels and will groom your dog right in your own driveway!

THE PET SHOP

Part-time or full-time work in a pet shop can help you make up your mind rather quickly as to whether or not you would like to have a shop of your own. For those who love animals and are concerned with their care and feeding, the pet shop can be a profitable and satisfying association. Supplies which are available for sale in these shops are almost limitless, and a nice living can be garnered from pet supplies if the location and population of the city you choose warrant it.

Best of Breed at the 1971 Irish Setter Club of Michigan Specialty Show was American and Canadian Ch. Rip Van Drake, C.D., owned by Dennis and Mary Laturie of Garden City, Michigan, and handled by Mr. Laturie.

Canadian and Bermudian Ch. Colnbrook Zodiac, owned by David E. Powell of Vancouver, British Columbia, Canada. Whelped April 23, 1970, his sire was Canadian and American Champion Jo-Ett's Marvelda Blazer **ex** Colnbrook Delight. His record in Canada, Bermuda and the United States includes 5 Bests in Show, 22 Group Firsts, 10 Group Seconds, 4 Group Thirds, 2 Group Fourths and 40 Bests of Breed.

DOG JUDGING

There are also those whose professions or age or health prevent them from owning or breeding or showing dogs, and who turn to judging at dog shows after their active years in the show ring are no longer possible. Breeder-judges make a valuable contribution to the fancy by judging in accordance with their years of experience in the fancy, and the assignments are enjoyable. Judging requires experience, a good eye for dogs and an appreciation of a good animal.

MISCELLANEOUS

If you find all of the aforementioned too demanding or not within your abilities, there are still other aspects of the sport for you to enjoy and participate in at will. Writing for the various dog magazines, books or club newsletters, dog photography, portrait painting, club activities, making dog coats, or needlework featuring dogs, typing pedigrees or perhaps dog walking. All, in their own way, contribute to the sport of dogs and give great satisfaction. Perhaps, where Samoyeds are concerned, you may wish to learn to train for racing, or sled hauling, or you might even wish to learn the making of the sleds!

Int. Ch. Red Star of Hollywood Hills, C.D.X., owned by the John Mc-Ateers of Bermuda.

26. GLOSSARY OF DOG TERMS

ACHILLES HEEL—The major tendon attaching the muscle of the calf from the thigh to the hock

AKC—The American Kennel Club. Address: 51 Madison Avenue, N.Y., N.Y. 10010

ALBINO—Pigment deficiency, usually a congenital fault, which renders skin, hair and eyes pink

AMERICAN KENNEL CLUB—Registering body for canine world in the United States. Headquarters for the stud book, dog registrations, and federation of kennel clubs. They also create and enforce the rules and regulations governing dog shows in the U.S.A.

ALMOND EYE—The shape of the eye opening, rather than the eye itself, which slants upwards at the outer edge, hence giving it an almond shape

ANUS—Anterior opening found under the tail for purposes of alimentary canal elimination

ANGULATION—The angles formed by the meeting of the bones

APPLE-HEAD—An irregular roundedness of topskull. A domed skull

APRON—On long-coated dogs, the longer hair that frills outward from the neck and chest

BABBLER—Hunting dog that barks or howls while out on scent

BALANCED—A symmetrical, correctly proportioned animal; one with correct balance with one part in regard to another

BARREL—Rounded rib section; thorax; chest

BAT EAR—An erect ear, broad at base, rounded or semicircular at top, with opening directly in front

BAY—The howl or bark of the hunting dog

BEARD—Profuse whisker growth

BEAUTY SPOT—Usually roundish colored hair on a blaze of another color. Found mostly between the ears

BEEFY—Overdevelopment or overweight in a dog, particularly hindquarters

BELTON—A color designation particularly familiar to Setters. An intermingling of colored and white hairs

BITCH—The female dog

Barbara Parks' Irish Setter, Gala Glen's Kerry Glen photographed against some local mountain greenery near their Lindale Kennels in Dillard, Georgia.

Ch. Verbu Missy Oogh, C.D.X. performing for the crowds at the premiere of the Disney film *Big Red* at the Chicago Theatre on State Street in Chicago. Missy was owned and trained by Emily Schweitzer, Verbu Kennels.

BLAZE—A type of marking. White strip running up the center of the face between the eyes

BLOCKY—Square head

BLOOM—Dogs in top condition are said to be "in full bloom"

BLUE MERLE—A color designation. Blue and gray mixed with black. Marbled-like appearance

BOSSY—Overdevelopment of the shoulder muscles

BRACE—Two dogs which move as a pair in unison

BREECHING—Tan-colored hair on inside of the thighs

Ch. McKendree's Bold Venture, Best of Breed winner at Westminster Kennel Club in 1975, and handled by Jan McKendree. Stanley, as he is called by his owners, was also #10 Irish Setter according to the Phillips System in 1974, has a Best in Show and several Group placings to his credit. Owned by Harold and Norma McKendree, McKendree Kennels, Jacksonville, Florida.

BRINDLE—Even mixture of black hairs with brown, tan or gray

BRISKET—The forepart of the body below the chest

BROKEN COLOR—A color broken by white or another color

BROKEN-HAIRED—A wiry coat

BROKEN-UP FACE—Receding nose together with deep stop, wrinkle, and undershot jaw

BROOD BITCH—A female used for breeding

BRUSH—A bushy tail

BURR—Inside part of the ear which is visible to the eye

BUTTERFLY NOSE—Parti-colored nose or entirely flesh color

BUTTON EAR—The edge of the ear which folds to cover the opening of the ear

CANINE—Animals of the family Canidae which includes not only dogs but foxes, wolves, and jackals

CANINES—The four large teeth in the front of the mouth often referred to as fangs

CASTRATE—The surgical removal of the testicles on the male dog

CAT-FOOT—Round, tight, high-arched feet said to resemble those of a cat

CHARACTER—The general appearance or expression said to be typical of the breed

CHEEKY—Fat cheeks or protruding cheeks

CHEST—Forepart of the body between the shoulder blades and above the brisket

CHINA EYE—A clear blue wall eye

CHISELED—A clean cut head, especially when chiseled out below the eye

CHOPS—Jowls or pendulous lips

CLIP—Method of trimming coats according to individual breed standards

CLODDY—Thick set or plodding dog

CLOSE-COUPLED—A dog short in loins; comparatively short from withers to hipbones

COBBY—Short-bodied; compact

COLLAR—Usually a white marking, resembling a collar, around the neck

CONDITION—General appearance of a dog showing good health, grooming and care

CONFORMATION—The form and structure of the bone or framework of the dog in comparison with requirements of the Standard for the breed

CORKY—Active and alert dog

COUPLE—Two dogs

COUPLING—Leash or collar-ring for a brace of dogs

COUPLINGS—Body between withers and the hipbones indicating either short or long coupling

COW HOCKED—when the hocks turn toward each other and sometimes touch

CRANK TAIL—Tail carried down

CREST—Arched portion of the back of the neck

CROPPING—Cutting or trimming of the ear leather to get ears to stand erect

CROSSBRED—A dog whose sire and dam are of two different breeds

CROUP—The back part of the back above the hind legs. Area from hips to tail

CROWN—The highest part of the head; the topskull

Ch. Knightscroft Erin Elan, or "Mickey," as he was called by his owner, Joseph P. Knight, Jr. This famous Irish Setter man is pictured above with Mickey on the day he finished for his championship at Saratoga in 1943.

CRYPTORCHID—Male dog with neither testicle visible

CULOTTE—The long hair on the back of the thighs

CUSHION—Fullness of upper lips

DAPPLED—Mottled marking of different colors with none predominating

DEADGRASS—Dull tan color

DENTITION—Arrangement of the teeth

DEWCLAWS—Extra claws, or functionless digits on the inside of the four legs; usually removed at about three days of age

DEWLAP—Loose, pendulous skin under the throat

DISH-FACED—When nasal bone is so formed that nose is higher at the end than in the middle or at the stop

DISQUALIFICATION—A dog which has a fault making it ineligible to compete in dog show competition

DISTEMPER TEETH—Discolored or pitted teeth as a result of having had distemper

DOCK—To shorten the tail by cutting

DOG—A male dog, though used freely to indicate either sex

English show dog Wendover Hope, photographed in 1967, and owned by Mrs. C.M. Girling, Dallinghoo Kennels, Beds., England. The sire was show Ch. Wendover Gentleman **ex** Wendover Jana.

Ch. Musbury Meteor, exported from Musbury Kennels (England), Best of Winners at the Atlanta Championship Show in April, 1967.

The top-winning Irish Setter in the breed for 1974, and #5 in the Sporting Group: American, Canadian and Bermudian Ch. Kincora Blazing Banner, pictured winning another Best in Show under judge Mildred Heald. Handled by Tom Glassford for owner Minnie Kiefer of Leola, Pennsylvania. Banner's sire was Ch. Tirvelda Earl of Harewood **ex** Wilson Farm Country Belle. John Ashbey photo.

DOMED—Evenly rounded in topskull; not flat but curved upward

DOWN-FACED—When nasal bone inclines toward the tip of the nose

DOWN IN PASTERN—Weak or faulty pastern joints; a let-down foot

DROP EAR—The leather pendant which is longer than the leather of the button ear

DRY NECK—Taut skin

DUDLEY NOSE—Flesh-colored or light brown pigmentation in the nose

ELBOW—The joint between the upper arm and the forearm

ELBOWS OUT—Turning out or off the body and not held close to the sides

EWE NECK—Curvature of the top of neck

EXPRESSION—Color, size and placement of the eyes which give the dog the typical expression associated with his breed

FAKING—Changing the appearance of a dog by artificial means to make it more closely resemble the Standard. White chalk to whiten fur, etc.

FALL—Hair which hangs over the face

FEATHERING—Long hair fringe on ears, legs, tail, or body

FEET EAST AND WEST—Toes turned out

FEMUR—The large heavy bone of the thigh

FIDDLE FRONT—Forelegs out at elbows, pasterns close, and feet turned out

FLAG—A long-haired tail

FLANK—The side of the body between the last rib and the hip

FLARE—A blaze that widens as it approaches the topskull

FLAT BONE—When girth of the leg bones is correctly elliptical rather than round

FLAT-SIDED—Ribs insufficiently rounded as they meet the breastbone

FLEWS—Upper lips, particularly at inner corners

FOREARM—Bone of the foreleg between the elbow and the pastern

FOREFACE—Front part of the head, before the eyes; muzzle

FROGFACE—Usually overshot jaw where nose is extended by the receding jaw

FRINGES—Same as feathering

FRONT—Forepart of the body as viewed head-on

FURROW—Slight indentation or median line down center of the skull to the top

GAY TAIL—Tail carried above the top line

GESTATION—The period during which the bitch carries her young; 63 days in the dog

GOOSE RUMP—Too steep or sloping a croup

GRIZZLE—Bluish-gray color

GUN-SHY—When a dog fears gun shots

GUARD HAIRS—The longer stiffer hairs which protrude through the undercoat

HARD-MOUTHED—The dog that bites or leaves tooth marks on the game he retrieves

HARE-FOOT—A narrow foot

HARLEQUIN—A color pattern, patched or pied coloration, predominantly black and white

HAW—A third eyelid or membrane at the inside corner of the eye

HEEL—The same as the hock

HEIGHT—Vertical measurement from the withers to the ground, or shoulder to the ground

HOCK—The tarsus bones of the hind leg which form the joint between the second thigh and the metatarsals.

HOCKS WELL LET DOWN—When distance from hock to the ground is close to the ground

HOUND—Dog commonly used for hunting by scent

HOUND-MARKED—Three-color dogs; white, tan and black, predominating color mentioned first

HUCKLEBONES—The top of the hipbones

HUMERUS—The bone of the upper arm

"Shannon," officially known as J-Mar Scarlet Thunder, is owned by Rudy and Marilyn De Mark, owners of the Woodland Acre Kennels in Dover, New Jersey.

INBREEDING—The mating of closely related dogs of the same standard, usually brother to sister

INCISORS—The cutting teeth found between the fangs in the front of the mouth

ISABELLA—Fawn or light bay color

KINK TAIL—A tail which is abruptly bent, appearing to be broken

KNUCKLING-OVER—An insecurely knit pastern joint often causes irregular motion while dog is standing still

LAYBACK—Well placed shoulders

LAYBACK—Receding nose accompanied by an undershot jaw

LEATHER—The flap of the ear

LEVEL BITE—The front or incisor teeth of the upper and lower jaws meet exactly

Canadian and American Ch. Draherin Bachelor Boy pictured winning Best in Show under judge Walter Jacob on the day of his retirement, June 22, 1974. Jeffrey has been the top-winning Irish Setter for 1969 through 1973, #2 Sporting Dog in 1969 and 1970, and #1 Sporting Dog 1971, 72 and 73. He was in the top 5 all-breed dog listing for 1969 through 1972. In Canada he is also the all time Best in Show winner in all breeds and has defeated more dogs than any other dog in the history of the Canadian Kennel Club to win the honor of 65 All Breed Bests in Show, 235 Group Placements and 245 Bests of Breed. He was shown 263 times under 106 different Canadian and American judges. His career in the States began in March, 1968 and he was handled here by Ken Murray. He completed his American championship in July, 1968 and won the Golden Leash award from the Irish Setter Club of America in 1968. He began his Canadian show career in April, 1969 winning Best in Show his first time out and finished for his Canadian championship in 4 shows with 2 Bests in Show. Owner-handled by Thomas G. Threlkeld, Halifax, Nova Scotia.

McKendree's Flint of Ireland, C.D. Flint got her first leg on her title when just 7 months old. Her C.D. title was won with three scores all over 195. Owned by Jan McKendree, Jacksonville, Florida, and photographed in 1969.

LINE BREEDING—The mating of related dogs of the same breed to a common ancestor. Controlled inbreeding. Usually grandmother to grandson, or grandfather to granddaughter.

LIPPY—Lips that do not meet perfectly

LOADED SHOULDERS—When shoulder blades are out of alignment due to overweight or overdevelopment on this particular part of the body

LOIN—The region of the body on either side of the vertebral column between the last ribs and the hindquarters

LOWER THIGH—Same as second thigh

LUMBER—Excess fat on a dog

LUMBERING—Awkward gait on a dog

MANE—Profuse hair on the upper portion of neck

MANTLE—Dark-shaded portion of the coat or shoulders, back and sides

MASK—Shading on the foreface

MEDIAN LINE—Same as furrow

MOLARS—Rear teeth used for actual chewing

MOLERA—Abnormal ossification of the skull

MONGREL—Puppy or dog whose parents are of two different breeds

MONORCHID—A male dog with only one testicle apparent

MUZZLE—The head in front of the eyes—this includes nose, nostrils and jaws as well as the foreface

MUZZLE-BAND—White markings on the muzzle

NICTITATING EYELID—The thin membrane at the inside corner of the eye which is drawn across the eyeball. Sometimes referred to as the third eyelid

NOSE—Scenting ability

OCCIPUT—The upper crest or point at the top of the skull

OCCIPITAL PROTUBERANCE—The raised occiput itself

OCCLUSION—The meeting or bringing together of the upper and lower teeth.

OLFACTORY—Pertaining to the sense of smell

OTTER TAIL—A tail that is thick at the base, with hair parted on under side

OUT AT SHOULDER—The shoulder blades are set in such a manner that the joints are too wide, hence jut out from the body

OUTCROSSING—The mating of unrelated individuals of the same breed

OVERHANG—A very pronounced eyebrow

OVERSHOT—The front incisor teeth on top overlap the front teeth of the lower jaw. Also called pig jaw.

PACK—Several hounds kept together in one kennel

PADDLING—Moving with the forefeet wide, to encourage a body roll motion

PADS—The underside, or soles, of the feet

Leslie Holvenstot with some Westwind puppies bred by her mother, Luz Holvenstot, Westwind Kennels, Long Valley, New Jersey.

The beautiful 14-month-old Bali's Kentucky Woman with her 15-year-old handler and co-owner, Karen Pfander. Jerry and Judy Ballantyne of Tacoma, Washington are the other proud owners.

PARTI-COLORED—Variegated in patches of two or more colors
PASTERN—The collection of bones forming the joint between the radius and ulna and the metacarpals
PEAK—Same as occiput
PENCILING—Black lines dividing the tan colored hair on the toes
PIED—Comparatively large patches of two or more colors. Also called parti-colored or piebald
PIGEON-BREAST—A protruding breastbone
PIG JAW—Jaw with overshot bite
PILE—The soft hair in the undercoat
PINCER BITE—A bite where the incisor teeth meet exactly
PLUME—A feathered tail which is carried over the back
POINTS—Color on face, ears, legs and tail in contrast to the rest of the body color
POMPON—Rounded tuft of hair left on the end of the tail after clipping
PRICK EAR—Carried erect and pointed at tip

Ch. Tirvelda Best Regards, C.D. handled by her owner, Edward Treutel, and Ch. Tirvelda Nor'wester, handled by Michelle Leathers for owner E. Irving Eldredge. Both of these magnificent dogs are pictured winning under the late judge Alva Rosenberg at an Asheville Kennel Club show. Graham photograph.

PUPPY—Dog under one year of age

QUALITY—Refinement, fineness

QUARTERS—Hind legs as a pair

RACY—Tall, of comparatively slight build

RAT TAIL—The root thick and covered with soft curls—tip devoid of hair or having the appearance of having been clipped

RINGER—A substitute for close resemblance

RING TAIL—Carried up and around and almost in a circle

ROACH BACK—Convex curvature of back

ROAN—A mixture of colored hairs with white hairs. Blue roan, orange roan, etc.

ROMAN NOSE—A nose whose bridge has a convex line from forehead to nose tip. Ram's nose

ROSE EAR—Drop ear which folds over and back revealing the burr

ROUNDING—Cutting or trimming the ends of the ear leather

RUFF—The longer hair growth around the neck

SABLE—A lacing of black hair in or over a lighter ground color

SADDLE—A marking over the back, like a saddle

SCAPULA—The shoulder blade

SCREW TAIL—Naturally short tail twisted in spiral formation

SCISSORS BITE—A bite in which the upper teeth just barely overlap the lower teeth

SELF COLOR—One color with lighter shadings

SEMIPRICK EARS—Carried erect with just the tips folding forward

SEPTUM—The line extending vertically between the nostrils

SHELLY—A narrow body which lacks the necessary size required by the Breed Standard

SICKLE TAIL—Carried out and up in a semicircle

SLAB SIDES—Insufficient spring of ribs

SLOPING SHOULDER—The shoulder blade which is set obliquely or "laid back"

SNIPEY—A pointed nose

SNOWSHOE FOOT—Slightly webbed between the toes

SOUNDNESS—The general good health and appearance of a dog in its entirety

SPAYED—A female whose ovaries have been removed surgically

SPECIALTY CLUB—An organization to sponsor and promote an individual breed

SPECIALTY SHOW—A dog show devoted to the promotion of a single breed

Mike, Pat and Flicka in a painting rendered in 1964 by Pat Detmold of New Jersey for owner Thomas G. Threlkeld of Halifax, Nova Scotia.

SPECTACLES—Shading or dark markings around the eyes or from eyes to ears

SPLASHED—Irregularly patched color on white or vice versa

SPLAY FOOT—A flat or open-toed foot

SPREAD—The width between the front legs

SPRING OF RIBS—The degree of rib roundness

SQUIRREL TAIL—Carried up and curving slightly forward

STANCE—Manner of standing

STARING COAT—Dry harsh hair, sometimes curling at the tips

STATION—Comparative height of a dog from the ground—either high or low

STERN—Tail of a sporting dog or hound

STERNUM—Breastbone

STIFLE—Joint of hind leg between thigh and second thigh. Sometimes called the ham

STILTED—Choppy, up-and-down gait of straight-hocked dog

STOP—The step-up from nose to skull between the eyes

STRAIGHT-HOCKED—Without angulation; straight behind

SUBSTANCE—Good bone. Or in good weight, or well muscled dog

SUPERCILIARY ARCHES—The prominence of the frontal bone of the skull over the eye

Ch. Conifer's Lance, sire of 15 champions, was sired by Ch. Red Rogue of Maple Ridge ex Canadian Ch. Conifer's Princess Acre. He is owned by Mr. and Mrs. Frank Wheatly. In 1961 Lance was 3rd ranking Sporting Dog in the nation according to the Phillips System and won 5 Bests in Show.

A photograph of classic beauty of a boy and his dog, from the Fishers, Needham, Massachusetts.

SWAYBACK—Concave curvature of the back between the withers and the hipbones
TEAM—Four dogs usually working in unison
THIGH—The hindquarter from hip joint to stifle
THROATINESS—Excessive loose skin under the throat
THUMB-MARKS—Black spots in the tan markings on the pasterns
TICKED—Small isolated areas of black or colored hairs on a white background
TIMBER—Bone, especially of the legs
TOPKNOT—Tuft of hair on the top of head
TRIANGULAR EYE—The eye set in surrounding tissue of triangular shape. A three-cornered eye
TRI-COLOR—Three colors on a dog, white, black and tan
TRUMPET—Depression or hollow on either side of the skull just behind the eye socket; comparable to the temple area in man
TUCK-UP—Body depth at the loin
TULIP EAR—Ear carried erect with slight forward curvature along the sides
TURN-UP—Uptilted jaw
TYPE—The distinguishing characteristics of a dog to measure its worth against the Standard for the breed

UNDERSHOT—The front teeth of the lower jaw overlapping or projecting beyond the front teeth of the upper jaw

UPPER-ARM—The humerus bone of the foreleg between the shoulder blade and forearm

VENT—Tan-colored hair under the tail

WALLEYE—A blue eye also referred to as a fish or pearl eye

WEAVING—When the dog is in motion, the forefeet or hind feet cross

WEEDY—A dog too light of bone

WHEATEN—Pale yellow or fawn color

WHEEL-BACK—Back line arched over the loin; roach back

WHELPS—Unweaned puppies

WHIP TAIL—Carried out stiffly straight and pointed

WIRE-HAIRED—A hard wiry coat

WITHERS—The peak of the first dorsal vertebra; highest part of the body just behind the neck

WRINKLE—Loose, folding skin on forehead and/or foreface

For those of you who declare your Irish Setters to be so intelligent that they seem almost human, recall this ancient Irish observation. . .

. . . it is not safe to ask a question of a dog,
for he may answer, and should he do so
the questioner will surely die.

INDEX